T3-BOG-208

PRIVILEGED COMMUNICATIONS IN THE MENTAL HEALTH PROFESSIONS

PRIVILEGED COMMUNICATIONS IN THE MENTAL HEALTH PROFESSIONS

Samuel Knapp

The Rosalie G. Handler Center
Millersburg, Pennsylvania

Leon VandeCreek

Psychology Department
Indiana University of Pennsylvania

VNR VAN NOSTRAND REINHOLD COMPANY

New York

Library of Congress Catalog Card Number: 86-24764
ISBN: 0-442-24055-4

Printed in the United States of America.

Van Nostrand Reinhold Company Inc.
115 Fifth Avenue
New York, New York 10003

Van Nostrand Reinhold Company Limited
Molly Millars Lane
Wokingham, Berkshire RG11 2PY, England

Van Nostrand Reinhold
480 La Trobe Street
Melbourne, Victoria 3000, Australia

Macmillan of Canada
Division of Gage Publishing Corporation
164 Commander Boulevard
Agincourt, Ontario M1S 3C7, Canada

16 15 14 13 12 11 10 9 8 7 6 5 4 3 2 1

Library of Congress Cataloging in Publication Data
Knapp, Samuel.
Privileged communications in the mental health professions.
Bibliography: p.
Includes index.
1. Confidential communications—Physicians—United States. 2. Mental health laws—United States. 3. Psychotherapists—Legal status, laws, etc.—United States. I. VandeCreek, Leon. II. Title. [DNLM: 1. Confidentiality—United States—legislation. 2. Forensic Psychiatry—United States—legislation. W 740 K67p]
KF8959.P4K58 1987 334.73'041 86-24764
ISBN 0-442-24055-4 347.30441

CONTENTS

PREFACE

The public welfare is the highest law.

Privileged communications is a legal term dealing with the admission of evidence into court. Privileged communication laws attempt to balance two important social values: the need for evidence in court and the need for privacy in psychotherapy. When privileged communication laws apply, psychotherapy patients may prevent their psychotherapists from testifying about them in court.

In recent years, legislators have created or revised many of the privileged communication laws for psychotherapy patients, and the number of court decisions interpreting them has increased. Mental health professionals now frequently offer testimony as expert witnesses. In 1966, Ralph Slovenko and Gene Usdin authored a definitive book on privileged communication, *Psychotherapy, Confidentiality and Privileged Communication* (Charles C. Thomas). In the last 20 years, however, their book has become outdated, and no other book has emerged to take its place. A comprehensive book summarizing and analyzing current privileged communication laws and cases is needed.

We have designed this book for both mental health and legal audiences. Virtually all psychotherapists will have cause to refer to this book at some point in their careers. Psychotherapists who specialize in forensics will find it useful. Similarly, many lawyers will have cause to refer to this book at some time. Lawyers who specialize in mental health litigation or who often rely on mental health expert witnesses can make this book a frequent companion. Graduate students in mental health professions or law school may use this book in a course on mental health and the law. Finally, we hope that those who are on the cutting edge of privileged communication laws will read this book. This book is also written for the legislators who write laws, judges who interpret them, and social scientists who research them.

We are indebted to the following libraries for use of their facilities in completing and researching this book: the State Law Library of Harrisburg, Pennsylvania, the law libraries of Dickinson Law School, the University of Pennsylvania, the University of Pittsburgh, Philadelphia County, and Lehigh County. We have used the extensive library at the Western Psychiatric Institute and Clinic of the University of Pittsburgh. We express appreciation to Cindy Herzog, a doctoral student in psychology, who did much of the legwork in searching and photocopying cases and checking references. And we thank Beverly Philippi who did the typing and reorganizing in the final days of manuscript preparation.

A comment is in order on the use of language. Mental health professionals differ in their use of the terms *psychotherapist* or *counselor* and the terms *patient* or *client.* For some mental health professionals, these terms reflect philosophical differences regarding the nature of the psychotherapeutic (counseling) relationship; for others, these terms merely reflect differences in customary usage. We have used the terms *psychotherapist* and *counselor* and the terms *patient* and *client* interchangeably. The application of privilege law does not hinge on the use of either term.

SAMUEL KNAPP
LEON VANDECREEK

Chapter 1

History of Privileged Communication

Mental health professionals are often led to believe that the information they obtain from clients is sacrosanct. They should not discuss it outside the professional setting except under most unusual circumstances. Nevertheless, relatives, third-party payers, police, or the courts will ask these professionals to reveal information about their clients. Unfortunately, many mental health professionals and clients do not know the limits of confidentiality and privilege.

Discussions of client information require the differentiation of the terms *confidentiality* and *privileged communications. Confidentiality* refers to the laws or rules of professional ethics that regulate the disclosure of information obtained in psychotherapy. Chapter 12 presents an overview of confidentiality. *Privileged communication* is a narrower term, referring only to the legal right that protects clients, under certain circumstances, from having their communications revealed in court without their permission. It is a legal term dealing with the admission of evidence into court.

BACKGROUND IN ENGLISH AND AMERICAN LAW

The effective administration of justice is one of the highest social values and a prerequisite for an ordered and civilized society. In order to aid the search for truth, the courts normally have access to all relevant evidence. A trial is only as good as the available evidence. The often-repeated maxim that "the public has a right to every man's evidence" was first articulated by Lord Hardwicke over 100 years ago, but it is still cited today (e.g., *United States v. Bryan,* 1950, p. 331). The importance of truth in the mission of the courts has been repeated in numerous notable ways. It has been said that "our system of criminal justice is a search for truth" (*Matter of Pittsburgh Action Against Rape,* 1981, p. 130); that "disclosure, rather than suppression of relevant materials ordinarily promotes the proper administration of criminal justice" (*Dennis v. United States,* 1966, p. 870); and that "the need to develop all relevant facts in the adversary system is both fundamental and comprehensive. . . . The very integrity of the judicial system and public confidence in the system depend on full disclosure of all the facts" (*United States v. Nixon,* 1974, p. 709).

All persons have a duty to testify because the proper administration of justice benefits all. In addition, when witnesses testify, they are required to tell the truth. The consequences of withholding evidence from the court are obvious. "We increase the risk of such a miscarriage of justice whenever we allow an important witness to keep any helpful facts away from the judge and jury" (Chafee, 1943, p. 609). The court may exonerate the guilty or punish the innocent.

Judicial rules of evidence aid the search for truth in court. Most rules of evidence facilitate truth discovery by excluding irrelevant, unreliable, or misleading evidence. Privileged communication laws differ from other evidentiary rules because the laws withhold otherwise admissible evidence from the court. "Their effect instead is clearly inhibitive; rather than facilitating the illumination of truth, they shut out the light" (Cleary, 1984, p. 171). The etymology of the word *privilege* gives further support for the uniqueness of the privileged communication law. Privilege derives from the Latin *privata lex* ("private law"), which means a law that does not apply to all persons equally.

This chapter will describe the background and origin of several common law and statutory privileges. Knowledge of these laws is important to understanding the full impact of privilege to psychotherapy patients. As will be described in later chapters, the psychotherapist-patient relationship often overlaps with other privileges. At times, persons covered under the physician-patient or clergy-penitent privilege will conduct psychotherapy. The background of the physician-patient privilege is especially important because past legislative and judicial experience with that privilege may explain the reluctance of some legal authorities to accept the psychotherapist-patient privilege. In addition, courts may sometimes look to precedents in the physician-patient privilege, especially if there is little case law or statutory guidance on that issue. Finally, a review of other privileges is important because during certain court proceedings, the psychotherapist-patient relationship may receive its only protection when psychotherapists are working as agents of attorneys and covered under their privilege.

COMMON LAW PRIVILEGES

According to the common law—or the judge-made legal tradition passed down by English and American courts—few communications were privileged. Most privileged communications were those found in the context of a special protected relationship. Other than government or state secrets, the common law privileges comprised only the attorney-client relationship and the husband-wife relationship. The clergy-communicant relationship had some common law precedent, although its primary legal status came from statutory law. The courts continually subject common law privileges to reinterpretation to meet the needs of a changing society.

Attorney-Client Privilege

According to Roman law, attorneys' loyalty to their clients prevented them from being a witness in their clients' cases. It is unknown how much this ancient Roman custom influenced the English court system, but by Elizabethan times, courts held that the honor of barristers or attorneys protected them from being required to disclose the secrets of their clients. By the eighteenth century, the emphasis on the code of honor had weakened, and a new rationale developed: full disclosure of the facts by clients to their attorneys would ultimately expedite trials. Clients can now speak freely to their attorneys because the courts can seldom compel the attorneys to testify against them.

In addition to the common law protection, some legal commentators believe that the Sixth Amendment (which guarantees the right to counsel) also protects the attorney-client relationship (e.g., Note, 1976a). Regardless of the origin of or rationale for this privilege, it is well established in American law and now has statutory protection in addition to the common law tradition.

Spousal Privilege

The common law also recognized a privileged relationship between husband and wife. The early common law automatically disqualified the husband or wife of a litigant as a witness regardless of the nature of the case or nature of the testimony. The spouse was incompetent to testify either for or against the partner. In more recent years, courts in the United States have permitted or required spouses to testify on some limited matters. For example, some states have no privilege in a proceeding in which one spouse is charged with a crime against the other or against a child. Privilege may be absent in proceedings designed to establish mental competence. In general, the privilege will now restrict only communications between spouses or information gained in the marital relationship (Cleary, 1984).

The rationale for this privilege is to preserve harmony and trust within the marriage. It is held that the possibility that one spouse may testify against another could lead to deceit or the lack of intimacy within the marriage. The validity of this assumption, however, is not universally shared. Cleary notes that "family harmony is nearly always past saving when the spouse is willing to aid the prosecution" (1984, p. 162).

STATUTORY PRIVILEGES

As a rule, Congress or state legislatures create other privileged relationships. Legislators usually weigh conflicting interests according to a utilitarian formula when considering privileged communications. On the one hand, it is argued that society benefits when certain relationships are fostered or protected. The privileged communication laws increase the effectiveness of these relationships by increasing privacy. On the other hand, it is argued that society is harmed when the courts cannot administer justice properly. Privileged communication laws decrease the likelihood of an accurate verdict because they permit persons to withhold information from the court. The group seeking the privilege must convince the legislature that the social benefits or nonlitigation values supported by protecting the relationship would compensate for the loss of information to the courts.

Legal scholars have often criticized the privileged relationships created by the legislatures (Chafee, 1943; Cleary, 1984; Curd, 1938; Morgan, 1943; Purrington, 1906; Wigmore, 1961). Yet despite these criticisms, most states include clergy, physicians, and psychologists within their privileged communication laws. Some states have privileged communication laws involving social workers, counselors, journalists, and nurses. A few states have privilege laws for detectives, trust companies, or accountants. Appendix A contains citations of privilege laws for clients of mental health professions in each state as of August 1985.

Clergy-Communicant Privilege

The clergy-communicant privilege is unique in that it has some common law background, although it is now primarily protected by statute. Early landmark cases in American jurisprudence highlighted the need for a clergy-communicant statute. In 1813 the New York case of *People v. Phillips* (1813) upheld a privilege for a priest without the benefit of a statute. In that case, a man confessed to the priest that he had stolen some goods. As part of his penance, he had agreed to take the property to the priest to return to the owner. The case was decided by the New York Court of General Sessions, which consisted of then Mayor DeWitt Clinton, the recorder, and two alderman. The court refused to compel the priest to reveal what the thief had confessed to him during penance. Four years later, however, a New York court denied the privilege to a Protestant clergyman because his denomination did not have the sacrament of confession. This judgment prompted the New York state legislature to pass the first clergy-communicant statute.

Now every state has a clergy-communicant statute except West Virginia (Gumper, 1984). Although the privilege is sometimes called the priest-penitent statute, the privilege is not limited to priests but applies to any clergy regardless of denomination. Some states have narrowly worded privilege laws for clergy that apply only to confessions by members of their own faith. Others have broadly worded statutes that protect any professional function of the clergy, including counseling (Gumper, 1984; Knapp and VandeCreek, 1985). We criticize the expansion of the clergy-communicant privilege to include counseling. The privilege for mental health counselees should apply only to relationships with professionals with specialized training in counseling or psychotherapy. Only a few specially trained pastoral counselors have the necessary qualifications. To date, only New Hampshire makes a distinction in the privilege between spiritual communications to general clergy and mental health or pastoral counseling with pastoral counselors.

Physician-Patient Privilege

According to the common law, medical patients had no privilege, and the court could compel their doctors to testify. The famous English bigamy trial of Elizabeth, duchess of Kingston, in 1776 dispelled any possibility of a common law privilege for physicians. Before the full Parliament sitting in assembly, the court had ordered the duchess's surgeon to testify whether the duchess had told him of a previous marriage. The surgeon was reluctant to testify, but the court ruled, "if a surgeon was voluntarily to reveal these secrets, to be sure, he would be guilty of a breach of honor and of great indiscretion; but to give the information in a court of justice, which by the law of the land he is bound to do, will never be imputed to him as any indiscretion whatever" (Duchess of Kingston's Case, 1776, p. 573). It is interesting to note that in the same trial, the court refused to allow a lord to claim the privilege as a gentleman (Purrington, 1906).

No common law privilege existed for physicians in the United States either. In 1828 New York became the first state to grant the privilege to medical patients. The statute allowed patients to reveal information necessary for proper medical treatment without fear of later disgrace before a public court. The legislators believed that this law would encourage patients to seek medical treatment, especially for communicable diseases such as venereal diseases, and would reduce the likelihood of a plague or an epidemic in the community. Most states passed physician-patient privileged communication statutes in the nineteenth century.

Although legislators originally created the physician-patient privilege to encourage persons with infectious disease to seek medical treatment, the privilege usually extended to all ailments treated by the physician. The medical privilege was of little consequence when it was first enacted. The impact of the medical privilege, however, expanded with the development of accident insurance, life insurance, and workmen's compensation. The privilege increasingly excluded relevant evidence from court. Critics also alleged that patients used the privilege as a vehicle to support or cover fraud. The eminent legal scholar Dean Wigmore concluded that "there is little to be said in favor of the privilege, and a great deal to be said against it. The adoption of it in any other jurisdiction is earnestly to be deprecated" (Wigmore, 1961, p. 832).

The physician-patient privilege subsequently became the object of much vehement criticism (Chafee, 1943; Curd, 1938; Morgan, 1943; Wigmore, 1961). Critics argued that patients did not need the physician-patient privilege before they would seek medical treatment with the thought that future litigation might be involved.

> Nor is there any objective evidence that the existence of the privilege has had any influence in promoting public health or that its absence has had any adverse influence. New York has had the privilege longer than any other state. Are residents of New York any more ready to consult physicians than residents of Massachusetts where the privilege has never been recognized . . . ? There is nothing to demonstrate any benefit to the public in the privilege, while law books are full of instances where its application has prevented the discovery of the truth to the damage of honest litigants. (Morgan, 1943, p. 291)

Furthermore, most patients do not have ailments that they consider intimate or overly personal. Patients often discuss their ailments freely with friends, relatives, or even strangers in the doctor's waiting room. "From asthma to broken ribs, from influenza to tetanus, the facts of the disease are not only disclosable without shame, but are in fact often publicly known and knowable by everyone—by everyone except the appointed investigators of truth" (Wigmore, 1961, p. 830).

Even the motives of physicians seeking the privilege have been questioned. Critics claimed that professional status, not social benefit, was a major motive behind the privilege. "The administration of justice ought not to be shaped by inter-professional jealousies and trivial claims to prestige" (Chaffe, 1943, p. 609). Subsequent amendments and strict interpretations of the law, however, have vitiated their importance, leading Slovenko to conclude that the physician-patient privilege is "much sound and fury signifying nothing" (1974, p. 656).

Psychotherapist-Client Privilege

Some critics of the physician-patient relationship failed to take into account the differences between the physician-patient relationship and the psychiatrist-patient or psychotherapist-client relationship, in part because psychiatry was not established as a professional activity until relatively recently. It was a novel and almost experimental profession when the eminent Professor Wigmore wrote his clear-cut criticisms of the physician-patient privilege. The activities of nonmedical psychotherapists received no more support than those of psychiatrists. "Those psychoanalysts who have been too busy to study medicine must have spicier facts to relate than physicians, but no court would yet bound them to secrecy" (Chafee, 1943, p. 611).

Gradually it became recognized that the psychiatrist and psychotherapist needed more privacy than the average medical practitioner. The early advocates of the psychotherapist-patient privilege did not defend the physician-patient privilege. Rather, they pointed out how the psychotherapist-patient relationship requires more confidentiality and privacy than is typically found in the physician-patient relationship (Comment, 1952; Cottle, 1956; Fisher, 1964; Guttmacher and Weihofen, 1952; Heller, 1957; Slovenko, 1960; Slovenko and Usdin, 1961). "Mental ill health, however, is still a matter which patients are likely to be more ashamed than physical ill health or injury, and there is a good deal more reason for supposing that a person who consults a psychiatrist intends to speak in more strict confidence than the automobile accident plaintiff" (Guttmacher and Weihofen, 1952, p. 34).

Over the years, state legislatures began to recognize the benefits of a psychotherapist-patient privilege. Before World War II, no state specifically dealt with the privilege within psychotherapy. Some psychiatrists, however, had limited coverage under the physician-patient privilege. After World War II, psychologists and social workers began to grow in prominence as nonmedical psychotherapists. Consequently, states gradually began to provide privileged communications for these practitioners.

Our review revealed that 47 states and the District of Columbia have privileged communication statutes for psychologists, and 28 states have privileged communication statutes for social workers. Psychiatrists are covered under specific statutes in 20 states. In addition, they are covered under the physician-patient privileges in 30 other states and the District of Columbia (DeKraai and Sales, 1982). Appendix A contains a complete state statutory citation listing for privilege laws for psychotherapists as of August 1985.

Readers are cautioned to consult local authorities for recent changes in their state's laws.

Mental health patients have no specific privilege in federal courts. When federal courts apply state law in civil proceedings, the applicable state privilege will apply. When federal courts apply state law in criminal proceedings, the courts will use the common law as based on "reason and experience." More details on the privilege for mental health professionals in federal courts can be found in Chapter 4.

Researcher-Subject Privilege

The psychotherapist-patient privilege was designed to encourage the treatment of emotional disorders. At times, however, mental health professionals will act as public scholars who research and investigate public issues. In these situations, mental health professionals may have a functional overlap with journalists in that they use confidential sources to create information that may be critical of existing public policies. Currently the only statutory protection comes from federal laws that protect research into drug abuse and issues of criminal justice (Nejelski and Lerman, 1971), laws in many states that protect drug research projects, and statutes in a few states that protect epidemiological or health surveys (Knerr and Carroll, 1978). Chapter 9 will discuss the researcher-subject privilege in more detail.

THEORETICAL RATIONALES FOR PRIVILEGE

Several arguments have been proposed to support the development of privilege for various relationships. The rationale traditionally advanced is that encouragement of special relationships serves the public more than the exclusion of information from court harms it. This is often referred to as the utilitarian view. Other rationales have also been proposed.

Utilitarian Views

According to the utilitarian view, legislatures should create a privilege only when the gains from the privilege outweigh the impact of loss of evidence available to the court. The gains envisioned by the legislature refer to gains or benefits to society. It is anticipated that society as a whole would benefit because the psychotherapists could minimize the adverse effects of mental illness, strengthen interpersonal relationships, and help prevent future litigation through preventing crimes and keeping families intact. Any gain by a client in a specific case is irrelevant as far as the rationale for privilege.

"Communication privileges, unlike the self-incrimination privileges, have never traditionally been concerned with the right of the person to avoid adverse use of confidential information" (Weisberg and Wald, 1984, p. 189).

Although the utilitarian view emphasizes the importance of the truth-seeking functions of the court, it realizes "that there is more to life than litigation" (Saltzburg, 1980, p. 600). Certain special relationships promote the overall welfare of society as much as the truth-seeking function of the courts. "Truth, like all other good things, may be loved unwisely—may be pursued too keenly—may cost too much" (*Pearse v. Pearse,* 1846, p. 951).

Wigmore's Criteria. Wigmore (1961) strongly advocated the utilitarian view for privileges. Courts and legislators have widely accepted and quoted his writings. His four essential criteria for justification for granting a privilege have been especially influential. Virtually every privilege statute enacted since the mid-1960s has been evaluated according to these criteria. These criteria ask: (1) Does the communication originate in the belief that it will not be disclosed? (2) Is the inviolability of that confidence essential to achieve the purpose of the relationship? (3) Is the relationship one that society should foster? (4) Is the expected injury to the relationship, through fear of later disclosure, greater than the expected benefit to justice in obtaining later testimony?

Wigmore believed that a negative answer to any of these questions would negate the justification for the privilege. Wigmore advocated a privilege status for the husband-wife, priest-penitent, and attorney-client relationships but opposed it for the physician-patient relationship because it failed the fourth criterion. Wigmore never evaluated the privilege for mental health professionals because he had developed his criteria before psychotherapy became well established as a professional activity. Nevertheless, it appears that the psychotherapist-patient relationship satisfies Wigmore's four criteria (e.g., Fisher, 1964; Foster, 1976; Green, 1980; Kennedy, 1973; Messersmith, 1984; Shah, 1969; Slovenko, 1960; Slovenko and Usdin, 1961; Stroube, 1979).

First, the communications originate with the belief that they will not be discussed outside the office. The relationship between the psychotherapist and patient implies a contract that the information will remain private. During psychotherapy, patients reveal the darkest aspects of their personality to a psychotherapist who gains confidences through promises of trust and shared secrecy. "The patient is called upon to discuss . . . the unspeakable, the unthinkable, the repressed" (Heller, 1957, p. 405). Publicity of these secrets could cause embarrassment, shame, or disgrace. Disclosure could blemish the patient's reputation in the community, cost the person employment, or undo intimate relationships (Slovenko and Usdin, 1961). Psychotherapy patients make themselves vulnerable through highly personal and intimate disclosures. The shield of confidentiality around psychotherapy gives them the security to make these disclosures.

The psychotherapy patient confides more utterly than anyone else in the world. He exposes to the therapist not only what his words directly express; he lays bare his entire self, his dreams, his phantasies, sins, and shame. Most patients who undergo psychotherapy know that this is what will be expected of them, and they cannot get help except on that condition. . . . It would be too much to expect them to do so if they knew that all they say—and all that the psychiatrist learns from what they say—may be revealed to the whole world from a witness stand. (Guttmacher and Weihofen, 1952, p. 34)

As discussed in Chapter 3, empirical studies have demonstrated the validity of the assumption that patients enter therapy with the expectation of confidentiality (Appelbaum et al., 1984; Schmid et al., 1983; Shuman and Weiner, 1982). The results of these studies are consistent with the interpretation of authors who stated that "the concept of the confidentiality of client-therapist communications is at the core of the psychotherapeutic relationship" (Jagim, Wittman, and Noll, 1978, pp. 458-459).

Second, successful psychotherapy requires the maintenance of confidentiality. Reductions in the secrecy afforded to patients would harm the psychotherapeutic relationship. It is believed that some persons might avoid psychotherapy, and those within psychotherapy might be more guarded about what they would reveal. Although the deterrence hypothesis has not yet received extensive empirical support, some evidence is consistent with it. The evidence, which is reviewed in Chapter 3, consists of analogue studies and surveys with patients (e.g., Appelbaum et al., 1984; Meyer and Willage, 1980; Schmid et al., 1983; Woods and McNamara, 1980).

Hague (1983) advocated the privilege to avoid a "cruel trilemma" in which psychotherapists must choose among three evils: harming their patient through the testimony, lying to the court, or facing contempt of court charges for refusal to testify. In fact, in several documented cases, psychotherapists have defied court attempts to require their testimony. These psychotherapists have been imprisoned, protested, or appealed their requirement to testify before the court, or both (*Binder v. Ruvell,* 1952; *Caesar v. Mountanos,* 1976; *Chidester v. Needles,* 1984; *In re "B,"* 1978; *In re Lifschutz,* 1970). At times psychotherapists have appeared to resist the courts' demands for information because of principled belief in the sanctity of confidentiality. At other times, the psychotherapists' resistance occurred when they were being investigated for welfare fraud and abuse. In these situations, any principled resistance may become mixed with attempts to avoid effective prosecution of alleged crimes. These are isolated examples, however, and overall it appears that mental health professionals will not present widespread resistance to testifying.

Third, the public fosters and supports psychotherapeutic relationships. The federal and state governments have authorized public moneys for state hospitals and community mental health centers. In addition, institutions such as the armed services, prisons, universities, and some industries make psychotherapy available. Also, states require psychiatrists and psychologists to meet minimum licensing requirements for independent private practice. This widespread support demonstrates the belief that mental health services remediate or prevent social ills and benefit the public. Advocates claim that psychotherapy has the potential to reduce the need for involuntary psychiatric hospitalization and acts to deter child abuse, suicide, juvenile delinquency, and criminal behavior. It is believed that psychotherapy can alleviate the emotional distress of patients and strengthen family relationships.

Finally, an increase in the effectiveness in the administration of justice will not compensate for the injury done to psychotherapy. Although no empirical evidence exists on this subject, it appears that the courts lose little information because of the psychotherapist-patient privilege. Much of the information obtained in psychotherapy deals with attitudes, feelings, or other psychological experiences irrelevant to the issue before the court (Slovenko and Usdin, 1961). Often the court may obtain the desired information elsewhere, such as from lay witnesses who know the patient.

The waivers and exceptions to the privilege greatly minimize its adverse impact. Patients may waive the privilege explicitly by their words or actions or implicitly by making nonconfidential disclosures of the same information. Also, patients automatically waive the privilege if they enter their mental health into litigation (see Chapter 6). Finally, states commonly make exceptions to the privilege in certain proceedings of high social importance such as suspected child abuse or involuntary civil commitments (Chapter 7).

Even if the privilege stands, courts can gain psychological information through a court-ordered independent examination. That examination may aid the court more than the psychotherapist's testimony because the court-appointed examiner will focus on questions at issue before the court (Rappeport, 1982). The independent examination does not harm the purpose of the psychotherapist-patient privilege because it has no pretext of treatment and does not deter the patient from seeking psychotherapy elsewhere.

One of the biggest difficulties in justifying the privilege is in proving the extent of harm to psychotherapy if the privilege did not exist. No doubt some patients would experience emotional damage as a consequence of unwanted judicial disclosures. The larger harm, however, would probably come from patients who fail to seek psychotherapy or who are inhibited in sharing information in their psychotherapy sessions.

The major argument for the deterrence hypothesis comes from its face validity or commonsense appearance. It is buttressed by the experiences of psychotherapists who have dealt with reluctant clients. Empirical evidence of the utility of the privilege (reviewed in Chapter 3) is supportive but not conclusive. The problem of perspective enters here. Judges and lawyers see first hand how privileges withhold evidence from court and thwart the fair administration of justice. By contrast, they cannot observe the benefits of privilege outside the courtroom. Psychotherapists see first hand how confidentiality concerns inhibit the progress of psychotherapy. By contrast, they do not observe its harmful effects on courtroom proceedings. More conclusive empirical demonstrations of how confidentiality promotes psychotherapy will increase legislative and judicial acceptance of the psychotherapist-patient privilege.

Saltzburg's Criteria. Saltzburg has been a leading expert on the law of evidence, and legal scholars frequently cite his work (Saltzburg, 1980; Saltzburg and Redden, 1982). Saltzburg, like Wigmore, takes a utilitarian approach to privileges, but Saltzburg emphasizes nonlitigation values more than Wigmore. Wigmore appears to stress the needs of the court for information, while Saltzburg emphasizes the societal benefit gained by protecting certain relationships.

Saltzburg claims that courts should consider four questions when attempting to balance the nonlitigation values found in privilege law. First, does the privilege concern a relationship that has typically received special solicitude from the government? Second, has the solicitude involved concern for the privacy of that relationship? Third, would reasonable persons find that disclosure of the information would threaten the relationship or cause the individual to suffer unwarranted harm? Finally, is the privacy claim still valued today? If the court answered "no" to any one of these questions, then the privilege would not be recognized. If the court answered "yes" to all these questions, then it should ask two additional questions to determine the appropriateness of the privilege. (1) Does the privilege conceal evidence that otherwise would be created or available to the court? (2) Is the loss of the information to the court an acceptable price to pay for the nonlitigation values? Saltzburg evaluated the psychotherapist-patient relationship according to his criteria, and he concluded that it merits privileged status.

Saltzburg correctly points out that privileged relationships create information that would otherwise be unavailable to the courts because it would not exist. At times courts can be criticized for focusing on the *ex post* question: now that this information exists, what would be the harm in this particular case if the information were revealed. Instead courts should consider the *ex ante* question: "To what extent will the privilege promote the creation of information that might otherwise not exist?" (1980, p. 600, n. 9). Although the court may enhance its fact-finding mission by creating an exception to a privilege in one case, it limits the ability of psychotherapists to create additional information in subsequent cases.

Nonutilitarian (Intrinsic) View

The nonutilitarian, noninstrumentalist, or intrinsic basis for the privilege states that the privilege of privacy should have legal significance regardless of its ability to achieve certain social goals. It rests on the belief that privacy is an end in and of itself. The intrinsic perspective holds that certain areas of human relationships are integral parts of human dignity and ought to be free from state interference (Black, 1975; Krattenmacher, 1973; Louisell, 1956; 1957; Louisell and Sinclair, 1971). The intrinsic rationale for the privilege differs from that of Wigmore and Saltzburg in that privacy need not have an ultimate utilitarian aspect in order to be justified. It is wrong, according to Louisell, to consider privileges only as exclusionary rules. They are primarily a protection of freedom of communication from state interference and become exclusionary rules by the chance litigation.

The intrinsic rationale for the privilege differs from that of Wigmore and Saltzburg in that justification for privacy need not have a utilitarian basis. Instead, Louisell argues that "there are things more important to human liberty than accurate adjudication" (1956, p. 110). It is difficult to compare the loss caused by the invasion of privacy with the loss caused by the lack of information in courts. No utilitarian argument is completely adequate here because the balance of privacy against accurate adjudication "involves value judgments, the testing of which, as far as known to this writer, is presently subject to no scientific technique" (Louisell, 1957, p. 750).

The area of privacy advocated by the intrinsic theorists is comparable to the area of privacy found in the tort theories for the invasion of privacy and in the decisions that have found a constitutional basis for the invasion of privacy. This area includes the intimate aspects of personal thoughts and acts, which Warren and Brandeis (1890) called the "inviolate personality." The average person desires to keep these topics from public disclosure. According to the constitutional theories of privacy, the government should not interfere unnecessarily in certain intimate areas, such as those dealing with marriage, sexual habits, or procreation. More detail on the constitutional decisions and their reasoning can be found in Chapter 2.

Absolutist Perspective

A final position that has been advocated is the absolutist position, which holds that "psychologists may not break the confidentiality of a patient or client under any circumstances" (Siegel, 1979, p. 249). Siegel does not encourage fellow psychotherapists to break the law but encourages them to work to change current laws so that they permit absolute confidentiality.

The absolutist position has little support within the legal profession, and we suspect that it has little support among mental health professionals as well. Among its shortcomings, it fails to consider nontherapeutic or litigation values, which may on occasion override the benefits of absolute confidentiality. Absolute confidentiality is costly in many ways. It means that reports of child abuse will not be made, that evidence will be withheld from courts, increasing the likelihood of any erroneous verdict, and that psychotherapists will be prohibited from breaching confidentiality to prevent assaults or suicides. If Siegel's position is taken to its logical extreme, then psychotherapists would stand by and do nothing while knowing that an innocent person is being harmed.

Despite its shortcomings, the absolutist position should not be dismissed in a perfunctory manner. It represents a dramatic statement of the importance of confidentiality. It also implies an empirical challenge that has not yet been addressed adequately. Will absolute confidentiality in the long run benefit society sufficiently to justify the loss of information to the courts? Unfortunately for Siegal's arguments, no evidence exists at this time to support the belief that absolute confidentiality or privilege will substantially improve the effectiveness of psychotherapy over the qualified confidentiality or privilege that currently exists. It should not be forgotten that psychotherapy has flourished in an atmosphere of qualified confidentiality.

Chapter 2

Constitutional Rulings Concerning the Privilege

Legislatures do not have absolute control over the nature of privileged communication laws. These and all other laws must not conflict with the standards of the U.S. Constitution or state constitutions as determined by the federal or state courts. Attempts have been made in the past 15 years to expand the privilege through the application of the constitutional right to privacy to privileged communication laws. Simultaneously, attempts have been made to restrict the privilege through the application of the Sixth Amendment right to confront adverse witnesses. This chapter will review these constitutional applications to the privilege.

CONSTITUTIONAL RIGHT TO PRIVACY

The right to privacy limits the degree of government intrusion into fundamental and sensitive areas of an individual's right. The right is not static, but court decisions have gradually developed it on a case-by-case basis. The exact parameters of the privacy zone will depend on the outcome of future court cases. Several courts have held that the psychotherapist-patient relationship falls within this constitutionally protected zone of privacy (e.g., *Caesar v. Mountanos,* 1976; *Hawaii Psychiatric Society v. Ariyoshi,* 1979; *In re Lifschutz,* 1970; *United States v. Layton,* 1981). These cases have been described in detail by several legal commentaries (Butler, 1971; Christensen,

1977; Davis, 1971; Maly, 1977; Note, 1972; Smith, 1980). Several other federal courts have discussed the constitutional basis for the privilege on privacy grounds. Each of these courts failed to reject categorically the possibility that the privilege may receive constitutional protection under certain circumstances (e.g., United States ex rel. *Edney v. Smith,* 1976; *Miller v. Colonial Refrigerated Transportation,* 1979; *Robinson v. Magovern,* 1979). In addition, justices in other courts have found that the privacy provisions within their state constitutions may provide grounds for acknowledging a psychotherapist-patient privilege (e.g., *Allred v. State,* 1976; *Falcon v. Alaska Public Offices Commission,* 1977; *In re "B,"* 1978; *Reynaud v. Superior Court,* 1982).

At first this may seem like a major expansion of the privilege for psychotherapy patients, but it is not. First, the Supreme Court has never addressed this issue. Consequently the lower courts will decide any constitutional basis for the privilege on a case-by-case basis. Although several courts have recognized the constitutional basis for the privilege, others have rejected it (e.g., *Bremer v. State,* 1973; *Felber v. Foote,* 1970; *Pratt v. State,* 1978; *State v. Enebak,* 1978). (*Felber v. Foote* is discussed in detail in Note, 1972.) In fact, only a few courts have recognized a constitutional basis for the privilege outside the California Supreme Court in *In re Lifschutz.* Furthermore, even if a court found a constitutional basis for the privilege, the courts would still subject it to the same waivers and exceptions as privileges created by statutes. Finally, a contrary constitutional trend has emerged by which some courts have overruled privilege laws when they conflict with the Sixth Amendment right to confront adverse witnesses.

BACKGROUND OF CONSTITUTIONAL RIGHT TO PRIVACY

The U.S. Supreme Court first articulated the constitutional right to privacy in *Griswold v. Connecticut* (1965). This decision struck down a Connecticut law forbidding the sale of birth control devices. Although no constitutional amendment specifically protects the intimacies within marriage, the Court held that the right to be left alone was a common theme running through several amendments (First Amendment: freedom of speech and religion; Fourth Amendment: prohibition against self-incrimination; Ninth Amendment: reserve power to people that is not explicitly granted to the states). It should be noted that the judges in *Griswold* reached a 5-4 decision, and each of the affirming justices had slightly different reasons for reaching his decision.

Subsequent court cases have expanded this right to privacy. In *Eisenstadt v. Baird* (1972), a person was allowed to distribute contraceptives to unmarried persons. In *Roe v. Wade* (1973), the court limited government intrusion into the right to have an abortion in certain situations. It is important to notice that these cases deal with the reproductive or marital relationship and the physician-patient relationship.

Although the protection of the right to privacy may be substantial, it is not unlimited, and it must yield when the state has a compelling and narrowly drawn interest. For example, in *Whalen v. Roe* (1977) the Supreme Court upheld a state law requiring pharmacists to furnish information about patient use of certain dangerous drugs. The control of these dangerous, but legal, drugs was considered a legitimate exercise of state authority.

Application of Constitutional Principles to Psychotherapist-Patient Privilege

Several cases resulted in federal courts' acknowledging that the constitutional basis of privacy applies to the psychotherapist-patient relationship. Some of the more notable cases are reviewed in detail here.

In re Lifschutz. This case arose out of a lawsuit initiated by Mr. Housek, a former client of Dr. Lifschutz, who was allegedly assaulted and suffered "physical injuries, pain, suffering, and severe mental and emotional distress" (p. 6). Housek stated that he had received psychiatric treatment from Lifschutz over a six-month period approximately ten years before. Although Housek neither expressly claimed nor waived the privilege, the court concluded that Housek had implicitly waived the privilege because he had entered his mental health into the proceedings.

Lifschutz refused to obey a court order to answer questions concerning his communications with Housek. Lifschutz claimed, *inter alia,* that the court order was invalid because it infringed upon the constitutional right to privacy of his patient. The court agreed with Lifschutz in part. It held that patients had a "zone of privacy" and that the psychotherapeutic relationship fell within that zone. The conclusion was based in large part on the Supreme Court case of *Griswold v. Connecticut* (1965). But the court held that the zone of privacy was not absolute and would have to yield to a narrowly drawn and compelling state interest. Here Housek had entered his mental health into the proceedings by claiming that the assault caused him severe mental distress, and therefore the patient-litigant exception to the privilege applied. (This exception is well established in privilege law and is discussed in detail in Chapter 6.) According to this exception, patients who enter their mental health as an issue in a legal proceeding cannot subsequently claim the privilege. They cannot claim harm and then deprive the court of means to evaluate adequately the claim of harm.

Caesar v. Mountanos. The controlling facts in *Caesar* are similar to those in *Lifschutz.* Dr. Caesar, a California psychiatrist, was treating a woman following a traffic accident. The patient was referred to Caesar because her attending physician thought that her condition might have been the result of a conversion reaction or depressive reaction. The patient then sued the driver of the vehicle, alleging that the accident caused her personal injury and pain, as well as emotional and mental distress.

The court subpoened Caesar, who acknowledged that he had treated the woman for depression, but he refused to answer questions regarding the relationship of the emotional condition to the accident. The court found Caesar in contempt, and he sought relief in federal court after having exhausted the state's remedies.

Caesar based his claim on grounds similar to *Lifschutz,* but it was strengthened by arguments that the subsequent Supreme Court cases of *Roe v. Wade* (1973) and *Doe v. Bolton* (1973) had extended the constitutional right of privacy to include the psychotherapist-patient relationship within its ambit. The court did not accept Caesar's claim. Both the *Roe* and *Doe* decisions spoke of a conditional right of privacy in the doctor-patient relationship, but, like *Lifschutz,* that right is not absolute and must yield to compelling state interest such as the need for information in court. The court ruled, "We have no doubt that the right of privacy relied on by Dr. Caesar is substantial. However, the right is conditional rather than absolute and limited impairment of that right may be allowed if properly justified" (p. 1068). Like Housek in *Lifschutz*, Caesar's patient had entered her mental health into the litigation and implicitly waived her privilege.

The *Caesar* case was notable for an articulate dissent by Justice Hufstedler, who parted company with her colleagues in interpreting the patient-litigant waiver in this case. The justice gave greater weight to the importance of privacy in psychotherapeutic communications than her colleagues. She stated that "although the right [of privacy] is not absolute, it enters the combat zone heavily armed" (p. 1072). Justice Hufstedler would have limited the information available under the patient-litigant exception to the fact of treatment, the time and length of treatment, the cost of treatment, and the final diagnosis unless the party seeking disclosure of the communications establishes a compelling need for more extensive information. Subsequent California cases have continued to hold that the psychotherapist-patient relationship falls within the constitutional zone of privacy (e.g., *Board of Medical Quality Assurance v. Gheradini,* 1979; *Britt v. Superior Court of San Diego,* 1978; *Jones v. Superior Court for County of Alameda,* 1981; *Roberts v. Superior Court,* 1973). These rulings, however, have not extended the scope of the privilege beyond that already found within the statutory language. They may, however, encourage courts to interpret privilege laws broadly to protect constitutional rights (*Roberts v. Superior Court,* 1973).

Hawaii Psychiatric Society v. Ariyoshi. The federal case of *Hawaii Psychiatric Society v. Ariyoshi* (1979) also found a constitutional right to privacy. In this case, the government investigated a psychologist in private practice, Dr. Willis, for possible Medicare fraud or abuse. The Hawaii attorney general produced a warrant and copied all of Willis's records. The investigators did not demonstrate any particular need to inspect Willis's records, nor had they requested him to produce the desired information voluntarily.

Willis acquired the support of the Hawaii Psychiatric Society (a majority of whom were Medicaid providers) and brought suit against Hawaiian state officials to enjoin the enforcement of the Hawaiian statute that authorized the issuance of administrative search warrants. They based the suit clearly upon the claim that these warrants violated the constitutional rights of privacy of the Medicaid patients. Willis and his fellow litigants found support in the federal court. The court ruled that the psychotherapist-patient relationship fell within the bounds of the constitutional right of privacy. It stated: "No area could be more deserving of protection than communications between a psychiatrist and his patient. Such communications often involve problems in precisely the area previously recognized by the Court as within the zone of protected privacy, including family, marriage, parenthood, human sexuality, and physical problems" (p. 1038). Like other courts, *Ariyoshi* did not consider the zone of privacy to be absolute. Relying on *Roe v. Wade,* the court held that the state may enter the zone of privacy if it has compelling interests that are narrowly drawn. In this case, the court restricted the enforcement of the search warrants to situations in which there is some individualized articulable suspicion.

Privacy Based on State Constitutions

In several cases, state courts have found a privilege based largely on state constitutional rights to privacy. State constitutions sometimes include provisions that make the right to privacy more explicit than found in the federal constitution. The first case, *Allred v. State* (1976), involved the confession of a murder by a mental health patient to his psychiatric social worker. This patient was also being seen concurrently by a psychiatrist, and the psychiatric social worker was obviously working under the direct supervision of the psychiatrist. The court recognized the communications to the psychiatrist as privileged, although the privilege was not found within Alaska's statutes. The court also held that the psychiatric social worker was working as an extension of the physician and would be covered by his privilege. The decision was based in part on common law principles, but other concurring judges sought provisions within the Alaska Constitution to justify their decision.

In *Falcon v. Alaska Public Offices Commission* (1977), the Alaska Supreme Court ruled on a conflict of interest law that required a physician who held a minor public office to disclose financial records, including the names of his patients. The court held that this provision of the law violated the right of privacy as found in the Alaska Constitution. It held that the potential damage to the patients outweighed the state's interest in the information. Some patients had seen the doctor for highly personal reasons, including psychiatric illness or abortions.

Another case, *In re "B"* (1978), is noteworthy because it involved a patient of a forensic psychiatrist, Loren Roth. In this case, the court wanted access to the mental health records of the juvenile's mother to help determine the optimal placement for the child. Roth appealed to the Pennsylvania Supreme Court and, in a footnote to the brief, mentioned that the physician-patient privilege should have federal constitutional protection. The supreme court issued a ruling in favor of Roth, which has been succinctly summarized in an article by Dr. Roth's attorney, Alan Meisel. The split ruling contained confusing language, and the different bases on which the judges made their ruling were not altogether clear. "This is a very confused opinion. First, it takes something akin to higher mathematics to determine which justices concurred in the reasoning of the court's opinion and which merely concurred in the result for other (nonconstitutional) reasons" (Meisel, 1982, p. 39, n. 168). The decision appears to be based in part on common law, in part on federal constitutional law, and in part on Pennsylvania constitutional law.

The *Allred, Falcon,* and *In re "B"* decisions have had limited impact beyond their specific cases. The Alaska legislature has since enacted a privilege law based on the proposed Federal Rules of Evidence (see Chapter 4), thus displacing the common law privilege created by the Alaska Supreme Court. The Pennsylvania courts have largely avoided challenges to *In re "B"* so that it is unclear whether subsequent courts would uphold the decision.

The California case of *Reynaud v. Superior Court* (1982) also sought to expand the psychotherapist-patient privilege on the basis of Article 1, section 1, of the California Constitution, which gives a right to privacy. It was unclear why the litigants based their claim on the constitutional right to privacy as found in the California Constitution alone instead of also relying on a federal constitutional right, which had been recognized by previous California courts. It is assumed that the litigants perceived the California constitutional right as broader or more explicit than any federal right.

In this case, a physician requested an adversary hearing to determine if the subpoena issued by the fraud unit investigators of Medi-Cal conflicted with the privacy rights of his patients. Although the *Reynaud* court recognized a constitutional right of privacy, it noted that the state did not have to have a preliminary hearing on the privacy rights of the patients:

> The scope of the privacy clause is potentially enormous and the variety of circumstances in which it might be invoked is essentially infinite. To require a noticed preliminary judicial determination whenever privacy rights are arguably involved would severely, and in our view unnecessarily, restrict the state's capacity to conduct

legitimate inquiries. Administration of the privacy clause, like the right of privacy itself, should take adequate account of all competing interests in the circumstances of each case. (p. 664)

It is prudent not to read too much into the application of a constitutional basis to psychotherapist-patient communications. Outside California, the case law has had little impact beyond the immediate case. Although California courts will recognize the psychotherapist-patient communications as falling within the constitutionally protected zone, it is doubtful that this added basis would have extended the protection beyond that already found in California's psychotherapist-patient privilege laws.

Three factors account for the limited impact of the constitutional basis arguments. First, it may not be desirable to freeze the privilege in constitutional ice. Privileges should grow or shrink in response to debates in courts or legislatures. To establish a fixed or unyielding basis for the privilege may prevent the experimentation, debate, and case law history necessary to the development of privilege law (Saltzburg, 1980; Weinstein, opinion in *United States ex rel. Edney v. Smith,* 1976; Weinstein, opinion in *Lora v. Board of Education,* 1977). Second, in certain situations, privileges may jeopardize other fundamental constitutional rights, such as the right of a criminal to get a fair trial and confront witnesses as stipulated in the Sixth Amendment. Finally, statutory laws provide an alternate basis for protecting these communications. Most noticeable in this regard has been the development of the privilege under Rule 501 of the Federal Rule of Evidence. This rule, which is discussed in detail in Chapter 4, allows the federal courts to acknowledge privileges, such as the psychotherapist-patient privilege, on the basis of "common law and experience."

CONSTITUTIONAL LIMITS TO THE PRIVILEGE

Not all of the constitutional arguments have been used to support or expand the privilege. At times, the privilege may interfere with the Sixth Amendment, which holds that criminal defendants have a right to a fair trial and a right to confront their accusers. At times, defendants have not had an opportunity to confront their accusers adequately because these witnesses have shielded information regarding their credibility from the courts through privileged communication laws. The U.S. Supreme Court has articulated limits to the privilege in cases unrelated to mental health (*Davis v. Alaska,* 1974; *United States v. Nixon,* 1974; *Washington v. State,* 1967). Despite the disparate issues involved in these cases, certain generalizations have emerged. The claim of privilege may be challenged when (1) the privileged material may exonerate an individual charged with a crime and (2) when the privileged material will cast doubt on the accuracy of the adverse testimony.

The privilege will not always be waived when a conflict appears between the right of confrontation and the privilege. The Supreme Court doctrine includes two important qualifications. First, the right to present an adequate defense depends to some degree on how critically the defense needs the privileged material. "The evidence sought by the defense must appear important to the defense and must not be available from other sources" (Smith, 1980, p. 56). The privilege may stand if the privileged material is cumulative (redundant) or of less probative value. Second, the legislature may rewrite the laws to allow the dismissal or modification of the case instead of violating the privilege. Although this may appear to be an extreme price to pay to maintain a privilege, the standards of the Supreme Court permit it (Cleary, 1984; Smith, 1980).

Several lower court cases have dealt with this Sixth Amendment limitation on the privilege in mental health cases. For example, in *State v. Hembd* (1975), a man was charged with false imprisonment after he tried to force a woman into his car. He argued that the woman had been speaking to him inside the bar and threatened suicide. He claimed that he was acting only to protect her life. The plaintiff acknowledged one suicide attempt but denied subsequent attempts. The defendant wanted her hospital records admitted into court to impeach her testimony. The Minnesota Supreme Court held that the medical privilege of the plaintiff's records must yield to the Sixth Amendment right to confront witnesses and remanded the case to the trial court for a new trial. One commentator did not quarrel with the principle followed by *Hembd* but suggested that the unique facts of this case made it appear that the medical records had little probative value and were unnecessary for a successful resolution of the case. Specifically, it was noted that the alleged assailant tried to elude the police after they arrived in response to the victim's cries. If the assailant really wanted only to protect the life of the woman, he would have welcomed the arrival of the police and not tried to avoid them (Note, 1976*a*).

Other cases have reached similar conclusions as *Hembd.* In *United States v. Lindstrom* (1983), the chief witness for the prosecution had a psychiatric history that included suicide attempts, threats to kill others, and several involuntary hospitalizations. The psychiatric reports described her as egocentric, immature, and manipulative in relationships with others. The defense lawyer claimed that she had told others that she was "out to get" the defendants. This statement was consistent with the vindictive and hostile nature described in her psychiatric reports. The court ordered a new trial, allowing the defendants access to her psychiatric records in order to impeach her credibility.

In *State v. Roma* (1976), the New Jersey Supreme Court ruled that the absolute privilege granted to marriage counselors in New Jersey was unconstitutional because it interfered with the right of the defendant to present an adequate defense. "Evidential limitations may be adopted by a state, but such limitations . . . must not impinge upon the provisions of the Constitution pertaining to due process. . . . When to sustain the exercise of a privilege, such as that here in issue, would compromise fundamental constitutional rights, judicial recognition of that privilege must be withheld" (p. 51).

New Hampshire cases have followed the Sixth Amendment qualification of the privilege but have noted that the waiver is not necessarily absolute. The Sixth Amendment "does not give the defendant a right to the blanket use of privileged information" (*State v. Farrow,* 1976, p. 1179). Instead, the defendant's right is limited to materials "found to be essential and reasonably necessary to permit counsel adequately to cross examine for the purpose of showing unreliability or bias" (p. 1179). Furthermore, the trial court should examine the records *in camera* to determine which parts, if any, the defendant may use "to protect the witnesses from unnecessary embarrassment" (p. 1179).

Other courts have recognized the principle of confrontation found in the Sixth Amendment but have found that it was not applicable in their cases. In *State v. Thresher* (1982), the trial court found that the state had developed an adequate case without the testimony of one witness. Consequently it refused to waive the privilege to impeach the testimony of the witness whose evidence was cumulative. In *State v. Bruno* (1984), the Appellate Court of Connecticut reached a similar conclusion and refused to allow an *in camera* inspection of the mental health records of the witness.

Past litigation had construed the Sixth Amendment as limiting the extent of the privilege in certain situations. A unique interpretation occurred in *M. v. K.* (1982) when a court ruled that the Fourteenth Amendment could be used to override a claim of privilege in a child custody case. Perhaps the critical element in this case was the possibility that the child had been a victim of sexual abuse. Thus the court was concerned not only with finding the best environment for the child but also with protecting the child from a substantially harmful environment.

The court noted that it has no higher duty than the "safety, happiness, and physical, mental, and moral welfare of [the] child" (p. 704) and said that the failure to create an exception to the privilege in this case could jeopardize the child's chance of having a minimally acceptable quality of life. It was held that the child's rights under the New Jersey Constitution and U.S. Constitution were implicated. Under the New Jersey Constitution, the child had the right of "pursuing and obtaining safety and happiness" (N.J.S.A. Constitution, Article 1, paragraph 1). Also, the court cited the Fourteenth

Amendment of the U.S. Constitution, which reads in part that no "state shall deprive any person of life, liberty, or property, without due process of law; nor deny to any person within its jurisdiction the equal protection of the law." Other statutory and common law rules regarding information in child welfare cases are discussed in Chapter 7.

Chapter 3

Empirical Research on Confidentiality and Privilege

Several theories have been used to justify privileged communication laws. The dominant scholars, Wigmore and Satzburg, base their theories largely on utilitarian grounds. The social benefits of the privilege will outweigh its harm, they believe. The utilitarian perspective assumes the privilege will encourage people to seek professional help or will encourage clients already in psychotherapy to disclose relevant information freely. DeKraai and Sales correctly concluded that "these are not legal questions but behavioral questions in need of empirical investigations" (1982, p. 376).

The research on the effects of privacy on disclosure or participation in psychotherapy is small but growing. Most studies do not directly address the effects of privileged communication laws but deal with disclosure in nonjudicial situations. The effects of disclosure in nonjudicial situations may provide clues to how disclosure in court would affect clients. This chapter will review the research on confidentiality in psychotherapy and, as much as possible, apply the research findings to the issue of privileged communications in court.

This area is difficult to investigate. It would be unethical to modify systematically the extent of confidentiality or privilege available to persons seeking psychotherapy or to persons already in psychotherapy. Such a design would have the potential to harm the participants, making it unacceptable. Consequently researchers have looked for less harmful means to evaluate the confidentiality premise. The common strategies are to survey psychotherapists, outpatients, or members of the public or to conduct analogue studies. Both the survey and analogue strategies have advantages and disadvantages. Surveys of psychotherapists are important because psychotherapists deal directly with their clients and should be able to judge the impact of privilege (or lack of privilege) on their clients. The shortcomings of surveys of psychotherapists are that psychotherapists may be blinded by preconceived notions concerning privilege, or they may be biased because they perceive privileges as enhancing their professional status. Surveys of patients or laypersons should help ascertain the effects of confidentiality on their willingness to benefit from psychotherapy. But the shortcomings of surveys are well documented in survey research (Bobbie, 1973; Dillman, 1978; Lockhart, 1984). Respondents often give socially desirable responses that do not reflect their true feelings. Also, because so few patients or laypersons have been to court on these issues, they may not know their reaction until such an event occurs.

The final research procedure, analogue research, systematically varies the conditions of confidentiality and privilege in an experimental situation. But these experiments are conducted with nonpatients, usually college students, who perform the studies in partial fulfillment of course requirements or for a small remuneration. Because these studies are simulations, they do not have all of the ethical problems of research with actual patients. They are useful only if the results are externally valid; that is, the results must generalize to actual patient populations. The results with students theoretically are analogous to the results that would be found with a patient population (Kazdin, 1978). No study has been conducted to measure the external validity of analogue studies of confidentiality.

SURVEYS OF MENTAL HEALTH PROFESSIONALS

Surveys of mental health professionals have found that they overwhelmingly endorse confidentiality as essential in maintaining a positive psychotherapeutic relationship (Jagim, Wittman, and Noll, 1978). A recent survey showed that psychologists considered the maintenance of confidentiality as their most important ethical responsibility (Crowe et al., 1985). In addition, psychologists and psychiatrists were less willing to breach confidentiality than a sample of internists (Lindenthal and Thomas, 1980) or a sample of patients and laypersons (Lindenthal and Thomas, 1982). These studies demonstrate the belief among mental health professionals that confidentiality is the sine qua non of the profession. This perception is apparently communicated well to the public because most psychiatric patients assume that their disclosures will be held in confidence and that their therapists are trustworthy with sensitive information (Appelbaum et al., 1984; Schmid et al., 1983; Shuman and Weiner, 1982).

Most professionals do not believe that confidentiality is absolute, and they believe that they may breach it in certain circumstances of high social importance. For example, research suggests that mental health professionals will sometimes breach confidentiality to protect third persons (Jagim, Wittman, and Noll, 1978; Muehleman and Kimmons, 1981; Weil and Sanchez, 1983, Wise, 1978). These surveys on the willingness to breach confidentiality, however, have a serious methodological flaw. They asked professionals if they are willing to breach confidentiality to protect a third person but failed to specify the factual circumstances or the alternatives to breaching confidentiality.

Lindenthal and co-workers (1984) attempted to remedy this flaw in the survey method. They requested mental health practitioners in U.S. medical schools to respond to ten vignettes representing a range of student problems. The respondents could select one of four to six alternatives for the vignette. Results showed that the mental health practitioners were reluctant to breach confidentiality in a wide range of situations, such as "escalating suicidal thoughts," "substance abuse," or "sexual seduction of a patient." They were much more willing to breach confidentiality when the lives of third persons were involved, such as in a "bomb threat." This study does not have the same limitations of the survey methods, but the conclusions are the same: mental health professionals are willing to breach confidentiality to protect third persons. Other than imminent danger to third persons, however, mental health professionals are extremely loathe to violate patient confidences.

SURVEYS WITH PATIENTS

Several surveys on confidentiality have been conducted among psychotherapy patients or counseling clients. Three of these studies dealt with possible disclosures with college student counselees. Simmons (1968) found that two-thirds of the college student counselees would not object to the release of certain kinds of information without explicit consent. The respondents, however, were selective about what kinds of information they were willing to have released and to whom.

Lewis and Warman (1964) administered a questionnaire concerning the release of counseling service information to three groups of students: those who had received vocational counseling, those who had received personal counseling, and those who had not received any counseling. The vocational and personal counseling groups differed significantly on 6 of 12 items. Students with personal counseling opposed the release of information without their permission more than did students with vocational counseling.

Anderson and Sherr (1969) extended this study by making a finer discrimination among the types of information that students would allow to be released. In general, students were more willing to have information released to friends or family and less willing to have it released to faculty or law enforcement agencies. Students who had received counseling, however, were less willing than noncounseled students to allow parental access to the data. On the whole, students were more willing to allow the release of less personal material such as aptitude test results or interest inventory results. They were less willing to release more personal material such as personality test results or information about personal problems. It can be concluded from these studies that college students are selective about what information they want released and to whom they want it released.

Miller and Thelen (1986) conducted a survey of mental health patients and nonpatient students concerning their attitude toward confidentiality. The majority of respondents believed that all communications to psychotherapists should be confidential. Almost all clients wanted to be informed of the exceptions to confidentiality, and most would react negatively to unauthorized breaches of confidentiality.

Two studies concerning patient attitudes toward disclosure were conducted at the Western Psychiatric Institute and Clinic in Pittsburgh (Appelbaum et al., 1984; Schmid et al., 1983). Although one study was conducted with inpatients and the other with outpatients, the results had a similar pattern. The vast majority of patients believed that confidentiality was important, and the fact that communications were confidential improved their relationships with the treatment staff. Most assumed that communications were confidential and would be upset by unauthorized disclosures. Patients' concerns about disclosure varied according to the nature of the disclosure (and presumably the degree of potential harm to the patient). For example, few patients felt concern if data were released to another physician to aid in treatment. Most, however, would be upset if the same information were released to their employer. Some patients responded that they would react to unauthorized disclosures by requesting another therapist, terminating psychotherapy, complaining to the psychotherapist's supervisor, or initiating a lawsuit.

A recent study by McGuire, Toal, and Blau (1985) assessed the factual knowledge and personal values that adult inpatients and outpatients placed on confidentiality and privilege. The usefulness of the results as presented, however, is limited because the authors combined factual knowledge with subjective value of confidentiality into one total score. The presentation of the data therefore does not further the understanding of the effects of confidentiality or privilege on psychotherapy.

ANALOGUE STUDIES

Several analogue studies have dealt with the issue of confidentiality. Meyer and Willage (1980) found that subjects who were instructed that their disclosures would not be confidential reported the most socially desirable responses. The students who were instructed that their responses were confidential produced the most pathological symptoms. The authors inferred that the lack of confidentiality influenced students to minimize their problems to "look good."

Woods and McNamara (1980) administered a battery of standard interview items to undergraduate students under three conditions: promised confidentiality, no confidentiality, or no mention of confidentiality. The students who received a promise of confidentiality were more open in their disclosures than those who were told there would be no confidentiality.

Contrary results were found by Kobocow, McGuire, and Blau (1983). Junior high school students were split into three groups of promised confidentiality, promised nonconfidentiality, and no mention of confidentiality. The three groups did not differ significantly in the number of problems reported. This study was flawed by the fact that many students reported that confidentiality instructions were given to them when in fact they were not. The authors surmised that the use of a secluded interview room may have led students to assume confidentiality although the actual instructions were to the contrary.

Merluzzi and Brischetto (1983) studied the effect of counselor breaches of confidences on trustworthiness. The students heard audiotapes of counselor-client interactions that culminated in the decision of the counselor to breach or to maintain confidentiality. The authors found that the counselors who breached confidentiality for highly serious problems lost trustworthiness in the eyes of the students. In addition, subjects were more likely to refer friends or to predict a favorable outcome when counselors maintained confidentiality. The authors concluded that any decision to breach confidentiality may result in a loss of influence with the client.

Finally, Tillinghast and VandeCreek (1985) studied the confidentiality expectations and preferences of college students regarding disclosure of counseling information. They presented the students with ten vignettes of clinical problems ranging from career and educational concerns, to drinking problems, to suicide and harm to others. Each clinical problem contained eight potential disclosure situations (e.g., disclosure to potential employer, parents, insurance company, journal article).

Subjects were asked how much information they would expect and prefer to be disclosed. In general, subjects preferred less information to be divulged than they expected their counselor to disclose. Disclosure of information, however, was dependent on the seriousness of the problem and the recipient of the information. They expected more information to be divulged about career and educational concerns than any other problem. They expected and preferred less information to be divulged to potentially harmful recipients and to persons outside the counseling agency. Finally, they preferred that their counselor share more information about their own case file than they expected their counselor would be willing to do.

What emerges from these survey and analogue studies is a pattern whereby clients strongly disapprove of unauthorized disclosures of information. These disclosures would have the "chilling effect" on psychotherapy that had been the basis of numerous commentaries (see Chapter 1). Unauthorized disclosures could interfere with the progress of therapy and even result in termination or legal suits. But for the most part, clients trust their psychotherapists with their personal information and do not expect their confidences to be breached.

Another pattern that emerges is that patients do not regard all information as equally sensitive. They are loathe to release highly personal information but less concerned about less personal information. It appears that any kind of "uniformity myth" with regard to client information should be avoided.

EMPIRICAL STUDIES OF PRIVILEGED COMMUNICATION

Several studies have dealt specifically with privileged communications and not confidentiality. In the first study, Meyer and Smith (1977) administered questionnaires to subjects in two groups, asking their preferred degree of involvement in group therapy. They told one group that their statements would not be confidential and the second group that their statements would be confidential but would not be privileged in case of a court order. Students preferred the confidentiality-but-no-privilege group over the no-confidentiality group. The study provides more support for the need for privacy in psychotherapy but no useful information on the benefits of a privileged communication law. To address that issue, it would have been better to compare a confidentiality-with-no-privilege group with a confidentiality-with-privilege group (DeKraai and Sales, 1982).

Four articles have provided survey information on privileged communications. In the first article (Comment, 1962), a survey found that most psychologists, marriage counselors, social workers, and psychiatrists favored a privileged communication law and believed clients would be less open if they thought there were no protective law. Laypersons were less likely to make free and complete disclosure to mental health professionals without such a law. The majority of lawyers who were interviewed favored a privilege for psychiatrists, and a minority favored the privilege for psychologists or marriage counselors. It may be relevant that this survey occurred about 25 years ago, before psychologists and psychiatrists were seen as functional equivalents to psychotherapists.

Shuman and Weiner (1982) conducted an extensive study on the effect of the privileged communication statute in Texas. In the first part of their study, they monitored the change in utilization of Blue Cross/Blue Shield insurance reimbursements for psychotherapy after the passage of Texas's privileged communication law. They found no change in the utilization rate. Their study, however, does not provide evidence that the presence of a privilege would not affect utilization rates. As they found in another part of their study, most of the lay public and most of the patients surveyed did not know there was a privileged communication law. In fact, some of the judges they surveyed did not know there was one either.

In the same study, Shuman and Weiner (1982) surveyed a number of laypersons, patients, psychotherapists, and judges. The laypersons stated that they would be less likely to discuss certain problems such as speeding, physical violence, income tax fraud, or theft with their psychotherapist if it were not for the privilege. Most of the patients surveyed did not know there was a privilege law, but only 8% would have started psychotherapy sooner if they knew there was such a law. Shuman and Weiner also surveyed 84 psychiatrists. Only 39 had ever received a request to appear in court, and only 13 ever had appeared in court. Although most patients were not bothered by the court appearance, two terminated therapy and two had therapy diverted because of the testimony. Only a few of the Texas judges surveyed recalled using mental health testimony in court, and at least one did not know the existence of the privilege law and several had only a vague familiarity with it.

Weiner and Shuman (1984) published a second empirical article concerning privilege. In this study, they surveyed a sample of psychiatric patients concerning their understanding of privileged communication laws and the impact of these laws on their willingness to participate in psychotherapy. The authors surveyed patients in two states without a psychiatrist-patient privilege (South Carolina and West Virginia) and patients in one state with a psychiatrist-patient privilege (Texas). They found that only a small percentage of patients would have started psychotherapy sooner if they had known of a privilege law. Most patients never asked about privilege or confidentiality at all. The authors concluded that "the existence or nonexistence of a privilege statute seemed to have little impact on the conduct of therapy" (p. 381).

A final study, by Corcoran, Breeskin, and Court (1977), investigated the impact of the lack of a privilege on the psychiatric help seeking of U.S. Air Force officers. The air force, like the other branches of the armed services, does not have a psychotherapist-client privilege. Anonymous questionnaires were sent to 1,048 air force officers. The proportion of officers stating that they would use mental health facilities if needed was comparable to a civilian population with an equal education level. Of those officers who would seek mental health services, 61% would seek them from a civilian psychotherapist. Of those preferring a civilian psychotherapist, 60% said that they did so because military psychotherapists lacked privilege protection. Neither cost nor money was the primary motivation. Over 80% of the respondents would go to a military psychotherapist if there was privilege protection. Many of the respondents who preferred the military psychotherapists were unaware of the lack of privilege. The authors concluded that the "lack of a psychotherapist privilege is one reason for under utilization of Air Force mental health facilities by officers" (p. 83).

This study appears to support the utilitarian basis of a privilege. It is not clear, however, how the results generalize to civilian populations. In addition to the lack of privilege, Air Force psychotherapists may also have different confidentiality regulations that are more porous than those of state governments. Perhaps the air force officers were responding in part to a lack of confidentiality in extrajudicial situations, as well as judicial situations. This wide difference in the privilege and confidentiality laws may explain the discrepancy found in the findings of Corcoran, Breeskin, and Court (1977), Shuman and Weiner (1982), and Weiner and Shuman (1984).

The research on the effects of confidentiality and privilege on psychotherapy is in its early stages. The research is replete with methodological problems, such as vagueness in defining terms, using different instruments to measure attitudes toward confidentiality, combining knowledge of confidentiality with attitudes toward it, and the use of nonrandom survey samples. Despite these problems, researchers should be commended for taking the first steps in studying this important issue. Future research can build on their initial foundations.

Despite the methodological limitations, a few generalizations emerge. First, the research indicates that clients value confidentiality, and it increases their amount of self-disclosure within psychotherapy. Second, the expectation of confidentiality makes laypersons more willing to seek psychotherapy. In addition, most clients appear to expect confidentiality and assume their psychotherapists will respect their wishes. When it comes to releasing information, clients do not view all information equally. They may be relatively unconcerned about the release of impersonal or less sensitive information if it does not appear to have the potential to harm them. On the other hand, they could react strongly to unauthorized releases with the potential to harm them.

This survey leaves plenty of room for the old adage, "More research is needed." The few studies in the area need replication to ensure external validity or application to different patient populations. In addition, future research can focus on whether the privilege affects all clients or potential clients equally. For example, a privilege statute may influence clients who are concerned about child custody, paranoid or suspicious, or with violent thoughts or tendencies more than clients with other types of problems. Shuman and Weiner are probably correct when they state that the privilege laws are inconsequential for the majority of patients. Most patients do not consider litigation when they seek psychotherapy. Of course, this does not mean that a privilege would not fulfill a utilitarian function. A privilege law might be quite important for a minority who need psychotherapy badly.

Chapter 4

Overview of Current Privileged Communication Laws

State or federal law may govern privileged communications law. Each state is sovereign under the federal system except for powers specifically reserved for the federal government. Consequently the United States does not have one legal system but 51. The wide differences in federal and state laws may appear unnecessarily confusing, but the federal system is one of the bulwarks of American government, and it has its advantages. As Justice Brandeis stated: "It is one of the happy incidents of the federal system that a single courageous state may, if its citizens choose, serve as a laboratory; and try novel social and economic experiments without risk to the rest of the country" (*New State Ice Company v. Liebmann,* 1931, p. 311). The courts are loathe to interfere with the legislative prerogative to write laws unless they violate constitutional principles. "We have frequently recognized that individual States have broad latitude in experimenting with possible solutions to problems of vital local concern" (*Whalen v. Roe,* 1977, p. 875).

State legislatures write most privileged communication laws. This chapter will discuss the general nature of these laws and will review the isolated cases of common law privileges. In addition, this chapter will discuss the rules of privilege as found in federal courts or as established through specific federal legislation.

STATUTORY BASIS FOR STATE PRIVILEGES

Except for a few constitutionally based cases discussed in Chapter 2 and a few common law cases discussed later in this chapter, the privilege rests almost entirely on statutory law. A listing of privileged communication laws for mental health professionals is found in Appendix A. We searched the indexes for the statutes in every state under numerous key words likely to produce citations concerning privileges for mental health professionals. In addition, we reviewed every case in the West Law Reporter System through August 1985. Although the list of state privilege laws is extensive, we cannot claim that it is exhaustive. Possibly statutory codes contain hidden privilege laws appended to larger bills. These possible provisions are obscure and are overlooked by litigants in a case. Also, state privilege laws are occasionally rewritten and revised. The laws in Appendix A were in effect as of August 1985, but readers should verify the current laws in their states.

The privileged communication statutes for mental health professionals vary considerably from state to state. At times the different professions are listed in separate statutes; at times they are included together. Sometimes the statutes specify the exceptions and boundaries of the privilege. At other times the statutes contain vague language that requires extensive judicial interpretation.

One common way of writing privileged communication laws was to model them on the attorney-client privilege laws. The phrasing of these statutes may take a form identical or similar to the state of Washington's law: "Confidential communications between a client and psychologist shall be privileged against compulsory disclosure to the same extent and subject to the same conditions as confidential communications between attorney and client" (Washington Revised Code Annotated, §18.83110, 1981). Such statutes were once considered favorable for psychotherapists because clients of attorneys receive broad privilege protection; however, psychotherapists have some activities with no parallel to the duties of attorneys, and the courts are forced to interpret the privileges according to strict common law precedents. Currently 14 states have the attorney-client model for clients of psychologists.

A second common form for privileged communication laws is that based on the proposed, but rejected, Rule 504 of the Federal Rules of Evidence, as discussed later in this chapter. These rules have advantages over the attorney-client model in that they specify the extent and limitations of the privilege with great precision and because they include both psychologists and physicians treating mental illness within their scope. Additional advantages of the proposed federal rules are discussed later. Currently eight states use the proposed federal rule model, and other states have adopted modifications that appear to have been influenced by it. The complete text of Rule 504 can be found in Appendix B.

A third model that deserves some attention provides for a privilege but allows judicial discretion in its waiver. An example of the wording of this model is found in North Carolina's law:

> No person, duly authorized as a practicing psychologist or psychological examiner, nor any of his employees or associates, shall be required to disclose any information which he may have acquired in rendering professional psychological services, and which information was necessary to enable him to render professional psychological services. Any resident or presiding judge in the district in which the action is pending may . . . compel disclosure, either at the trial or prior thereto, if in his opinion disclosure is necessary to a proper administration of justice. (General Statutes of North Carolina, §8-53.3, 1983)

North Carolina courts hold that the privilege is important and that the judicial waiver provision "was intended to refer to exceptional rather than ordinary factual situations" (*Lockwood v. McGaskill,* 1964, p. 67). These statutes have the advantage that they prevent the privilege from being used to deter the court from a correct verdict. The disadvantages are that the petitioners do not always know the extent or limitations of the privilege, and the effect of the privilege on the public perception of confidentiality is not known.

Other state statutes are idiosyncratic and do not follow any special pattern or logical grouping. Readers interested in detailed case law histories of the psychotherapist-patient or physician-patient privilege will find the following commentaries of use: Arkansas (Note, 1983), Florida (Newman, 1981), Illinois (Herst, 1979), Indiana (Olson, 1973), Kansas (Kennedy, 1973; Woods, 1978), Louisiana (Guidry, 1984), Mississippi (Carraway and Currie, 1977), North Carolina (Brooks, 1980), Oklahoma (Cosden, 1971), Oregon (Byrnes, 1976), Texas (Green, 1980), Washington (Hague, 1983), Utah (Heffernan, 1980), and Virginia (Williams, 1979).

COMMON LAW PRIVILEGES

In a few cases, courts have recognized privileges without relying on statutory authority. These common law privileges are rare and have little value as precedents. Usually they can be explained by the unique circumstances of the case or the idiosyncratic interpretations by the judge. For example, in the Saskatchewan, Canada, case of *In re Kryschuk v. Zulynik* (1958), a magistrate refused to require a social worker to testify in a paternity case. The magistrate noted that privacy was important for the social worker to fulfill her functions, and the magistrate did not want her to violate that duty.

In 1952, a trial judge refused to require a psychiatrist, Dr. Roy Grinker, to take the witness stand. In this suit for alienation of affection (*Binder v. Ruvell,* 1952), the opposing attorney desired to have Grinker take the stand to testify concerning the psychotherapy of one of the spouses. Grinker refused and was prepared to stand in contempt of court, but this was not necessary. The judge, however, stated, "I am persuaded that the courts will guard the secrets which come to the psychiatrist and will not permit him to disclose them. I am persuaded that it is just one of those cases where the privilege ought to be granted and protected. And the social significance of it is probably even greater than that which comes from the protection of the communications between lawyer and client" (p. 1242). Although *Binder* had little impact on the development of case law, it was the subject of commentaries that focused attention on the need for a psychotherapist-patient privilege (Comment, 1952; Guttmacher and Weihofen, 1952).

In another well-publicized case, *Mullen v. United States* (1959), a District of Columbia court granted a privilege for a clergy-communicant relationship that involved religious counseling with a woman accused of child abuse. A minister told the judge that his communicant-client had confessed to him that she had abused her infant child but was making attempts to rehabilitate herself. Although the District of Columbia did not have a clergy-communicant privilege statute, the court created one in this case. Judge Fahy ruled that "when reason and experience call for recognition of a privilege, which has the effect of restricting evidence, the dead hand of the common law will not restrain such recognition" (p. 275). Judge Edgerton, in his concurring opinion, wrote that courts should recognize a privilege "in such circumstances that disclosure is shocking to the moral sense of the community . . . whether the trusted person is or is not a wife, husband, doctor, lawyer, or minister" (p. 281). The opinion appears to have been motivated in part by a concern for religious freedom.

In *State v. Evans* (1969), the Arizona court refused to require a psychiatrist to testify as to the self-incriminating statements made by the criminal defendant in an insanity evaluation. The judge noted that the Arizona legislature had recently passed a law stating that the court could not use self-incriminating statements made in insanity evaluations to determine guilt. The law, however, would not go into effect until after the trial. The judge limited the scope of the psychiatrist's testimony to the determination of sanity. In making this ruling, the judge avoided a constitutional challenge on the basis of the Fifth Amendment right against self-incrimination.

In *Allred v. State* (1976), the Alaska Supreme Court held that the communications between a social worker and her client were privileged, although Alaska did not have a specific privileged communication law. The reasons for the decision were mixed. Some judges based their decision solely on the fact that they believed that this privilege met the criterion established by

Wigmore. Others relied on an expansive interpretation of the antigossip provisions in the psychologist-licensing law in Alaska and on the privacy guarantees of the Alaska and federal constitutions.

Probably the best interpretation is to consider these common law privileges as anomalies with little impact upon subsequent cases. Virtually all courts follow legislative directives closely in determining privileges. For example, "The statutory psychiatrist-patient privilege is absolute in absence of legislated and recognized exceptions, and it is not for the Court of Appeals to take it upon itself to waive the privilege for someone or to carve out exceptions" (*Amburgery v. Central Kentucky Regional Mental Health Board,* 1984, p. 952).

PRIVILEGED COMMUNICATIONS IN FEDERAL COURTS

Federal courts have rules for privileged communications that differ from those found in state courts. These rules are found in the Federal Rules of Evidence. In addition, several federal statutes provide for privileged communications in highly specific situations.

Federal law prohibits the use of information gained in pretrial mental examinations for use on the issues of guilt in criminal trials. Also, federal law provides a privilege for persons receiving treatment for drug abuse or alcohol abuse. Finally, there is a privilege for research subjects in mental health, drug, or alcohol abuse projects authorized by the secretary of health and human services.

Proposed and Current Federal Rules

State courts will decide most cases involving privileged communications issues. Some litigation, however, will appear in federal courts, such as for cases on appeal from state courts dealing with constitutional issues, cases dealing with federal facilities, or diversity cases (involving citizens of different states). In 1975 Congress enacted comprehensive rules of evidence for federal courts that involved a general privilege rule, Rule 501. Rule 501 reads in its entirety:

> Except as otherwise required by the Constitution of the United States or provided by Act of Congress or in rules prescribed by the Supreme Court pursuant to statutory authority, the privilege of a witness, person, government, State, or political subdivision thereof shall be governed by the principles of the common law as they may be interpreted by the courts of the United States in the light of reason and experience. However, in civil actions and proceedings, with respect to an element of a claim or defense as to which State law supplies the rule of decision, the privilege of a witness,

person, government, State, or political subdivision thereof shall be determined in accordance with State law. (Federal Rules of Evidence, 501).

The passage of Rule 501 followed much controversy and debate. In addition, case law that developed out of Rule 501 is in considerable confusion (Saltzburg and Redden, 1982).

In 1965, Supreme Court Chief Justice Earl Warren appointed the Advisory Committee on Rules of Evidence to propose new rules of evidence for federal courts. The Supreme Court generally favored the new rules developed by the committee, although it did not supervise or monitor their writing. The committee introduced proposed Rule 501, which excluded state privileges and recognized only those found in the Constitution, acts of Congress, or the Federal Rules as adopted by the Supreme Court. The committee also introduced Rules 502 through 510 for nine nonconstitutional privileges. (Rule 504, a privileged communication provision for psychotherapists, appears in its entirety in Appendix B.)

On November 20, 1972, the Advisory Committee transmitted the proposed rules to Congress. They created controversy immediately. Justice Douglas dissented from the other justices and stated that the Supreme Court lacked the authority to submit proposed rules because they were beyond the scope of powers given to the Court. He argued that the courts or Congress should develop the rules of evidence on a case-by-case basis. In addition, the proposed rules raised the issue of federalism. Proposed Rule 501 would have ignored all state privileges in the federal courts. Finally, there was controversy because government privileges were given more weight than individual privileges.

Congress responded to these criticisms by amending existing legislation to require its approval for any amendment on the rules of privilege, although its approval was not required for the amendment of any other rules. The final Rule 501 differed from the proposed rule in that the former allows for the application of relevant state law in civil cases. Congress adopted the present Rule 501 and eliminated Rules 502 through 510.

Relevant Case Law on Rule 501

There is considerable controversy concerning the proper interpretation of Rule 501. Some comments in the congressional debates about the proposed Rules of Evidence indicate that the elimination of Rule 504 did not necessarily mean a rejection of the psychotherapist-patient privilege. In these debates, Congress made clear that it did not want to freeze or limit the privilege law. Rather, Congress wanted to provide the courts with flexibility to decide rules of privilege on a case-by-case basis (Messersmith, 1984).

Federal courts have differed in their interpretation of Rule 501. Some courts have interpreted it to freeze the law of privilege. They have interpreted Rule 501 to mean that the courts will recognize only the privileges found in traditional common law: the attorney-client privilege or certain government secret privileges. Because the psychotherapist-patient privilege does not exist in common law, these courts have ruled that the federal courts cannot recognize it (*In re Grand Jury Subpoena,* 1983; *Slakan v. Porter,* 1984; *United States v. Lindstrom,* 1983; *United States v. Meagher,* 1976).

Other courts have interpreted Rule 501 differently and held that it gives the courts the opportunity to use reason and experience to weigh the benefits of a new psychotherapist-patient privilege. Several courts rejected the psychotherapist-patient privilege. Several courts did so in their instant cases, but their commentary makes it clear that they would recognize a privilege in other factual situations. In *Lora v. Board of Education* (1977), the plaintiffs sought access to the file of a school to see if the school discriminated against minority children in special education placements. The *Lora* court used a balancing test by which the privacy interests of the individual and the public policy of promoting the psychotherapist-patient relationship were weighed against the "need for full development of the facts in federal litigation in order that the paramount interest in the fair administration of justice be served" (p. 578). The court stated that Rule 501 did not prohibit it from following the guidelines of rejected Rule 504.

In two cases (*In re Pebsworth,* 1983; *In re Zuniga,* 1983), courts refused to find a psychotherapist-patient privilege applicable to nonconfidential information, such as names of patients, dates of treatment, length of treatment, and billing dates. A majority of courts have considered this kind of information, which does not intrude into the content of the psychotherapist-patient relationship, as unprivileged.

The *In re Zuniga* court adjudged two psychiatrists in civil contempt for failing to produce patient records subpoenaed by a grand jury in an investigation of a scheme to defraud the Michigan Blue Cross/Blue Shield. The court stated that it had an obligation to interpret Rule 501 and to participate in the continuing development of privilege law. It noted that Congress did not intend that 501 would preclude the development of a psychotherapist-patient privilege. Instead 501 provided the courts with common law powers to create privileges. The court stated that it would be likely to find in favor of a common law psychotherapist-patient privilege in federal courts. In this particular case, the court did not find the privilege applicable because the grand jury wanted only the names of patients, dates of treatment, and length of treatment. In a similar case *(In re Pebsworth),* a federal court held that the privilege did not apply to the billing records of psychotherapy patients, especially because the patients had already authorized a limited waiver of the privilege by seeking insurance reimbursement for psychotherapy. The court noted, however, that "we might well have decided differently if the information sought under the subpoena involved detailed psychological profiles of patients or substantive accounts of therapy sessions" (p. 263).

In two cases, the federal courts refused to recognize a privilege for cases involving the investigation of allegedly sham script mills. Their analyses, however, did not categorically reject a psychotherapist-patient privilege. In *United States v. Witt* (1982), the federal government was investigating an alleged front clinic for the illegal distribution of Quaaludes. The physician, whose training was in obstetrics, claimed the psychotherapist-patient privilege because physicians treating mental diseases were considered psychotherapists under the proposed, but rejected, Rule 504. The court held that this type of activity did not qualify for a psychotherapist-patient privilege because it was a conspiracy to commit crimes—in this case, distribute controlled substances in an illegal manner and evade taxes.

In the second case, *In re Doe* (1984), the drug enforcement authorities investigated a private sleep clinic that was allegedly a front to allow the widespread, illegal, and wholesale distribution of controlled drugs to consumers and street dealers. Dr. Doe (a pseudonym), a psychiatrist, claimed the privilege for his contacts with patients. The court analyzed Doe's privilege claim according to Wigmore's four criteria and found that the relationship Doe claimed did not meet the fourth criterion: that the harm to the relationship would be unbalanced by the harm to the judicial process. The court noted that the doctor's files contained little of a confidential nature to protect. "The 70 patient per day assembly-line technique involving only a brief interview is scarcely a psychiatrically nurturing event for a patient, much less one worth fostering" (p. 1193). In addition, the court did an *in camera* examination of patient files and found that "there are no communications in these files of the intensely personal nature that the psychotherapist-patient privilege is designed to protect from public scrutiny" (p. 1193-1194). Consequently there would be no privilege because "there is substantial evidence indicating that no real psychotherapist-patient relationship existed between Doe and the persons whose identities appear in the files" (p. 1194). Even if *Witt* and *Doe* had specifically recognized a psychotherapist-patient privilege, the privilege would not have applied to them because of the "future crime exceptions." (Chapter 8 explains how this exception is implicit in Rule 504.)

One federal court (*Jennings v. D.H.L. Airlines,* 1984) upheld the psychotherapist-patient privilege by following the standards established in proposed Rule 504. They found that the previous mental health treatment of an airline attendant was not relevant in this sexual harassment suit and did not fall under any of the exceptions to the privilege found in proposed Rule 504.

The Privilege and Federally Funded Drug and Alcohol Facilities

On August 1, 1975, new regulations went into effect concerning the confidentiality of alcohol and drug abuse patient records (Comprehensive Alcohol Abuse and Alcoholism, Prevention, Treatment, and Rehabilitation Act of 1970 (42 U.S.C. 4582); Drug Abuse Office and Treatment Act of 1972 (21 U.S.C. 1175). The regulations apply to both extrajudicial and judicial releases of information. The confidentiality of records applies to any drug or alcohol clinic that receives federal support in any manner, including a direct subsidy, revenue sharing, or tax-exempt status. Also, prevention and treatment programs conducted by the criminal justice system such as the Treatment Alternatives for Street Crime are included. (Appendix C contains the complete text relevant to privileged communications.)

Patients in drug and alcohol facilities are granted a broad privilege that applies to any civil or criminal proceeding in any state or federal court. The privilege covers any interviewing, counseling, or related activity in the treatment of addictive diseases. The court can make an exception to the privilege where there is a reasonable likelihood that the disclosure of the records will further the public interest and outweigh the potential adverse consequences to the program or similarly situated programs. The disclosure must be limited to the narrowest divulgence necessary to achieve the purposes of the court order.

In addition, the law prohibits the employment or enrollment of undercover agents or informants in a drug or alcohol facility without first obtaining a court order. The only exception would occur if the agents or informants voluntarily sought treatment for themselves. The prohibition against informers refers only to official informers. Other patients in the program may serve as ordinary witnesses and may testify as to the misconduct they saw (*United States v. Goffman,* 1977).

Special procedures regulate the investigation of crimes committed on program premises or against program personnel. In such circumstances, program personnel may, but are not required to, report the crimes to the police. The program personnel must obtain a court order before an official investigation into the crime may occur. The program personnel may report the fact of a crime without a court order, but they must make a court order before giving any identifying patient information concerning the crime.

Law enforcement agencies may obtain records if necessary to conduct an investigation concerning an "extremely serious" crime against a person. As with crimes committed on program premises or against program personnel, a court order must be obtained. These rules have been summarized in several reviews (Harms, 1981; Human, 1983; Roach and Harms, 1981).

Subsequent court decisions have clarified the courts' definition of "extremely serious" crimes under the terms of the law. In *United States v. Hooper* (1977), the court ruled that the crime of distributing heroin was sufficiently serious to allow a waiver of the privilege. Two courts have ruled that the proceedings for the custody of children or the neglect of children (*In the Matter of the Doe Children,* 1978; *Matter of Baby X,* 1980) were of sufficient social importance to waive the privilege.

Another court refused to create an exception to the privilege in *National Health Laboratory v. Mora* (1980) because the crime was not serious enough. In this case, the patients had failed to make payments to their methadone maintenance clinic.

The fact that an "extremely serious" crime was committed does not automatically waive the client privilege. In numerous cases involving serious crimes, judges have found grounds to exclude drug and alcohol records when they were not crucial to the case. In a child neglect proceeding, the drug and alcohol records of the mother were not admitted into testimony because the drug abuse occurred before the birth of the child (*In the Matter of Stephen F.,* 1982). In *State v. Walker* (1982), the drug and alcohol records of the presecutrix in a rape trial were not admitted into evidence after the court conducted an *in camera* review and found that they would not assist the defense. Also, in *United States v. Graham* (1977), the records of the government's chief witness were similarly excluded because they would aid the defendant's case. In *Commissioner of Social Service v. David S.* (1982), the court would not admit the records of a woman in a paternity suit to attack her credibility when the putative father had evidence from other sources to attack her credibility.

Drug and Alcohol Regulations and Child Abuse

An apparent conflict exists between the state laws mandating the reporting of child abuse and federal statutes regulating the confidentiality of drug and alcohol patient records. A joint statement of guidelines by the National Center on Child Abuse and Neglect and the Alcohol, Drug Abuse, and Mental Health Administration (Confidentiality, 1979; Roach and Cosgrove, 1981) resolved this apparent conflict.

The Child Abuse Prevention and Treatment Act (42 U.S.C. 5101) encourages the reporting of child abuse by providing federal grant assistance to states that comply with minimum standards for preventing and treating child abuse. One of those minimum standards is that the act requires the reporting of child abuse by persons, such as mental health or drug and alcohol treatment professionals, who are likely to have contact with children or abusing parents. Although the federal guidelines on confidentiality with drug- and alcohol-abusing persons are strict, Congress never intended that the confidentiality statutes should preclude alcohol or drug abuse personnel from reporting suspected child abuse.

If drug abuse and alcohol service providers believe that cases of child abuse or neglect may come to their attention, then the service provider may enter into a qualified service organization agreement (QSOA) with the appropriate child abuse protective agency. This agreement will allow the facility to comply with both the drug and alcohol provisions and the state child abuse and neglect reporting requirements. Under the QSOA, the child protection agency agrees to follow federal guidelines with regard to its confidentiality regulations, including agreeing to resist any judicial attempt to violate the federal guidelines on the release of drug and alcohol patient records into court.

Court orders for the release of records will not be required if the child welfare agency is attempting only to seek protective services in civil court. But if the child abuse protection agency wants to use the information for initiating or substantiating any criminal case, it must obtain a court order. According to this provision, the court may order the production of drug and alcohol records for proceedings that are serious crimes. Previous courts have included child abuse or neglect in this category.

Chapter 5

Applications of the Privilege

Courts may vary as to whether they adopt a broad (liberal—to expand the privilege) or narrow (strict—to restrict the privilege) interpretation. Ideally the courts should receive direction from the legislature or from common law precedent to decide cases. In a few situations, courts have created or extended privilege laws in the absence of legislation. But for the most part, judges follow the legislatures' directives and do not subvert the privilege law. When the "words in a statute are clear, there is no room for speculation as to [the] meaning thereof" (*Corcoran v. S. S. Kresge,* 1943, p. 257). "The court must interpret a statute in accordance with its plain and ordinary meaning" (*Rosegay v. Canter,* 1982, p. 611).

No court, however, can anticipate every conceivable set of circumstances that could emerge in a case or every series of legal theories, rights, or interests that could conflict. At times the instant court must decide to apply or reject the privilege in the absence of clear statutory language or judicial precedent. In these situations, they may interpret the law according to the legislative intent as determined by the history of the legislation.

The common law tradition has been to interpret privilege laws strictly so as to minimize the impact of the privilege. The common law tradition holds that the privilege laws are in derogation of the common law because they run counter to the tradition of admitting all evidence into court. Consequently the facts must fit every letter and comma of the statute before the privilege will stand. The strict interpretation has been applied especially to the physician-patient privilege. Judges saw only that the privilege withheld information, and they were skeptical of any societal benefit from the privilege. Instead the opinion developed among legal scholars that the privilege often served to perpetuate fraud (Chafee, 1943; Curd, 1938; Wigmore, 1961).

More recent decisions have not taken such a strict approach to the privilege. Instead several courts have interpreted the privilege according to the public policy on which it rests. The purpose of the privilege is to promote psychotherapy through the protection of privacy in that relationship. Consequently "protective statutes are to be read broadly where necessary to preserve the public policy they reflect" (Justice Roberts, concurring opinion in *In re "B,"* 1978, p. 429). But Saltzburg has pointed out that "privileges should extend no further than the underlying policies require. Unwarranted extension of these privileges may bring forth equally unwarranted cries for total abolition of the privileges" (1980, p. 602).

DEFINITION OF A PRIVILEGED RELATIONSHIP

A professional relationship must exist in order to have the privilege apply. The privilege occurs when clients seek treatment for an emotional disorder or receive diagnostic tests for use later in treatment from a mental health professional. There is no privilege for court-ordered examinations. (See Chapter 8 for details on this exception.)

Little case law could be found regarding the extent of the involvement that a client must have with the mental health professional before a professional relationship is said to be established. Precedents from other privileged relationships may provide the court with direction. For example, communications with the view of employing an attorney are privileged even if the attorney was not subsequently employed. When attorneys are consulted for matters other than the law, there is no privilege (Cleary, 1984). If the analogy were to apply, the privilege should cover the initial communications of the patient seeking treatment or information about treatment, though a further relationship might not develop. The policy of protecting initial contacts of persons seeking help for emotional problems appears consistent with the purpose of the privilege. It was followed in *State v. Miller* (1985) when a prospective patient called the nearest state hospital to seek mental health treatment. The initial statements of the prospective patient to the psychiatrist were privileged, even though the man did not become a patient at the hospital.

Most state statutes are mute on the situation in which persons fraudulently present themselves to the community as qualified mental health professionals. In most states, the law does not specify whether the client would have the protection of the privilege. Those states that followed Rule 504 of the proposed Federal Rules of Evidence are an exception, however, because they protect the communications of clients to anyone whom they reasonably believe to be a psychologist or physician. States that follow the attorney-client model have a similar precedent from that relationship to follow. The privilege applies to clients who consult persons fraudulently holding themselves out as an attorney. It appears that this special rule applies only to situations in which a fraudulent actor dupes the client. It does not apply to situations in which a mental health professional promises confidentiality out of ignorance of the law but is later forced to divulge information in court.

The burden of proof in claiming the privileged relationship lies with the persons who claim the privilege. The privilege runs contrary to common law, and the court will admit testimony unless the client can demonstrate that the privileged relationship exists. Consequently in *Mahoney v. Superior Court* (1983), the participants in a marital therapy session were required to testify and could not claim the privilege. The litigant who objected to the introduction of the testimony could not produce the name of the psychotherapist, and the court could not verify that the person met the statutory definition of a psychotherapist under California's privileged communication law. A similar result was reached in *State v. Stotts* (1985).

The communications must occur in the context of a professional relationship in order to be privileged. For example, in *Jones v. Department of Human Resources* (1983), a pastor was allowed to testify in a child custody hearing because he obtained the information through his role as a foster parent and not through the clergy-penitent relationship. In *Fahlfeder v. Commonwealth of Pennsylvania Board of Probation* (1984), a clergyman was required to testify over objection concerning conversions with a parolee. In this situation, the clergyman was a volunteer and auxiliary supervisor assisting in the petitioner's rehabilitation or parole and was not acting as a religious confessor. Also, in *In re T.L.S.* (1984), a psychologist could testify in a child custody hearing about the mother because the psychologist did not have a professional relationship with the mother and the "opinion was limited to personal observations in a nonprofessional capacity" (p. 1038). Finally in *State v. Sands* (1985), an Arizona psychologist engaged in extensive negotiations with a man who was holding his children hostage. Although the psychologist and the man had long discussions, the psychologist had informed him that he was working for the police and that the conversations were not confidential.

The psychotherapist-patient privilege will not apply when psychotherapists are using the relationship as a front for criminal activities. Thus, in *In re Doe* (1984) the court held that no psychotherapeutic relationship existed where the physician used assembly-line techniques to distribute dangerous drugs. In *Ascherman v. Superior Court* (1967), a physician was charged with engaging in the unethical solicitation of other patients. No privilege was held to exist because no professional relationship existed. "Any unethical solicitation by an interlope is quite unrelated to information communicated to enable the physician to 'prescribe or act for the patient' " (p. 553).

In the case of *People v. Doe* (1982*b*), a court correctly held that the information obtained by a nurse was not privileged because it was not obtained from her relationship with a patient. The nurse at a hospital in Illinois had overheard a rumor that a patient, who matched the police composite sketch of an ax murderer, had told other patients of committing the murder. Although the Illinois psychotherapist-patient statute included nurses, the court held that this nurse had to testify "because the therapist made no claim that her knowledge was obtained through conversations with him or someone else, so that answering questions would not have been a disclosure of communications" (p. 696).

Although the situations in the cases cited were clear-cut, the definition of a nonprofessional communication has been strained at times, especially when it involves communications to persons working within a hospital. Communications to nurses acting as agents of physicians are privileged. The court must determine when the nurses, or other nonprivileged workers, are acting as agents of the physician and when they are not.

DISTINCTION BETWEEN TYPES OF PSYCHOTHERAPY AND RESEARCH

The utilitarian rationale for the psychotherapist-patient privilege is that it will increase the effectiveness of psychotherapy. It will encourage mentally ill persons to seek psychotherapy and will encourage those within psychotherapy to disclose facts openly that are relevant to their condition. The Alaska court in *Allred v. State* (1976) tried to create a legal division of psychological methods into counseling and psychotherapy. The court claimed that psychotherapy deserved a privilege because it has a deeper "penetration into the psychic processes of the patient or client" (p. 419). This deeper penetration requires a privilege to ensure complete openness. It argued on the other hand that counseling is a superficial activity, and important revelations are "more in the nature of an unintended byproduct of the counseling activity" (p. 419). It concluded that the success of this superficial activity requires no privilege.

This distinction of the *Allred* court does not appear useful. Although some may argue that counseling and clinical psychology are distinct entities, they overlap a great deal, and both are involved in the treatment of mental disorders. The privilege should apply whenever the practitioner is treating a mental disorder—whether the procedure has the label *counseling* or *psychotherapy.* The courts should not be concerned with the hypothetical depths of a person's psyche but whether the professional has treated a mental disorder.

It appears that the *Allred* court attempted to limit the psychotherapist-patient privilege to exclude unqualified persons with limited education and experience. The court has a valid concern because the privilege should protect the relationship only with highly trained psychotherapists or counselors with adequate qualifications. It is not the purpose of the privilege to protect practitioners who lack the proper credentials to treat mental illness. Unfortunately, few states have defined the terms *psychotherapist* or *counselor* in a rational or systematic manner. (Recommendations will be made in Chapter 11 to define professionals who should fall within the purview of psychotherapist-patient privilege.)

A question remains if the privilege should apply whenever the mental health professionals are not treating mental disorders. Psychologists often do industrial consultation, teaching, or research. Counseling psychologists and counselors often perform educational or vocational testing. Social workers may work for child welfare, public welfare, or departments of aging and do not provide psychotherapy as part of their employment.

In a few states, the statutes read that the mental health professional should be involved in the treatment of a mental disorder for the privilege to apply. For example, in *State ex rel. Pflaum v. Psychology Examining Board* (1983), the state psychology licensing board of Wisconsin compelled the psychologist to reveal the names, addresses, and telephone numbers of volunteers in a research project. The court noted that the Wisconsin psychologist-client privilege law specified that the patient had to seek treatment for mental disorder in order to qualify for the privilege. Other states, such as those that model their psychotherapist-patient statute on the attorney-client model, may simply state, for example, that the "communications between psychologist and client are privileged." The word *patient* or *client* (and not *research subject*), however, should direct the courts that the privilege requires treatment or contemplation of treatment. Although the legislatures may have intended for privilege laws to apply only to the treatment of mental disorders, the present wording of many statutes includes a loophole whereby clients of the professional may invoke a privilege even though they are not being treated for a mental disorder. Often privilege laws apply to professions that have obtained licensure laws, and these laws include a section on the privilege. A remedy to this loophole would be to include a functional privilege statute that provides protection for several professions engaged in psychotherapy. Of course, the privilege would apply to any situation where the research was done simultaneously with the treatment of a mental disorder, such as in a psychotherapy or psychiatric outcome study. This does not mean, however, that a researcher-subject privilege cannot be justified. Such justification and statutory authority, however, should come separately from any psychotherapist-patient privilege.

WHAT INFORMATION IS PRIVILEGED?

Numerous courts have wrestled with the question of whether, when the privilege applies, it is absolute as far as the amount of information it covers. That is, is all the information acquired by the psychotherapist included in the privilege? Most courts hold that the privilege includes all information and will not distinguish between communications received by the patient and mental impressions obtained by the psychotherapist. Many courts, however, hold that the mere fact of being a client is not privileged, and the courts may have access to other nonconfidential information, such as times and dates of treatment, if there is an overriding public need.

Observations or Communications

In the past, courts looked at the physician-patient privilege with hostile eyes and interpreted it with extreme strictness. Most judicial authorities saw the medical privilege as an obstruction to justice that served no compensatory underlying social purpose. Consequently the courts would sometimes go into tortuous interpretations to secure the information necessary for an accurate verdict. The courts could circumvent the privilege by distinguishing between the content of the communications and the observations and opinions of the professional. For example, doctors could be barred from reporting what the patient said but could be required to give their opinions and diagnoses of the patient. In other cases, the court ruled that there was no privilege because, in the opinion of the court, the information requested was unlikely to embarrass the patient. Finally, a few courts granted the privilege only to that kind of information derived from professional knowledge. Observations that could have been made by any layperson were not privileged (*American Jurisprudence*, 1976; Best, 1972).

The court of appeals in Arkansas still follows this distinction between communications and observations. The interpretation occurs in part because Arkansas has a unique feature of including the psychotherapist-client and physician-patient privilege in the same statute. The privilege law includes "confidential communications made for the purpose of diagnosis or treatment of his physical, mental or emotional condition, including alcohol or drug addiction, among himself, physician or psychotherapist" (Arkansas Statutes Annotated, §28-1001, 1985. In an attempt to circumvent the physician-patient privilege, the court held in *Baker v. State* (1982) that the privilege applied only to "communications" and not to "any information" obtained through the treatment of the patient. Consequently the state could introduce evidence of the defendant's treatment for venereal disease in a rape trial.

In a subsequent case, *Horne v. State* (1984), the Arkansas Court of Appeals applied the same distinction to the information and communications obtained by a psychologist. In this case, the psychologist was required to testify as to the credibility of his patient, who was a witness in a murder trial. The defendant had wanted to show that the witness "suffered from a histrionic personality, causing her to fantasize events that never happened" (p. 859). This distinction by the *Horne* court may have been unnecessary. If the witness's testimony was a crucial element in the conviction of the defendant, then the court may have obtained the testimony of the psychologist because the Sixth Amendment guarantees the right to confront adverse witnesses.

In another isolated case, *People v. Dean* (1984), the court allowed a psychiatrist to testify concerning the nature of the prescription he wrote for a woman on probation. The defendant had altered the prescription written by the psychiatrist so that she could acquire a controlled substance. The pharmacist noticed that the prescriptions appeared to have been altered and notified the police. At the hearing to revoke her parole, the court permitted the testimony of the treating psychiatrist. The psychiatrist was not required to disclose any information he had obtained from the defendant but only to establish "a variance between what was prescribed and what was presented to the pharmacist" (p. 353). Although the court reached the correct conclusion, it could have used a more persuasive reasoning. It should not have attempted to distinguish between information that the client revealed to her psychiatrist and information that was at variance with what she revealed to others. Instead the information could have been acquired through the future crimes exception, which holds that information is not privileged when it is used in the furtherance of a criminal act.

Fortunately, these interpretations are rare as applied to the psychotherapist-patient privilege. Courts see that psychotherapy has a unique rationale independent from that of the physician-patient privilege and generally follow the spirit as well as the letter of the privileged communications laws. Today the general rule is that any information acquired by the psychotherapist in the course of the treatment or diagnosis of the patient is privileged. Distinguishing among the types of information gained in psychotherapy would undercut the privilege. In addition, it would tie the court up in a morass of judgments to distinguish observations in psychotherapy from communications (communications that would embarrass the client and those that would not) or professional judgments and that which any layperson could make. All communications and observations in psychotherapy should be treated as equally privileged.

Fact of Being a Client as Privileged

It would be nearly impossible to distinguish among the types of information gained in psychotherapy. Also, it would effectively undercut the function of the privilege to try to make these distinctions. The content of psychotherapy, however, can be distinguished from the knowledge of the mere fact of being a client. A body of law has arisen concerning the issue of whether the mere fact of being a mental health patient is privileged.

The states that have statutes based on the attorney-client model will follow their rule regarding the privacy of the fact of having an attorney. This rule holds that the mere fact of having an attorney is not privileged. It is assumed that most persons involved in litigation will have an attorney, and the mere fact of having an attorney does not impute guilt or wrongdoing on the part of the litigant or tarnish their reputation or stature in the community.

No other statute could be found that specifically addressed the issue of whether the fact of being a client is privileged. Nevertheless, this question has arisen in a number of court cases. Most courts have held that the fact of being a client is not privileged. This decision has occurred in cases where government investigations have requested the names and billing dates of patients as part of the investigation of welfare or insurance fraud or abuse (*Doe v. Hynes,* 1980; *In re Doe,* 1984; *In re Pebsworth,* 1983; *In re Zuniga,* 1983; *State v. Washington,* 1978). Also, it has occurred when divorcing wives wanted information on the billing of patients so they could ascertain their husband's income and determine appropriate alimony and support payments (*Cranford v. Cranford,* 1969; *Scherz v. Scherz,* 1981; *Zilborg v. Zilborg,* 1954), and it has occurred when a group representing handicapped children wanted information regarding the demographic features of the children to develop a class action suit against the school district (*Lora v. Board of Education,* 1977). The usual rationale is reflected in the decision of *In re Zuniga* (1983): "The essential element of the psychotherapist-patient privilege is its assurance to the patient that his innermost thoughts may be revealed without fear of disclosure, mere disclosure of the patient's identity does not negate this element" (p. 640).

Usually the disclosure of the identity of the patients is limited to the action before the court, and the courts take precautions to protect the privacy of the patients. For example, in *State v. Washington* (1978), the judge reviewed the records *in camera* and obliterated the medical parts of the records, and in *In re Pebsworth* (1983), the court stated that the trial court should take "scrupulous measures to ensure that there occurs no unnecessary disclosure of patients' names or diagnoses" (p. 264).

A few courts have considered the fact of receiving mental health treatment as privileged. In *Smith v. Superior Court* (1981), the California court held that a divorcing spouse could not have information on the billing procedures of her psychotherapist husband if it meant revealing the names and billing dates of his patients. Also, the Alaska Supreme Court held that a physician elected to the school board did not have to reveal the names of all his patients as part of the disclosure of his income records because "disclosure of the mere fact that an individual has visited a certain physician may have the effect of making public certain confidential or sensitive information" (*Falcon v. Alaska Public Offices Commission,* 1977, p. 479).

Empirical evidence may help the courts in this situation. It would be helpful to learn how patients or prospective patients view the disclosure of the fact of being a patient and if that would deter their participation later in psychotherapy. Differing court decisions have been based in part upon differing perceptions of the social stigma of the fact of being a mental patient. To some courts, the mere fact of being a patient substantially harms the purpose of the privilege (*Smith v. Superior Court,* 1981; *Falcon v. Alaska Public Offices Commission,* 1977). Other courts minimize the effects of this limited disclosure: "By and large, people are today satisfied that . . . there is no more disgrace in being mentally ill than there is in suffering a heart ailment, poliomyelitis, or cancer" (*Reid v. Moore-McCormack Lines,* 1970, p. 94).

Although no studies have specifically addressed this issue, evidence has accumulated that patients do not view all the information about their psychotherapy with an equal degree of sensitivity. Patients are more likely to object when the information has the potential to harm them. Although the evidence is scanty, it cannot be proved that a limited disclosure of names and dates of treatment to a judicial body with confidentiality regulations would severely harm patient willingness to participate in psychotherapy.

REFUSAL TO EXTEND BEYOND ENUMERATED PROFESSIONS

Courts may interpret the privileged communication laws strictly and refuse to recognize privileges outside of the professions enumerated in the statutes. Consequently the definitions of the terms *psychologist, physician,* or *social worker* in the statutes will determine which mental health professionals are included. The case law is replete with cases in which the courts have denied the privilege to psychotherapists or counselors who were not included in the privileged communication laws. At times these restrictions appear to fulfill a legitimate purpose in that the legislature did not intend to provide the privilege to "psychotherapists" with limited education and experience. Instead, the legislature wanted to promote psychotherapy with psychotherapists of acceptable credentials. Consequently, the privilege has been denied to unlicensed psychotherapists (e.g., *Commonwealth v. Clemons,* 1981; *In re Brenda H.,* 1979; *Lipsey v. State,* 1984; *State v. Gotfrey,* 1979) and unsupervised student interns (*People v. Gomez,* 1982). Also, the client of a caseworker at a residential facility for delinquent boys was denied the privilege because the caseworker did not qualify under either the school counselor or psychologist privilege statutes of Indiana (*In the Matter of L.J.M.,* 1985).

At other times, the exclusion of certain professionals from the privilege laws does not appear to reflect a systematic policy toward psychotherapy. In previous court decisions, psychiatrists have been denied the greater protection often found in the psychologist-patient privilege (*Miller v. Colonial Refrigerated Transportation,* 1979; *Ritt v. Ritt,* 1967; *State ex rel. Juvenile Department v. Brown,* 1974). Psychologists have been denied the greater protection afforded patients of psychiatrists (e.g., *Elliot v. Watkins Trucking Company,* 1969).

Most states are silent about whether a mental health professional licensed in other states will qualify for the privilege. The proposed Rule 504 of the Federal Rules of Evidence was broad in this respect and required only that the psychotherapist be a "person authorized to practice medicine in any state or nation, or reasonably believed by the patient so to be" or "a person licensed or certified as a psychologist under the laws of any state or nation" (Appendix B). The rule with regard to states following the attorney-client model differs on the state and federal level. Ordinarily the privilege applies only to attorneys qualified to practice in the state, but the privilege has extended to attorneys consulted in other states in isolated transactions. The Federal Revised Uniform Evidence Code holds that attorneys consulted qualify for the privilege if the client reasonably believes them to be qualified in any state or nation (Cleary, 1984).

Most state statutes are silent on this issue, and the courts will have to interpret the law. In the only appellate court case found addressing this issue, a patient was not allowed to invoke the privilege for communications made to a physician who was not licensed to practice in the state (*State v. Fouquette,* 1950). The privilege in that case was also disallowed on other grounds.

Courts have been consistent in their rationale for denying the privilege to professionals outside of those enumerated in the statutes. Privileged communication laws run counter to the common law tradition of admitting all evidence into court and must be strictly construed. The effect of all privilege statutes is to "close another window to the light of truth" (*State v. Gotfrey,* 1979, pp. 1327-1328). In addition, other courts have noted that they are obligated to follow the plain language of the statute and may not "change the express language of its scope and applicability" (*State v. Driscoll,* 1972, p. 855).

Mental health professionals cannot rely on confidentiality provisions of their professional code of ethics to have standing in court (*Belmont v. State Personnel Board,* 1974; *Falcon v. Alaska Public Offices Commission,* 1977). Courts cannot allow pledges of privacy or oaths of secrecy to avail against the demand for the truth (Wigmore, 1961). As the *Falcon* court has noted, to allow privileges to rest on the ethical guidelines of professional organizations could lead to professional groups' effectively exempting themselves from the law.

A few comments are appropriate concerning the definition of *psychologist*. In four states, the licensing provisions for psychologists are such that persons with a Masters' degree in psychology might qualify for a license and the privilege (Missouri, Kentucky, West Virginia, and Pennsylvania). Also, most states had grandfather clauses when they enacted their licensing laws, which allow persons with less than minimal credentials to become licensed if they were practicing psychology at the time that the new licensing law was passed. Other states have psychologist licensing laws that allow persons with doctorates in fields closely aligned to psychology, such as counseling, to qualify for the license. Three other states put additional requirements on psychologists beyond that found in the license. Hawaii requires a doctorate in clinical psychology, Massachusetts requires a doctorate in psychology (thus excluding grandfathered nondoctorate psychologists), and Connecticut requires that the psychologist practice in clinical psychology. The proposed Rule 504 of the Federal Rules of Evidence did not distinguish between privileged or nonprivileged professionals on the basis of credentials beyond that required of a license. Rule 504, does however, require that the physician or psychologist be "engaged in the diagnosis or treatment of a mental or emotional condition, including alcohol or drug addiction" (Appendix B). This additional requirement appears reasonable. Medical practice and psychology licensing laws are generic and cover all aspects of medicine (obstetrics to pediatrics) and psychology (community to physiological). It is reasonable to restrict the law to the treatment of mental disorders because the intent of the law is to promote mental health, not to promote certain professions.

In some situations, protection from forced disclosure may come through the agency where the mental health professional is employed. Some agencies have comprehensive regulations governing confidentiality that also extend to judicial proceedings. For example, drug and alcohol facilities that receive federal funds may be eligible for the privilege. Nevada provides some degree of agency privilege to state agencies. The protected professionals include "a person employed by a public or private agency as a psychologist or psychiatric social worker, or someone under his guidance, direction or control, while engaged in the examination, diagnosis or treatment of a patient for a mental condition" (Nevada Revised Statutes, 1979, §49.215).

In some states, clergy have broad privileged communication laws that could include counseling within their purview. Three jurisdictions—Alabama, Delaware, and the District of Columbia—have privileged communication laws that specifically include marital counseling. Other states have broadly written laws that could be construed as including counseling. The Pennsylvania law, for example, states that the privilege will apply to any secret or confidential information acquired by the clergy in the course of their employment. Although the statute does not specifically mention counseling, it could fall within the statute because some clergy frequently counsel parishioners as part of their job.

EXTENSION BY TEAM APPROACH

The case law dealing with the extension of the physician-patient privilege to nurses or other physician agents has had mixed results. Some courts interpret the statutes strictly so as to nullify the privilege for any communications made in front of the physician's agents. This strict interpretation may have been motivated in part by the general antipathy courts had for the physician-patient privilege, an antipathy that does not always carry over to the psychotherapist-patient privilege.

Under certain circumstances, the privilege may extend to persons working under the direction of members of protected professions. For example, states that follow the attorney-client model have a precedent by which agents or subordinates of the attorney working with the client may fall under the privilege. In addition, statutes based on proposed Rule 504 of the Federal Rules of Evidence state that the privilege extends to "persons present to further the interest of the patient in the consultation, examination or interview, [and to] persons reasonably necessary for the transmission of the communication, or persons who are participating in the diagnosis and treatment under the direction of the psychotherapist" (Appendix B). This would cover psychiatric nurses or social workers working directly with the protected psychologist or psychiatrist. It would also cover secretaries, clerks, or stenographers who record information.

In states without clear statutory direction, the courts may extend the privilege to nonprotected professionals working with members of the protected profession. For example, the court in *Allred v. State* (1976) held that the communications to a social worker were privileged. Although Alaska law did not consider communications to social workers as privileged, the social worker had worked in conjunction with a physician (who was protected under Alaska common law). Because both the social worker and physician had kept regularly scheduled appointments with the patient, the court viewed the social worker as an extension of the physician and considered communications to her as falling under the physician-patient privilege. The court noted that the treatment center utilized a team approach. It described the social worker as the "eyes, ears, and spokeswoman for a therapy group consisting of staff members of various specialties" (p. 425, n. 2), and it referred to her as the "alter ego" (p. 426) of the psychiatrist.

In *Ex Parte Day* (1979), Day was arrested following his assault upon guests during a party. In preparation for a defense of not guilty by reason of insanity, his attorney arranged for his evaluation by the University of Alabama Psychological Clinic. The trial court held that the communications to the psychologist were privileged because Alabama had a psychologist-client privilege, but Day's communications to the psychiatrist were not privileged because Alabama had no psychiatrist-patient privilege at that time. Upon appeal, the Alabama Supreme Court disagreed and stated that Day's communications to the psychiatrist were also privileged because the clinic had hired the psychiatrist as a consultant on the same case: "A psychiatrist with whom a psychologist is required by law to maintain 'effective intercommunication' is covered by the same privilege extended to licensed psychologists by statute" (p. 1160).

This collaborative relationship and joint coverage of the privilege can work both ways, though. When a defendant waived the privilege for the psychiatrist who examined him, he also waived the privilege for the communications made to the psychiatrist's social worker assistant (*Harris v. State,* 1984).

A distinguishing feature of the *Allred, Day,* and *Harris* cases was that both psychotherapists had a direct professional relationship with the client. In several cases, however, the question of the privilege has arisen for clients of unlicensed psychotherapists where the supervising licensed professional has no direct contact with the client. Courts have differed on their interpretation of this situation.

In the California case of *Luhdorff v. Superior Court* (1985), the court granted the privilege to the client of an unlicensed social worker by virtue of his supervision by a licensed psychologist. The psychologist provided regular supervision to the social worker, approved all of his treatment plans and methods, and regularly read his treatment notes. The court ruled that the communications to the social worker were privileged because the "defendant's case was ultimately controlled and supervised by a person to whom privilege attached" (p. 516).

Another California case ruled that it would recognize communications to student interns as privileged if they were working under a protected psychotherapist (*People v. Gomez,* 1982). In this case, however, the family court student interns had no professional supervision by a protected professional and were required to testify as to the communications to them.

Other courts in factual situations similar to *Luhdorff* have reached different conclusions. In *Commonwealth v. Clemons* (1981), the court refused to grant the privilege to the clients of an unlicensed psychotherapist, even though he received weekly consultation with a psychotherapist to whom the privileged attached. The Massachusetts court held that the privilege did not apply because the licensed psychotherapist had no direct professional contact with the client. The court left open the possibility that it could recognize a privilege if both psychotherapists had a professional relationship with the client.

Finally, in *State of Georgia v. Reid-Hall* (1984), a client was denied the privilege for the psychotherapy sessions with a graduate student of psychology despite the fact that a licensed psychologist supervised the student and listened to tape recordings of her sessions. The court held that the client of the student did not have the benefit of the privilege because he had no direct relationship with the licensed psychologist. The restrictive ruling by the Georgia court was not necessary to obtain the full facts because the defendant had been referred to treatment involuntarily and had signed a waiver with the Greene County Juvenile Court. Thus the courts would have had access to the contents of the tapes anyway.

In the absence of statutory direction, the application of the privilege may depend upon how the courts interpret *supervision.* Currently the definition of "under the supervision" falls into a legal no-man's-land without consistent definition. It appears, however, that the privilege will apply to clients of the supervised professional if the protected professional also has a relationship with the client. It is uncertain if the privilege will apply to clients if the protected professional has no direct relationship with the clients.

The communications to the supervised professional must further treatment in order to be considered privileged. The nature of privileged versus nonprivileged communications has become an issue in several court cases dealing with nurses in hospitals. In *Myers v. State* (1984), an accused murderer had made damaging statements to a nurse while she was in the mental health unit of a hospital. The court held that the communications were not privileged because the nurse at the time was not working under the direction of the patient's psychiatrist. In fact, the nurse did not even know who the defendant's psychiatrist was and had never discussed the case with her psychiatrist. Also, in *State v. Sweet* (1982), the statements to a nurse performing clerical functions were not privileged. A nurse asked a prospective patient to sign a consent to treatment form before admitting him to the ward. The patient's response that he was "too drunk" to sign was not privileged.

The state and federal laws create a wide patchwork of laws that vary considerably even within the same jurisdiction according to profession. One general consequence that emerges is that the statutory wording tends to deny equal privacy to patients of the public mental health facilities that are staffed primarily by social workers, psychiatric nurses, or unlicensed psychologists who are less likely to be covered under the privilege. These inequalities could be remedied through a functional privilege statute by which the function of psychotherapy is protected for several types of mental health professionals with different kinds of professional training.

Chapter 6

Waivers and Exceptions to the Privilege

Even in the presence of privilege statutes, courts can often acquire information through waivers by the clients or exceptions written in the statutes. Technically *waivers* refer to situations in which clients voluntarily relinquish the privilege. *Exceptions* refer to situations in which the statutory language or common law requires the relinquishment of the privilege. The distinction between the two terms can become blurred. For example, the exception when clients lose the privilege through entering their mental health into litigation is sometimes called an *automatic waiver.* At times writers will not follow the strict definition of the terms and use them interchangeably.

The waivers and exceptions keep the privilege from being absolute. "We do not face the alternative of enshrouding the patient's communication to the psychotherapist in the black veil of absolute privilege or of exposing it to the white glare of absolute publicity. Our choice lies, rather, in the grey area" (*In re Lifschultz,* 1970, pp. 7-8). One of the biggest problems of the state legislatures and courts is in determining the scope of the waivers and exceptions.

Generally the client or guardian controls the privilege. But the waiver of privilege is more complex than it might at first appear because clients can unknowingly waive the privilege by their actions.

WHO CONTROLS THE PRIVILEGE?

The privilege belongs to the client or to the guardian of the client. The psychotherapist has no independent right to assert the privilege (*Romanowicz v. Romanowicz,* 1968; *San Francisco v. Superior Court,* 1951; *Touma v. Touma,* 1976). California courts have also asserted this rule in two well-publicized cases, *Caesar v. Mountanos* (1976) and *In re Lifschutz* (1970). When the client waives the privilege, the psychotherapist must testify and, like any other witness, would be in contempt of court for refusing to do so.

In unusual circumstances, the psychotherapist may assert the privilege on behalf of a client. Illinois' statute provides that a psychologist may independently assert the privilege in the absence of a client, although the therapist cannot override the client's waiver of the privilege (Illinois Annotated Statutes, ch. 111, §5306, 1985). States that have adopted the proposed Rule 504 of the Federal Rules of Evidence also allow a limited psychotherapist control over the privilege. The rule states: "The person who was the psychotherapist may claim the privilege but only on behalf of the patient. His authority so to do is presumed in the absence of evidence to the contrary" (see Appendix B).

Even without a protective statute, the courts will allow hospitals (e.g., *Tucson v. Rowles,* 1974; *Grand Jury Investigation of Onondaga County,* 1983), psychotherapists (e.g., *Town of Lafayette v. City of Chippewa Falls,* 1975), or even drug companies that had possession of patient records (*Rudnick v. Superior Court of Kern County,* 1974) to assert the privilege on behalf of clients in their absence. The privilege can be asserted only on behalf of the client and not for the benefit of the record holder. For example, a nursing home had no right to invoke the physician-patient privilege to prevent the disclosure of medical records when it was being investigated concerning its treatment of its patients. The privilege in this situation would not have benefited the patients, who were alleged victims of mistreatment. Instead the privilege could have acted only to protect the nursing home from effective investigation (*People v. Doe,* 1978). Also, a hospital being investigated in connection with possible crimes against its patients could not assert the patient's privilege as a bar to a grand jury subpoena (*People v. John Doe,* 1982).

The general rule that the client controls the privilege may present a conflict for the psychotherapist. Psychotherapists may be required to testify and risk the possibility that their testimony will harm their patient psychologically. The decision for this risk rests with the client, not with the psychotherapist. As the court found in *Cynthia B. v. New Rochelle Hospital* (1982), "The ultimate responsibility for any inconvenience or embarrassment resulting from the revelation of her records is with plaintiff, and it is for her alone to balance any distressing consequences of such disclosure upon her sensibilities against what effect the non-compliance with the rules will have upon the outcome of her lawsuit" (p. 758).

Other interested parties, including those who pay for the psychotherapy, have no control over the privilege. In *Bieluch v. Bieluch* (1983), a father tried to prevent the testimony of a psychologist who was treating his wife and children. Although the father had paid for many of the sessions, he was not allowed to invoke the privilege because he had no professional relationship with the psychotherapist. In *Hampton v. Hampton* (1965), a husband tried to prevent the testimony of the psychiatrist who was treating his wife. Although the husband had attended the sessions, he could not invoke the privilege because his wife, who had a paranoid disorder, was the obvious patient, and the husband had no professional relationship with the psychiatrist.

Control for Minors and Incompetents

The waiver generally belongs to the parent or guardians of a minor child. This control rests on the assumption that the parent will be acting to benefit the child. The parents or guardians may not control the privilege if the court believes they are acting for their own interests and against the interests of the child. For example, in *People v. Lobaito* (1984), a court held that the father could not assert the privilege for his infant child. The 3-year-old child was home when his mother was killed. The babysitter testified that the child had told her that three men came into the house and injured his mother. The child's psychologist, however, testified that the child consistently denied ever seeing his mother get hurt and that the child's narrative as related by the babysitter was inconsistent with the boy's speech patterns. The court ruled that the father was attempting to assert the privilege only to aid his defense and not to advance the welfare of the child. Thus the court will use its discretion in determining what constitutes the welfare of the child.

In recent years, courts have faced several controversial situations when parents disagreed about the waiver for a minor child, when adolescents disagreed with their parents about the waiver, or when both spouses were clients together in psychotherapy and disagreed about the waiver. Often the courts lack clear statutory direction in these situations.

Only a few relevant cases could be found concerning situations in which parents disagree concerning the testimony of the child's psychotherapist. The court waived the psychologist-client privilege in *Last v. Franzblau* (Psychotherapist/Medical Records, 1979). Of importance is the fact that this case occurred in New York, which allows wide judicial discretion in waiving privileges in child custody cases. A Maryland court used a different procedure in *Nagle v. Hooks* (1983) by appointing a guardian *ad litem* to determine the best interests of the child. The court noted that usually the parent with custody would control the privilege, but in a custody case, the guardian or parent may be motivated by concerns other than what is the best interests of the child. With so little case law or statutory direction, it appears that the ruling in any case will depend on the predilections of the judge or the unique circumstances of the case.

Traditionally adolescents have no more control over the privilege than infants. Melton (1981) suggested that adolescents who seek treatment on their own should control the release of information obtained in psychotherapy. The right to seek treatment voluntarily implies the right to control the information generated by that treatment. Although one New Jersey court has upheld this rationale (Weinapple and Perr, 1981), it is largely untested in other courts. In another case, the court refused to waive the privilege in a proceeding to have a teenage girl committed to a psychiatric school (*In re Sippy,* 1953). Some courts view commitment proceedings for adolescents as adversarial in nature; thus the court may not necessarily presume that the waiver will be in the best interest of the child. Because courts have so little guiding precedent or legislation to support the concept that the adolescent controls the privilege, it is prudent to assume that parents will retain control.

Most cases have dealt with situations in which only one person was the client. In a few recent appellate court cases, the parents received treatment together through marital or family psychotherapy. No consistent principles have emerged concerning the waiver when spouses disagree about the waiver. In some jurisdictions, the court may make an exception to the privilege, not because one party or another controls the privilege but because the mere presence of a third person in psychotherapy allegedly indicates that the client did not intend the communications to be confidential or privilege.

Expressed and Implied Waivers

Clients may expressly or implicitly waive the privilege. In an expressed waiver, clients openly allow the testimony of the mental health professional by actively placing their mental health into litigation. In an implied waiver, the actions of the client imply that the communications were not confidential. Patients or their legal representatives implicitly waive the privilege if they fail to assert it when another attempts to enter their mental health into litigation. Implied waivers are sometimes controversial because clients may not knowingly waive the privilege by their actions.

Traditional privilege analysis holds that material disclosed to others is no longer privileged. There is no privilege for "that which is already known, for when a secret is out, it is out for all time and cannot be caught again like a bird and put back into its cage" (*People v. Bloom,* cited in *People v. McHugh,* 1984, p. 756).

Courts should not, however, treat all disclosures equally. Most disclosures should waive the privilege, but otherwise confidential disclosures intended to further treatment should not waive the privilege. In several situations, courts have properly held that clients have implicitly waived the privilege through their actions. For example, information waived in a previous hearing may not be privileged in a later hearing dealing with the same set of facts. In *Hamilton v. Verdow* (1980), a minister who had released his records in a civil suit was considered to have waived the privilege to his records in a subsequent criminal suit. The Maryland court held that a "prior waiver of the privilege is generally regarded as a waiver to the subsequent discovery or use of that information at a later trial of the same issues, or even unrelated issues" (p. 914). The mere mention of seeing a psychiatrist in a previous hearing, however, without mentioning any details or content of the sessions does not constitute a waiver (*Schaffer v. Spicer,* 1974; *Simpson v. Braider,* 1985). Most courts hold that the mere fact of being a patient, as well as the dates and times of treatment, are not privileged. Conversely, disclosure of this unprivileged information does not waive the privilege.

Clients waive the privilege when they examine their mental health professionals in court. A few courts have held that when multiple physicians have been consulted, the client may silence all but the one testifying in court (Cleary, 1984). However, this formula does not appear adequate for mental health testimony. The waiver should be absolute and complete. This is especially important in mental health matters where the diagnosis is made with less accuracy than in physical examinations because the cumulative knowledge of more than one mental health professional may shed important light on the facts and diagnosis of the case. Also, a malingering patient may conceivably deceive one professional. The possibility of deluding more than one is less, thus allowing the court greater likelihood of reaching the truth. More important, however, the client may have made highly relevant communications to one psychotherapist but not to others. We agree with Cleary (1984) and Slovenko (1974) that clients should not use the privilege as both a sword and a shield. When clients seek benefits in court by entering their mental condition into the proceedings, the court should have access to all relevant information.

Clients may also waive the privilege implicitly through their actions in court. At times clients will present testimony on their own mental condition. General or global statements about health or the mere mention of having received treatment will not waive the privilege. But the court should create an exception to the privilege if clients testify about the nature of the treatment.

In contrast to other disclosures, those intended to further treatment should be confidential. *Roberts v. Superior Court* (1973) stated that the "delivery of psychotherapists" reports to patient's other physicians did not waive psychotherapist-patient privilege" (p. 310). Also, in *Huelter v. Superior Court for County of Santa Clara* (1979), the court held that a woman had not waived the privilege in regard to her psychiatrist's records. The woman had waived the privilege to her internist's records. Although the internist had possession of the records of her psychiatrist, the woman had not specifically waived the privilege in regard to these records. This decision contrasts to *In re Fred J.* (1979), where a mother requested that two psychiatrists examine her children and report the findings to a social service agency. In a later custody hearing, the court refused to consider the psychiatrists' evaluations as privileged because the mother had allowed the psychiatrist to send the report earlier to the agency. Presumably this problem would not have existed if the agency itself had completed the evaluation. According to a strict judicial interpretation, the privilege may no longer exist once the client has divulged the communication to anyone.

The court in *Fred J.* made the right decision, although it should have clarified its reasoning. The waiver in *Fred J.* should have been permitted because of the nature of the proceeding (a proceeding to determine the custody of a neglected child) and because the mother had permitted release of her records to agencies unrelated to her mental health treatment. As we discuss in Chapter 7, proceedings to protect abused children are of high social importance and warrant a waiver of the privilege. Also, communications should be confidential only if they are intended as such. In this case, the mother had released her records to a number of different agencies, some of which had nothing to do with her mental health treatment. The release of records to agencies that further treatment should not in and of itself be considered sufficient to waive the privilege. Information exchanged with other treatment sources facilitates treatment and is not intended to publicize it.

PATIENT-LITIGANT EXCEPTION

Courts have held, either through explicit statutory law or through common law interpretations, that clients waive the privilege when they enter their mental health as an issue in litigation, a common procedure in malpractice suits, civil commitments, child custody suits, criminal cases when there is an insanity plea, or suits involving emotional pain or suffering. (The statutory and case law regarding civil commitments, child custody suits, and criminal cases are reviewed in Chapters 7 and 8, respectively.)

General Rules

Patients automatically waive the privilege when they claim emotional damage in a lawsuit. The bringing of a malpractice suit against a psychotherapist automatically creates a waiver to the privilege. Here the court must have details on the patient's condition and the treatment provided so that experts can testify if the conduct of the psychotherapist was acceptable. Conversely, one court held that the privilege laws will not prevent a provider from collecting a bill from a patient because the records of the cost did not disclose any confidential material (*State ex rel. Etc. v. Estate of Stephens,* 1981).

Automatic waivers of the privilege frequently occur as a result of an accident, assault, or other trauma or impact. For example, in *In re Lifschutz* (1970), the only reason that the psychiatrist's records became an issue is because his former patient had claimed emotional damage as a result of an assault. After the patient modified his claim to an ordinary claim of suffering, the psychiatrist's records were no longer needed.

Most courts properly hold that clients do not automatically enter their mental health into litigation when they sue for normal distress arising out of a physical trauma. For example, in *Webb v. Quincy City Lines, Inc.* (1966), a woman claimed she was "stick, sore, lame and disordered and permanently injured" (p. 166) when her arm was caught in the door of the defendant's bus. She did not allege psychiatric harm and did not enter her mental health records into the litigation. Justice Smith refused to allow the defendants to enter her mental health records into litigation: "To now open a pandora's box of inquiry into the mental condition of the claimant where it is not specifically made a part of the claim or defense is to permit time consuming excursions into the hinterlands of speculation and to lose sight of the main event in the big tent while fiddling around with the side shows" (p. 167).

Similarly, in *Tylitzki v. Triple X Service, Inc.* (1970), the court refused to admit psychiatric records into litigation when the claim was only for physical suffering. The court noted that interpreting the term *mental condition* in an exceedingly broad manner would effectively vitiate the privilege:

> The ability to observe, to concentrate, to relate our knowledge to others in a comprehensible manner, to tell the truth under oath, and many other phenomena, are all partially dependent upon what would be called one's "mental condition." Thus the extension of defendants' argument is to urge that whenever a plaintiff who has been under psychiatric care testifies at a trial, the defendant should be allowed to call the plaintiff's psychiatrist to the stand so that he could give a detailed analysis of the plaintiff's mental condition to aid the trier of fact in evaluating the merit of plaintiff's testimony. The important purpose of the creation of a patient-client privilege, however, was not meant to be paid lip service while being effectively eroded by judicial construction. (p. 536).

The case of *Ideal Publishing Corp v. Creative Features* (1977) provides an example of how claims for emotional pain do not necessarily imply a waiver of the privilege. A woman sued a publisher for slander. Although the woman claimed to suffer "embarrassment, humiliation, upset and feelings of distress and anguish" as a result of the slander, the court ruled that she did not waive the privilege by placing her mental health into litigation. The court noted that "she had merely set forth the natural consequences which the law presumed to result from slander" (p. 119).

In some situations, it takes a measure of clinical judgment on the part of the judge to determine when psychiatric records become relevant. For example, in *Roberts v. Superior Court* (1973), the judge refused to admit the psychiatric records of the patient when she filed for physical suffering following a car accident. The judge maintained the privilege even though the woman's back pain had started before the accident (and just after an attempted suicide) and her pain was out of proportion to the physical findings. Also, in *Britt v. Superior Court of San Diego County* (1978), the court held that the plaintiffs did not enter the psychiatric records into litigation when they complained of "shock and injury to the nervous system, emotional upset, [and] irritability" (p. 772) caused by the noise of the airfield close to their homes. This case involved a strong dissent by Justice Richardson, who noted that charges of the plaintiffs were made in broad and general terms. Justice Richardson said that the defendants should have had some opportunity to show that factors other than the airport noise might have caused the variety of physical and mental complaints.

One final pain and suffering case deserves mention. The Supreme Court of Colorado issued a balanced and sensitive decision in *Bond v. District Court in and for Denver City* (1984). In this case a 4-year-old child was severely injured when she fell off a truck owned and operated by the YMCA. The child, Erin, and her parents filed suit against the Y for negligence and sought recovery for damages for "physical pain and suffering, mental pain and suffering, past and future medical and psychiatric expenses, loss of enjoyment of life, and loss of earnings" (p. 36). Although the Bond family had entered its mental health into litigation, the court did not require a carte blanche access to psychiatric records. Instead, the court adopted a middle position and ruled that the trial court should use procedures such as "*in camera* hearings, *in camera* inspection of documents, and employment of court-appointed experts when appropriate" (p. 35). This was done largely in response to an affidavit of the director of the Foothills Clinic where the petitioners were receiving treatment. The affidavit included the following remarks:

> The Bonds are in a high degree of turmoil and confusion. The clarity and stability in their lives at the present time is in their psychiatric treatment. If notes or other records in connection with this treatment were used against them in an adversary proceeding, it could destroy a major portion of that clarity which would be highly detrimental to their emotional health and further treatment. . . . Very significant is the fact that the issues relating to the injury to Erin are complicated and involve distortions. If details of distorted perceptions become part of a legal proceeding, for example, Erin could become seriously and unnecessarily ladened with guilt to her severe detriment. . . . Further, it is my opinion that it would be a serious mistake to turn over notes and other detailed material to either the attorney for Plaintiffs or the Defendants for the reason that the Bonds have been hurt enough and this would only serve to hurt them more. (p. 39)

The court's decision carefully balances the competing interests in that it avoids unnecessarily harming the Bond family, including Erin, while at the same time providing the court with some access to the materials necessary to ensure a fair verdict.

Waiver of Non-Litigant Records

Several cases have emerged in which the plaintiffs in a malpractice action have sought the records of other patients to bolster a lawsuit. The information is apparently sought so that the plaintiffs can compare the procedures used with them with those used on other patients with similar medical problems. This search for information conflicts with the privacy rights or the statutory privilege for the nonlitigant patients. No cases involving this conflict could be found with psychiatric patients, although some courts have discarded the admission of psychiatric records because they were not directly relevant or material to the issues before the court (e.g., *Campbell v. State,* 1980).

Precedents with medical patients, however, may provide direction for the courts in these situations. Courts have either rejected the use of nonlitigants' records because they were too intrusive, allowed the plaintiffs to contact the non-litigant patients to ask them to waive the privilege, or released the records while concealing the identity of the patients.

Three Florida courts failed to admit records of nonlitigant patients into malpractice actions although Florida did not have a physician-patient privilege to cover the records (*Argonaut Insurance Company v. Peralta,* 1978; *Teperson v. Donato,* 1979). Although *Argonaut* used language suggesting that a physician-patient privilege existed in Florida, such comments were extraneous to the outcome of the case. *Argonaut* stated, "The question in medical malpractice is whether or not the doctor, in treating the plaintiff, used a standard of care commensurate with that used in the community and that question can be answered by utilizing other methods of proof than the invasion into medical records of strangers" (p. 233).

Two courts sought a middle ground to this problem by telling the defendant physician to turn over the names and addresses of the nonlitigant patients so that the injured patient could contact them and ask them to waive the privilege (*King v. O'Connor,* 1980; *Payne v. Howard,* 1977).

Most courts will allow access to the privileged information by concealing the identity of the patients (*Community Hospital Association v. District Court in and for the County of Boulder* 1977; *Hyman v. Jewish Chronic Disease Hospital,* 1965; *Osterman v. Ehrenworth,* 1969; *Rudnick v. Superior Court of Kern County,* 1974; *Williams v. Buffalo General Hospital,* 1967; *Ziegler v. Superior Court in and for the County of Pima,* 1982). The rationale for this limited disclosure is that it will not violate the spirit of the privilege law, which is to protect patients from embarrassment of personal details. As noted in *Rudnick v. Superior Court,* "If disclosure reveals the ailments but not the patient's identity, then such disclosures would appear not to violate the privilege" (p. 651). The *Rudnick* court noted that disclosure of patients' names without identifying the nature of the ailment does not violate the privilege. The privilege is violated only when the patient's name is associated with a specific ailment.

Not all courts have held this way, though. *Parkson v. Central DuPage Hospital* (1982) held that the privilege covered information even if the patient's name did not accompany that information. The *Parkson* court stated that it would not be deterred from a literal interpretation of the Illinois statute because a broadening of the interpretation of the statute "would neither serve a public interest nor the private interests of those non-party patients" (p. 143). Also, it held that the mere disclosure of the ailments would contain "information that in the cumulative can make the possibility of recognition very high" (p. 144).

The arguments of the *Parkson* court, however, do not appear persuasive. First, nonparty litigants and the public in general do benefit when justice is administered properly. Public interest is furthered when hospitals and medical staff perform their duties more scrupulously and can be held accountable for malpractice for conduct that is below the minimum standards of their profession. Second, it is highly speculative that the identity of patients may be surmised by a perusal of their medical records, especially in large, urban hospitals. This remote possibility, however, can be controlled by removing names and any other nonessential identifying information about the patients and by requiring that the records by completely confidential except for the limited purpose of litigation and then sealing or destroying the copies used by the litigants.

The privilege should extend no further than necessary to protect the patient. The psychotherapist-patient privilege, like the physician-patient privilege, "might be so literally construed as to work great mischief in the administration of justice. The ultimate object of every judicial inquiry is to get at the truth. Therefore no rule of law standing in the way of getting at the truth should be loosely or mechanically applied. The application of such law must be with discrimination, so that it may have the legislative effect intended for it, and yet the investigation of truth be not unnecessarily thwarted" (*Green v. Terminal R. Association of St. Louis,* cited by *Benoit v. Randall,* 1968., p. 110).

THIRD-PARTY RULE

The privilege may be waived or maintained according to the statutory wording or court interpretation of the third-party rule. According to this rule, the communications made in the presence of disinterested third persons are not confidential. The common law tradition holds that the presence of third persons suggests that the communications were not intended as confidential. This rule appears reasonable if it is applied to casual conversations made in public places. Obviously, communications made to a psychotherapist or counselor at a party with other guests present do not qualify as privileged communications. This rule, however, may provide difficulty for psychotherapy conducted in the presence of assistants, group therapy, or other family members.

Assistants of the Psychotherapist or Counselor

The application of the privilege with assistants present such as interns, paraprofessionals, or unlicensed mental health professionals may depend on the wording of the state statute. Some statutes, such as those that follow Rule 504 of the proposed Federal Rules of Evidence, specifically ensure the privacy of communications made with assistants present. Proposed Rule 504 says that "a communication is 'confidential' if not intended to be disclosed to third persons, except persons present to further the interests of the patient in the consultation . . . including members of the patient's family" (See Appendix B).

Statutes based on the attorney-client model may provide some direction. According to the general rules of the attorney-client privilege, communications in the presence of the agents of the attorney, such as paralegals or secretaries, are as private as if they were made directly and privately to the attorney. By applying the same rationale to psychotherapists with privileged modeled after the attorney-client relationship, communications in the presence of assistants of the psychotherapists or counselors would be privileged if they furthered treatment.

Unfortunately, most state statutes provide no direction concerning communications to assistants. In these situations, the courts must rely on common law precedents. No case could be found in which the privilege was challenged because the communication to the psychotherapist occurred with an assistant present. However, there have been precedents in which communications have been made to physicians with nurses, medics, or other medical technicians present. The court rulings in these situations have been mixed. Some courts, following their general antipathy toward the physician-patient privilege, have used any means at their disposal to waive that privilege. The presence of a third person provided that excuse. Other courts have held differently and stated that the circle of confidence may be extended to third persons "if the third person is present as a needed and customary participant in the consultation" (Cleary, 1984, p. 250). Consequently nurses or other medical assistants working directly with the doctor were considered to be agents, and communications made in their presence were privileged.

The case law concerning communications to psychotherapy or counseling assistants when the psychotherapist was not present was reviewed in Chapter

5. There is little case law in this area, but it appears that the privilege may extend to an unprivileged worker if the patient also had a direct professional relationship with the privileged professional.

Marital or Family Therapy

Similar to the situation with psychotherapy assistants, the application of the rule for marital or family therapy may depend on the wording of the state statute. States that follow Rule 504 allow for the privilege in marital or family therapy by protecting communications to "persons present to further the interest of the patient in the consultation . . . including members of the patient's family" (See Appendix B).

States that model the psychotherapist privilege on the attorney-client relationship have a precedent to follow. According to the attorney-client model, "When two or more persons employ or consult the same attorney in the same matter, communications made by them in relation thereto are not privileged *inter sese*. By selecting the same attorney, each party waives his right to place those communications under the child of professional confidence. Either party may introduce testimony concerning the same as against the other" (*American Jurisprudence,* 1976, sec. 190). By applying this principle, a court in Arizona (*Hahman v. Hahman,* 1981) held that the privilege communication laws on the attorney-client model could possibly rule similarly.

Most state statutes, however, do not provide the courts with specific directions for communications in marital or family therapy. Consequently the courts in such states must decide on common law grounds whether to admit these communications. To date, the case law has been mixed. One court upheld the privilege when parents were present in therapy with their children (*Grosslight v. Superior Court,* 1977). The *Grosslight* court recognized that the participation of family members may be crucial for effective therapy. The court held that "the communications from petitioner's parents are necessary for the proper performance of the psychotherapist's duties" (p. 282). The court relied in part on precedents whereby the communications of a parent to an attorney were covered by the attorney-client privilege when the client was a minor child (*In re Terry W.,* 1976). The *Grosslight* interpretation was followed in *Simpson v. Braider* (1985), which further stated that the communications of the psychotherapists to the parents of the patient were equally privileged.

Several courts have recognized a privilege in marriage counseling. *Clausen v. Clausen* (1983) held that the lower court had improperly admitted the testimony of a marriage counselor in a divorce case, noting that the marriage counselor fell under the provisions of Utah's counselor privilege law. In *Sims v. State* (1984), the court refused to waive the privilege for marital counselors, noting "that there is a strong public policy in favor of preserving the confidentiality of psychiatric patient confidences where a third party is present as a necessary or customary participant in the consultation and treatment" (p. 165).

Other courts have interpreted privileged communications in family or marital counseling differently. One court held that the privilege was waived because the spouse was a third person who nullified the effect of the privilege (Virginia Court, 1979). A Tennessee court in *Ellis v. Ellis* (1971) adopted a different standard. The communications made by the spouses to their psychiatrist were privileged, and the psychiatrist could not be made to testify as to the statements made to him or as to his diagnostic impressions. But the spouses could testify as to the statements made by the other spouse.

New York courts have had two cases dealing with marital privileges. The court in *In the matter of Humphrey* (1974) found that the communications were not privileged between a client and her social worker in the presence of the putative father of her child. The court relied on the model of the attorney-client privilege but noted that little case law could be found on this issue. A subsequent case (*Yaron v. Yaron,* 1975) overruled *Humphrey* and held that the communications between a husband and wife were privileged when made in the presence of a social worker. The court noted that to hold otherwise could cause the privilege to "be reduced to a meaningless act of the Legislature" (p. 524). It held that the "privilege granted by the Legislature was not meant to be a myth. It was meant to cure the evil which had resulted from social workers either voluntarily or by court direction being forced to disclose communications given them of an intimate nature by people desperately in need of help" (p. 524).

The New Jersey marriage counselor privilege law is absolute except for charges against the marriage counselor (New Jersey Statutes Annotated, §45:8B-29, 1985). In *Wichansky v. Wichansky* (1973), the court held that the marriage counselor privilege would extend to a psychologist who was licensed as a psychologist but not as a marriage counselor. The court noted that the purpose of the marriage counselor privilege section was to promote the function of marriage counseling and not to promote one profession over another. A subsequent New Jersey case (*Touma v. Touma,* 1976) held that the parties may mutually agree to a waiver. Another New Jersey case decided by a different New Jersey court implied differently because in that case it appeared that the privilege conflicted with the Sixth Amendment right to confront adverse witnesses (*State v. Roma,* 1976).

Often marriage counseling is provided by clergy who are covered by clergy-communicant statutes (*Kruglikov v. Kruglikov,* 1961; *LeGore v. LeGore,* 1963; *Pardie v. Pardie,* 1968; *Spencer v. Spencer,* 1983). The nature of the clergy-communicant statutes varies considerably. Some statutes expressly cover marital counseling, some could conceivably permit marital counseling under their purview, and some clearly reject marriage counseling under their umbrella. The California court in *Simrin v. Simrin* (1965) provided a unique interpretation of marital counseling. In this case, a rabbi had agreed to participate in marriage counseling with members of his synagogue but only if they promised to keep the counseling sessions confidential. Later an attempt was made to enter the rabbi's testimony into the court. Although the court rejected the clergy-communicant privilege for the marriage counseling, it held that the communications were privileged because they were similar to that of a mediator attempting to negotiate an out-of-court legal dispute.

It appears consistent with the purpose of the privilege to include communications of family members within the privilege. The preservation and improvement of marriages and family life are important goals that society needs to promote. Stability and continuity in family life are important contributors toward mental health, and family and marital therapy are designed to promote healthy family environments.

For some clients, family and marital psychotherapy are necessary to achieve therapeutic benefits. It would make little sense, for example, to treat the disordered child in individual therapy when faulty parenting practices cause the disorder. Similarly, it would make little sense to treat only the disordered spouse when the behavior of the other spouse causes or aggravates the disorder. Even if the parents or spouses do not cause the problems, the therapist can often incorporate them into therapy as allies who can greatly facilitate the treatment process.

Protection by a privilege statute would encourage family members to participate without fear that their participation would cost them later in court. Even in medical privilege cases, some case law recognizes an affirmative action to acquire background information and current facts from other family members (*Bassil v. Ford Motor Company,* 1936; *Denaro v. Prudential Insurance Co.,* 1913; *State v. Gibson,* 1970). The protection of marital counseling appears to have support from other common law countries as well. For example, the Federal Divorce Act of Canada reads, in part, "evidence of anything said or of any admission or communication made in the course of an endeavor to assist the parties to a marriage with a view of their possible reconciliation is not admissible in any legal litigation" (Federal Divorce Act of Canada, 1970). One Canadian commentator (Dickens, 1979), however, stated that the privilege could be waived in a child custody suit or some other set of unusual circumstances. The rationale for this marital privilege presented by a Canadian court (*Theodoropoulas v. Theodoropoulas,* 1963) is similar to that articulated by the California case *Simrin v. Simrin* (1965). The Canadian court concluded,

> The common law favoured reconciliation of parties whose marriage was marred by disputes and preferred to take a position that would encourage the spouses to engage in honest discussion as to their problems which might rise to a better understanding between them and a renewal of the marital status .... The analysis thereof must be in

an atmosphere of mutual trust with each one believing and acting upon the implied understanding that everything said on such an occasion directed towards resumption of their cohabitation must be completely confidential between themselves and not subject to repetition in a court of law or otherwise. (p. 774)

Group Psychotherapy

Group psychotherapy has some similar problems as family and marital psychotherapy in that communications are made in front of third persons. A few states, such as those that follow the proposed Federal Rules of Evidence, specifically provide for the confidentiality of group psychotherapy sessions. Most state statutes are silent on this issue. Only one appellate court case could be found on this issue, and it held that the communications within group psychotherapy would be privileged (*State v. Andring,* 1984). Although some commentators appear concerned about the issue of confidentiality and privilege in group psychotherapy (Braman, 1967; Cross, 1970; Foster, 1976; Meyer and Smith, 1977; Morgan, 1978; Slovenko, 1977), such concerns have not yet been accompanied by much litigation.

Group psychotherapy can be an effective mode of treatment, and for some individuals it may be the preferred mode. The purpose of group treatment is to enlist other group members as therapeutic agents for each other. The interactions of group members create a therapeutic effect for some clients that individual psychotherapy alone could not provide. In addition to the therapeutic advantages, group therapy costs less than individual therapy, thus making it more available to the public at large.

As in individual therapy, group members need to feel free to discuss problems. The need for disclosure is as great in group therapy as in individual therapy. Consequently group leaders usually require the participants to hold their discussions and the information they receive from other members in strict confidence.

Because group psychotherapy is an effective and sometimes optimal mode of treatment, its members should receive the benefit of the psychotherapist-patient privilege. One legal scholar asks, "Can the anticipated purpose [of the therapy] be carried out in the absence of such third persons?" (Morgan, 1978, pp. 75-76). The answer is "no," at least not as effectively. The interactions and participations of other third persons (group members), as well as their cost sharing, make them necessary for the effectiveness of group therapy.

OTHER WAIVERS

Death of Client

The common law tradition says the privilege does not end with the death of the patient but continues (Cleary, 1984). Several states have specific statutory instructions for control of the privilege after the death of the patient (e.g., Massachusetts, Maryland, Michigan, District of Columbia). In Massachusetts and the District of Columbia, judges may use their discretion as to whether the interests of justice override the privilege. Other states stipulate only that the legal representative of the patient controls the privilege.

States lacking statutory direction are likely to follow a common law interpretation that the legal representative of the deceased may assert the privilege on behalf of the patient (e.g., *State ex rel. Calley v. Olsen,* 1975). The court decides who the legal representative is, and it need not be the executor of the estate (e.g., *Boling v. Superior Court,* 1980). The privilege may not be waived by one who has an interest adverse to the estate. Some courts have allowed the privilege to be waived in the context of a validity of a will (Cleary, 1984; *Hayerstick v. Banet,* 1978; *Lembke v. Unke,* 1969; *Will of Postley,* 1984). On a few occasions, courts have asserted the privilege on behalf of dead patients who were not party to the action before the court (Best, 1972).

There is controversy concerning the admission of mental health records of deceased persons in insurance cases. In *Grey v. Los Angeles Superior Court* (1976), Dr. Grey had died when his car ran into a parked truck. The insurance company wanted to look at the records of his psychiatrist to learn if there was a possibility of suicide. There was no evidence that the accident might have been suicide, except that a policeman at the scene of the accident stated that it could have possibly been suicide. The court ruled that the insurance company could not have access to the psychiatrist's records. The "right of party to existing or prospective lawsuit to invade psychotherapist-patient privilege is limited in cases in which something more than mere speculation supports invasion" (p. 318).

This finding contrasts to the result found in *Prink v. Rockefeller Center, Inc.* (1979). A man had opened a defective window and fell to his death, and his wife sued the architects for defective workmanship. The court held that the bringing of the lawsuit was enough to waive the spousal or physician-patient privilege. The court held that "as a matter of common knowledge . . . many apparently accidental deaths are in fact suicides and that wrongful death complaint in issues . . . was sufficiently equivocal in that respect to put in issue husband's mental condition" (p. 519). The court noted that the man would have had to have waived the privilege through the patient-litigant exception if he had lived.

Insurance Company Waivers

Jurisdictions have developed different standards in regard to the waiver of the privilege in court on the grounds that the patient signed a broad waiver when participating in an insurance policy contract. Most courts have adopted a strict common law standard and held that the waiver signed by the patient with the insurance company is evidence that the communications were not intended as confidential and could not be privileged in court (e.g., *Jones v. Prudential Insurance Company,* 1978; *Leach v. Millers Life Insurance Company of Texas,* 1968; *Wright v. American General Life Insurance Company,* 1982). Also, in *United States v. Radetsky* (1976), the fact that Medicare patients gave explicit consent to disclose records to obtain reimbursement meant they had waived the privilege. Another court held differently and found that the mental health of the insured was not waived because it was not specifically mentioned in the waiver (*Boggess v. Aetna Life Insurance Company,* 1973).

In two New York cases, the application of the privilege in insurance cases depended on the wording of the contracts. In *Greene v. New England Mutual Life Insurance Company* (1981), the contract specified that the patient waived the privilege for any physician who "has attended or examined me." Because the wording of the contract was in the past tense, the patient did not waive the privilege to future physician relationships. This interpretation contrasts to *Lynch v. Mutual Life Insurance Company of New York* (1967), where the wording of the contract waived the privilege for any physician "who may attend or examine me."

One judicial interpretation that has emerged in recent cases dealing with insurance company waivers is the principle of the mutuality of purpose, which holds that the insurance company waiver and the privilege law have the same purpose: encouragement of persons to seek psychotherapy. By following this principle, the court in *Blue Cross of Northern California v. Superior Court of Yolo County* (1976) refused to allow a waiver. The rationale for the mutuality of purpose principle was well articulated by Justice Gray in his concurring opinion in *In re Pebsworth* (1983). Although Justice Gray advocated a waiver of this privilege on other grounds, he argued that the insurance waiver should not necessarily abrogate the privilege:

> It seems to me that the traditional waiver doctrines are inappropriate in the context of present day medical insurance. Such insurance plans . . . are designed to lessen the considerable financial burdens that, in the absence of insurance, would force many people to gamble with their health. Since the doctor-patient privilege exists to encourage such relationships and protect them when they are made, policies behind health insurance and privilege go hand in hand. (p. 264)

Mandated Reports

Physicians or other health professionals are sometimes required to report to government agencies matters of public health and safety such as fetal deaths, gunshot wounds, cases of venereal disease, the dispensation of controlled drugs, and suspected child abuse. Two of these areas, suspected child abuse and the prescription of controlled drugs, may affect mental health patients. (Child abuse reporting is discussed in detail in Chapter 7.) Few cases could be found dealing with the reporting of controlled drugs, and those dealt with the legality of the law. Perhaps the provision in some laws (e.g., Connecticut; *Felber v. Foote*, 1970) that explicitly states that the reports cannot be used in criminal prosecutions eliminates the need for frequent challenges in court.

Previous litigation has upheld the constitutionality of these reports. A federal court upheld Connecticut's drug reporting law in *Felber v. Foote* (1970) and specifically rejected the physician-patient privilege as having any constitutional basis. The Supreme Court also addressed this issue concerning the New York law in *Whalen v. Roe* (1977). Physicians in New York were required to report every prescription of certain dangerous but legal drugs, such as those used for "epilepsy, narcolepsy, hyperkinesia, schizo-affective disorder, and migraine headaches" (p. 873, n. 8). The Court stated that these and other mandated reporting laws did not violate the constitutional privacy of the patients. It noted that the reporting scheme was a legitimate attempt by the state to control the distribution of dangerous drugs. The Court rejected any physician-patient privilege as prohibiting the reporting law. Although the Court did not specifically reject a constitutional basis for the privilege, it stated that privilege laws are dependent on legislative enactment, and legislatures usually subject the privilege to many waivers and exceptions. The state power to regulate health concerns is an important and legitimate concern that does not unnecessarily invade privacy.

The question emerges as to the statutes of these mandated reports in courts. Generally most statutes hold that these mandated reports are confidential or not available to the public. No cases could be found in which the physician-patient privilege conflicted with the mandated report of controlled drugs, primarily because of the wording of those statues. Case law concerning other mandated reports may provide direction in case such a conflict should emerge with controlled drugs.

Two courts have held that the content of the mandated report cannot be withheld from court. In *State v. Fears* (1983), the court allowed records of venereal disease to be entered into a rape trial. Although a statute made the reports confidential, it did "not protect them from courts and public officers . . . in the performance of their official duties" (p. 371). Also, in *Freeman v. State* (1975), a physician could testify as to the nature of the wounds of his patient. His testimony, however, was restricted to the matters found within the mandated reports, and he could not testify to facts beyond that.

One final case dealt with the records of nonlitigants. In *Carr v. Schmid* (1980), the court held that the venereal disease records of nonlitigants could be entered into court; however, they would be limited in scope and would be available only for an *in camera* inspection to minimize the adverse effect on a "publicly desirable program" (p. 807).

RELEVANCE OF INFORMATION

Even in the absence of a privilege, some psychiatric information can be eliminated from court because it does not meet the judicial criterion of relevance. This common law holding of state and federal courts is reflected in the Uniform Rules of Evidence: "All relevant evidence is admissible, except as otherwise provided by statute or by these rules or by other rules applicable in the courts of this state. Evidence which is not relevant is not admissible" (Uniform Rules of Evidence, 402). The legal definition of relevance contains two components: materiality and probative value. Evidence is immaterial if the evidence supports a proposition that is not an issue in the case. Evidence is not probative if it does not establish the proposition that it is offered to prove (Cleary, 1984; Rothstein, 1981).

The most common situation in which psychiatric information is excluded on the basis of relevance appears to be when attempts are made to admit old and remote psychiatric records. For example, *Lukaszewicz v. Ortho Pharmaceutical Corporation* (1981) was a products liability suit alleging that the oral contraceptives produced by Ortho Pharmaceuticals were unreasonably dangerous and caused the plaintiff to have a cerebral accident. The defense argued that the cerebral accident was a psychological event caused by the plaintiff's emotional condition. The plaintiff planned to enter the testimony of nine nontreating physicians but sought to prevent the disclosure of 40 pages of records dating from 1960. Ten pages of those records were a psychological profile of her family. The court held that the manufacturer could have access to those portions of the records dealing with the plaintiff but not those dealing with her family. The court noted that the privacy interests of the family were important and that the records were of "minimal relevance" to the defendant's planned defense. The court noted that this profile was developed 15 years before the cerebral accident. "The records are of tangential relevance at best and the defendant will in all probability suffer no prejudice whatsoever if not permitted to review them" (p. 709).

Other courts have reached similar conclusions. In *Sampson v. Missouri Pacific Railroad Company* (1978), the seven-year-old records concerning the plaintiff's alcoholism were not relevant in a negligence action. In *U.S. v. Glover* (1978) the 12-year-old psychiatric records of a man accused of heroin possession were not related to the issues before the court. In *Greene v. Greene* (1972), a North Carolina court refused to admit the testimony of a psychiatrist who saw the parties briefly 13 years earlier and kept no notes of that contact.

Chapter 7

Application of Privilege to Civil Proceedings

This chapter will discuss common types of civil proceedings in which privilege will arise as an issue: child custody proceedings, child abuse proceedings, civil commitments, and regulatory proceedings of health professionals. The distinction between civil and criminal cases becomes blurred in the case of child abuse because this activity can sometimes result in criminal prosecutions. But because most child abuse cases end up only in civil court, it has been included in this chapter.

CHILD CUSTODY CASES

In child custody disputes, the courts attempt to make decisions in the best interest of the child (Guernsey, 1981). The best-interest test is a general principle that alerts all parties that the child's interests are important, but it does not indicate the relative weight paid to the various determinants of the child's interests. Although the criteria used in the best-interest test vary from state to state, they often include such factors as the love and affection existing between the child and other parties; the ability of the other parties to give the child love and guidance; the capacity of the other parties to provide material needs; the moral, physical, and psychological fitness of the parties; and the preferences of the child. Slovenko (1974) has noted that "these are sweeping, slippery words which may say much and at the same time say nothing" (p. 371).

The courts or adversarial parties may rely on the testimony of psychotherapists in trying to clarify the facts against which they apply the best-interest test. The question of privileged communication is not raised if the court has requested an independent evaluation because these evaluations are to provide information to the court, and treatment is not contemplated. Here the examiner should tell the parents that they will share the information with the court. Privilege is more likely to be asserted when one or more of the adversarial parties has received assessment or psychotherapy prior to or separate from the child placement dispute. In fact, under certain circumstances, some states mandate a period of counseling, prior to granting a divorce. In such counseling it is common for both parties to be present throughout the sessions, and one spouse may later attempt to use the therapeutic communications for personal advantage against the other spouse. In other instances, one of the parties in the dispute may have received prior treatment for concerns unrelated to custody. But because psychotherapists encourage clients to share their innermost secrets, it is possible that the prospect of therapist testimony will now threaten the client. Similarly an angry spouse may desire to hear that therapist's testimony in hopes that the other spouse will appear unfit for custody.

The application of the privilege in child custody cases, as in other cases, varies according to the wording of the state statute, the common law traditions within each state, or the interpretations of the court. The courts generally interpret privileged communication laws strictly. In addition, the courts value the welfare of children highly and will attempt to include all testimony that may help them make a proper placement. As a whole, the courts value the welfare of children more than the privacy of their parents (Foster, 1978). Various courts have reflected this attitude in their opinions: "Regardless of the desires of the parents, in making an award of custody the polar star is to determine what is for the best interest of the child" (*Atwood v. Atwood,* 1976, p. 466). "This court has no higher calling than to preserve and protect the best interests and welfare of a child" (*M. v. K.,* 1982, p. 708). "If need be, parental rights must be sacrificed to promote the child's best interest" (*Shipman v. Division of Social Services,* 1981, p. 104). Unless a statute clearly protects the privacy rights of parents, the courts will tend to rule in favor of admitting testimony.

Even in the presence of a privileged communication statute, a judge may obtain the psychotherapist's testimony in four ways. First, the client may waive the privilege and permit testimony in court. Second, the courts may nullify the privilege for communications made in the presence of third persons (see Chapter 6). Third, the wording of the state statutes may allow an exception to the privilege in certain child custody cases. Finally, the parents may automatically waive the privilege if they introduce their mental condition into the proceedings. The privilege applies only to psychotherapy and not to court-ordered mental examinations.

Statutes in several states have specific exceptions to the privilege. The most common statutory exception occurs when the child custody case is initiated as a result of suspected child abuse. (The following section presents details on this exception.)

Massachusetts has a waiver rule that applies only to child custody cases. Massachusetts law specifically allows a waiver if the judge, upon a hearing in chambers, "determines that the psychotherapist has evidence bearing significantly on the patient's ability to provide suitable custody, and that it is more important to the welfare of the child that the communications be disclosed than the relationship between the patient and psychotherapist be protected" (Massachusetts General Laws Annotated, ch. 233, 1980).

North Carolina, New Hampshire, New York, and Virginia allow the judges in child custody cases to waive the privilege when they believe that the interests of justice outweigh the client's need for privacy. New York state courts have ruled that privileges may not "cavalierly be ignored or lightly cast aside" (*Perry v. Fiumano,* 1978, p. 383). To permit the waiver, the mental health of the parents must be raised as a relevant issue in the child's placement, and this information must be unavailable from other sources (*State ex rel. Hickox v. Hickox,* 1978). Also, the courts must attempt to look for less intrusive ways to acquire the information such as requiring psychiatric evaluations of the parents or by viewing the psychiatric records *in camera* to determine if they are relevant to the case. For example, one court disregarded four-year-old psychiatric records because they were too old to be relevant to the present mental status of the parent (*Application of Do Vidio,* 1968).

Clients waive the privilege when they enter their mental health into the proceedings. The major problem is determining when mental health has been raised as an issue. States disagree on whether parents automatically enter their mental condition into litigation in child custody cases (Guernsey, 1981). Most states hold that the privilege is maintained and that parents do not automatically enter their mental condition into child custody cases (e.g., *Gillespie v. Gillespie,* 1982; *Husgen v. Stussie,* 1981); *Kristensen v. Kristensen,* 1981; *Matter of Atkins,* 1982; *Wing v. Wing,* 1980).

Florida courts have taken a middle ground regarding when to make exceptions to the psychotherapist-patient privilege. On the one hand, most Florida courts have held that the privilege applies in child custody cases (*Mohammad v. Mohammad,* 1978; *Roper v. Roper,* 1976), but some other courts have made an exception to this rule when the psychiatric information was "vital to the proper determination of permanent custody" (*Critchlow v. Critchlow,* 1977, p. 455; followed in *Miraglia v. Miraglia,* 1984).

The final determination of when the information becomes vital depends on the trial judge, who views the totality of the litigation. Consequently, one Florida judge waived the privilege when the parent had a psychiatric hospitalization (*Critchlow v. Critchlow,* 1977), and another judge did not (*Khairzdah v. Khairzdah,* 1984).

Courts in Kentucky (*Atwood v. Atwood,* 1976) and New Jersey (*Fitzgibbon v. Fitzgibbon,* 1984), however, have ruled that parents automatically enter their mental health into litigation in child custody cases. In *Atwood,* a mother was awarded custody of three children. She remarried and later obtained psychotherapy with her children and new husband. Her first husband then sought custody. The Kentucky Supreme Court refused to exclude the testimony of the psychotherapist. The court concluded that custody investigations require an "extensive and acute investigation" (p. 467) and that the parents made their mental condition an issue. The court would exclude no relevant information automatically. The *Atwood* and *Fitzgibbon* decisions are binding only in Kentucky and New Jersey, respectively; most other states will not automatically waive communication laws in child custody cases.

CHILD ABUSE AND PRIVILEGED COMMUNICATIONS

Child abuse is a general term that covers four kinds of harm to children: nonaccidental injury, neglect, sexual molestation, and emotional damage. Every state has statutes that define and identify abused children. Every state also includes nonaccidental injury and neglect within its definition of abuse. States vary on their inclusion of sexual molestation or emotional harm within the definition of child abuse (Education Commission of the States, 1979).

Child abuse is a social ill that concerns all responsible citizens. Legislators have attempted to increase control over abusing families through the establishment of child welfare services and mandatory reporting laws. Mandatory reporting laws attempt to increase the identification of abused children by granting immunity for reporters who act in good faith and by imposing penalties on those who fail to report suspected abuse. Nothing in the privileged communication laws prohibits a mental health professional from making a report of suspected child abuse. No court has ever allowed the privilege to hinder the filing of such a report.

Most states hold that privilege laws will not apply to proceedings arising out of reports of suspected child abuse. This is as it should be, because it would make little sense to require psychotherapists to report suspected abuse and then bar their testimony at a proceeding designed to protect the child. But the laws of some states have shortcomings and ambiguities. Not all states have abrogated the privilege in proceedings arising out of suspected child abuse. In states that have abrogated the laws, the abrogation is often done for some mental health professions and not for others. Finally, even when the privilege is abrogated, it is not always clear if the waiver applies to all subsequent proceedings or only certain ones.

Maryland and New Jersey laws do not abrogate the privilege in cases of suspected child abuse, but in these two states, an exception for child abuse proceedings is highly probable. The Maryland legal code includes an opinion of the attorney general, which holds that psychiatrists who learn of child abuse during treatment may report it, although they may not testify in criminal cases arising out of the report. Also, the New Jersey courts have a common law tradition of making an exception to privileged communication laws for any proceedings involving the custody of children. Certainly custody proceedings arising out of reports of child abuse would receive a similar exception in New Jersey courts. Also, a New Jersey court has held that the Fourteenth Amendment of the U.S. Constitution and Article 1 of the New Jersey constitution overrode the privilege in a case where the safety and happiness of an allegedly abused child was at issue (*M. v. K.,* 1982).

Not all states apply the abrogation laws to all categories of mental health professionals. Although no case has been reported to date, it is conceivable that the law may prohibit some mental health professionals from testifying in court in a child protective services hearing. It is hoped that in such a case, the court would seek an interpretation based on public policy grounds to admit that testimony.

In addition to specific laws that abrogate the privilege in child abuse cases, the courts may obtain evidence by several other legal avenues in certain states. Several states have "dangerous patient" exceptions, which hold that the privilege would not apply to communications of the patient dealing with harmful acts or crimes or the contemplation of harmful acts or crimes. In *Commonwealth v. Collett* (1982), a social worker had to reveal information given to her by a man who had killed his girlfriend's infant child. The court noted, however, that the dangerous patient waiver was not unlimited and would not be used to justify a fishing expedition or a convenient discovery rule by the prosecution. The court would limit the testimony to matters dealing with the issue of guilt. A subsequent case, *Commonwealth v. LeCain* (1985), followed the relevancy standard developed by *Collett.* In this case a social worker was prohibited from testifying at a murder trial because her information "did not relate directly to fact or immediate circumstance of a crime" (p. 208).

The dangerous patient exception in California's privilege law applies to child abuse proceedings. In *In re Courtney S.* (1982), a mother told her psychotherapist that the man she was living with had sexually molested her daughter. The court held that the dangerous patient exception would apply to sexual as well as physical harm.

Several states have laws that permit the judge to balance the need for evidence against the harm that could occur to the relationship with the psychotherapist. In other states the regular waivers and exceptions apply to child abuse proceedings as they do to other proceedings. Evidence can be admitted if the parents enter their mental health into proceedings. Also the court may admit evidence derived from court-ordered examinations of parents. The fact that the examination may have benefited the parents is secondary to their court-ordered purpose. If the court is to use the evidence from the evaluation for incriminating purposes, then the examiner must give *Miranda*-type warnings as in other criminal cases.

A shortcoming of the abrogation laws is that they are often unclear as to the types of proceedings to which the abrogation applies. The initial report of child abuse could conceivably be used in a number of different hearings: a hearing for protective services, termination of parental rights, modification of parental visitation rights, or civil or criminal suits against the abusing parents. For example, some courts hold that the child abuse abrogation clause does not apply to deprivation (parental termination) proceedings (*In Interest of Zappa,* 1981; *In Interest of R.D.S.* 1977), while other courts hold that it does (e.g., *In re Welfare of Dodge*, 1981; *Matter of Parental Rights of P.P.,* 1982).

The Privilege Applied to Criminal Cases of Child Abuse

One major controversy concerns the abrogation of privilege laws in criminal cases against abusing parents. The following section will review recent cases that addressed this issue. One court held that the privilege applies to criminal proceedings arising out of reports of child abuse. Other courts have held that the reports of child abuse take precedence over the privilege even in criminal cases, although they have limited the available information to the actual report of abuse.

The Alaska court ruled on the relationship of privileged statutes to criminal prosecution for child abuse in *State v. R. H.* (1984). A girl, identified only as S.H., had been the victim of sexual abuse by her father for several years. At the age of 15, she ran away from home and then saw a counselor who reported the sexual abuse that she and her sister had endured over the years. The child welfare agency investigated the report and brought the family before the children's court. The master of the children's court, Mr.

Hitchcock, ordered the family to undergo a psychological evaluation by Dr. Wetherhorn, a clinical psychologist. The family also agreed to participate in counseling. Hitchcock's statement read in part, "I do want to emphasize that the emphasis in these proceedings is one of getting to the root of whatever problems exist and dealing with them in a treatment sense, trying to get the family back together if at all possible" (p. 273). One month later, a family court judge reaffirmed Hitchcock's orders and told the family to continue in counseling.

Three months after the initial report of abuse, R. H., the father, was charged in criminal court for sexual activity with his children. The state wanted to enter the testimony of Wetherhorn, but he contended that the communications were confidential. The Alaska Appellate Court eventually ruled on the status of the family's communications to Wetherhorn.

The state rested its argument on two major points. First, it argued that the mandated initial report created an exception to the privilege because it made the communications public. Second, it argued that the court-ordered nature of the treatment made the information available to the court just as if it were a court-ordered examination.

Before ruling on the issue of the privilege, the court noted that the statute dealing with the issue of reports arising out of suspected child abuse was vague. It noted that "ambiguous statutes affecting criminal proceedings should be strictly construed in favor of criminal defendants" (p. 270). The court also noted that the Alaska Supreme Court had previously ruled that it valued highly the privacy of the psychotherapist-patient relationship because of its close nexus with the state constitutional right to privacy (*Allred v. State,* 1976).

The court rejected each of the state's arguments and held that Wetherhorn's testimony was privileged. First, the mandated reports did not waive confidentiality. The mandated reports were not made public, but rather their use was restricted to certain designated individuals dealing with child abuse. Furthermore, the mandatory reports were intended to protect children, not to prosecute criminals. The court noted that Hitchcock properly interpreted Alaska law in child abuse proceedings as desiring to "preserve family life whenever possible." Criminal prosecutions do not aid in the preservation of family life.

The court also rejected the argument that the court-ordered nature of the treatment made the information acquired by Wetherhorn available to it. Such an interpretation would have raised Fifth Amendment issues. If Wetherhorn was to provide information to the court about the H. family, then he should have issued a *Miranda*-type warning to them before the sessions started. The waiver of the privilege in these situations would have a chilling effect on the effectiveness of psychotherapy: "People who in the past had committed acts of child abuse would fear that the psychotherapist would testify against them in a criminal case" (p. 283).

Privilege Abrogated in Criminal Suits or Suits for Civil Damages

Most courts have permitted psychotherapists to testify as to the content of child abuse reports in criminal cases or civil suits for damages against abusing parents. These courts, however, often limit the waiver to the initial report and maintain the privilege for subsequent information.

One case that limited the extent of the waiver in criminal prosecution of child abuse occurred in California (*People v. Stritzinger,* 1983). During a 15-month period, a defendant allegedly engaged in various sexual acts with his stepdaughters. When the mother learned of these activities, she arranged for her husband and daughter to see Dr. Walker, a licensed psychologist. After interviewing the stepdaughter alone, Walker complied with the child abuse act and reported the sexual activity. Later, under pressure from police investigating the report, Walker made a subsequent and more detailed report. The father was subsequently convicted, in part on the basis of the information that Walker provided to the police.

The defendant appealed the verdict and won a reversal of the judgment. The core issue was the interpretation of the waiver provided by the child abuse reporting act. All parties agreed that Walker had properly notified the child welfare agency of the sexual abuse. The court ruled, however, that the information Walker subsequently gave the police fell under the psychotherapist-patient privilege. It noted that the police had inadvertently misled Walker into revealing more than the law required.

The court made it clear that it was concerned about the impact of subsequent reports on the values of psychotherapy. Judge Kaus wrote in a separate opinion:

> Since it is fair to assume that child molesters like to avoid being prosecuted just as much as other criminals, it obviously impedes the objective of cure if therapists who are supposed to effect it are legally bound to testify against their patients in court. Those who do so a few times should not plan on specializing in pedophilia. (p. 751)

Although subsequent communications (those in addition to the initial report) may be privileged, the report itself is not privileged. This fact was reestablished in the California case of *People v. Battaglia* (1984). Battaglia allegedly forced his stepdaughter to take a trip with him, where he repeatedly molested her. Later Battaglia entered a walk-in psychiatric clinic and was interviewed by William Ruiz, a clinical social worker. During this discussions, Ruiz suspected that Battaglia had engaged in sexual molestation and contacted the police, who subsequently detained Ruiz.

Battaglia was convicted of lascivious acts with a child under 14. He appealed the verdict claiming, *inter alia,* that the psychotherapist-patient privilege applied. He also claimed that he should have received a *Miranda*-type warning before his admissions of sexual molestation could be admitted into court.

The appeals court rejected these claims. Ruiz did not fit under the psychotherapist-patient law, but even if he did, the court ruled that the report and the information in it were not privileged. The court also dismissed the claim that the Fifth Amendment should have applied to his conversations. According to recent interpretations of the Fifth Amendment, the court may not use inculpatory statements stemming from custodial interrogations of the defendant unless *Miranda*-like warnings have been given. Here Battaglia was not under police custody, and the discussions with Ruiz could not be called interrogation. Battaglia was under no obligation to stay and speak to Ruiz and had voluntarily given the information.

Two Minnesota cases have held that the privilege is waived for the initial report of abuse but that the privilege covers subsequent information. In *State v. Andring* (1984), a man was tried in criminal court for sexual molestation of his stepdaughters. The state attempted to acquire his treatment records from a drug and alcohol facility to aid in the prosecution, apparently hoping to find confessions of guilt within his psychotherapy sessions. Although the judge did not rely on the joint regulations regarding the apparent conflict between the privacy of the drug and alcohol act and child abuse regulations, the judge correctly ruled that the drug and alcohol regulations did not prohibit that facility from reporting child abuse. The court also ruled that the exception to the privilege held only for the initial report; subsequent records were privileged. The court attempted to balance the need for evidence in court with the purpose of the privilege to encourage abusing parents to seek psychotherapy. The court noted that

> the central purpose of the child abuse reporting statutes is the protection of children, not the punishment of those who mistreat them. . . . This policy, which recognizes that the child may return to the same home environment in which the maltreatment occurred, is best effectuated by continued encouragement for child abusers to seek rehabilitation treatment. (p. 132).

Among the other issues decided, *State v. Andring* also held that the fact that many of the communications occurred in group psychotherapy did not automatically waive the privilege.

The *Andring* decision was followed in *State v. Odenbrett* (1984). The initial report of child abuse was not privileged in a criminal trial for sexual molestation, but information about other sexual activity unrelated to child abuse was protected medical privilege information. "This disclosure, though distressing, has no bearing on the conviction here" (p. 268, n. 2).

In *State v. Brydon* (1981) Brydon was convicted of deviate sexual assault on his foster daughter and sent to prison. He appealed, in part on the basis that his incriminating confessions to a licensed psychologist should not have been admitted into testimony. He argued that the mandated reporting laws should apply only to proceedings that protect the child. The court rejected this argument, noting that one of the goals of the law was punishment of offenders, as well as protection of children. The court also noted that Brydon's Fifth Amendment rights were not violated because the psychologist had told him that he would report any statements of abuse to the child welfare authorities.

In two cases, the courts abrogated the privilege for civil suits for damages arising out of abuse (*Carson v. Jackson,* 1984; *State v. Hoester,* 1984). The *Hoester* court refused to exclude the communications made to the physician. It stated that the legislature had not authorized any exception to the mandated reporting law, which waived the privilege in proceedings arising out of reports of abuse. The "Supreme Court was not at liberty to add by interpolation, or otherwise, limiting provisions not plainly written or necessarily implied from language used in statute limiting invocation of privileges in child abuse proceedings" (p. 449).

Carson also refused to apply the privilege to criminal proceedings or proceedings for civil damages. It also refused to allow the defendant to invoke the Fifth Amendment for self-incriminating statements she made to the court-ordered psychotherapist. The alleged abuser knew that the psychotherapist would convey her statements to others. Furthermore, she could have asserted her rights under the Fifth Amendment at any time during her psychotherapy sessions but failed to do so. Her statements to the psychotherapist were voluntary and not compelled.

Indirect Evidence

Most of the court decisions to date have dealt with direct evidence—that is, evidence that psychotherapists used to initiate or substantiate a report. Weisberg and Wald (1984) have commented on the importance of indirect evidence—information that by itself does not show abuse but might aid the court or agency in the disposition of the case—in child custody proceedings. It is more often relevant in the disposition of child custody after abuse has already been founded. Indirect evidence may include five general categories: (1) the parent's mental conditions (such as alcoholism or psychosis), which may impair the ability to act as a capable parent; (2) the parent's responsiveness to treatment; (3) statements concerning the parent's feelings toward the child; (4) background of violent behavior; (5) history of ill treatment of the child that in isolation does not constitute abuse or neglect but whose cumulative impact when combined with other sources provides evidence of abuse or neglect. Although the court may accept direct evidence under certain circumstances, the privilege protects the indirect evidence in many cases (e.g., *Matter of Atkins,* 1982).

Weisberg and Wald have no systematic data on the amount of information the courts lose because indirect evidence is excluded. Their clinical experience, however, suggested that it is substantial and is limited by the failure of many attorneys to protect parental privacy interests vigorously.

Weisberg and Wald recommend changing the statutes to require mental health professionals to disclose any information to the courts that is relevant to the adjudication of abused or neglected children. They are cognizant, however, of the problems involved with this exception to the privacy of the parents and suggest that mandatory reporting laws should be altered so that they are narrower and more uniform, thus reducing the number of unfounded reports.

The viewpoint of Weisberg and Wald is not without some support. For example, in *Shipman v. Division of Social Services* (1981), a judge ruled on the admission of indirect evidence into the court. The court did not believe that an independent psychiatric evaluation would provide the court with the information it needed. The judge stated, "I do not agree that merely permitting a present examination obviates the necessity for producing previous medical records. It would not be unlike the task of trying to judge the import of today's world without the knowledge of earlier history" (p. 105).

Also, in *Matter of A.J.S.* (1981), a Montana court permitted Dr. Gustafson, a psychologist, to testify concerning his treatment of an abusing mother. The court had ordered the mother to receive an evaluation from Gustafson, thus eliminating any privilege in their relationship. But the issue was more complicated because Gustafson had previously treated the mother for an unrelated matter. The court did not distinguish between the previous treatment and the court-ordered evaluation and simply allowed Gustafson's testimony. It opined that "the best interests of the child require some degree of flexibility in procedure to insure that all evidence pertaining to the best interests of the child may be considered" (p. 221).

Clearly the status of the privilege in child abuse reporting laws is in turmoil. Part of the turmoil is due to conflicting attitudes concerning the need for information in court versus the instrumental benefits of encouraging abusing parents to seek psychotherapy. Unfortunately, however, part of the turmoil is due to the haphazard way that privilege laws have been written and enacted. The laws are replete with inconsistencies so that the requirement to testify varies according to the professional affiliation of the psychotherapist or nature of the proceedings. The laws seldom reflect a consistent legislature policy.

PRIVILEGED COMMUNICATION IN CIVIL COMMITMENTS

Every state has legal procedures for the involuntary treatment of mentally ill persons. These laws have been the subject of significant debate in the last decade and have undergone legislative modifications and judicial challenges. To a large extent, these debates have centered on the role of due process in the commitment proceedings. The procedures regarding the availability of information to the court have been implicated.

Three situations may occur whereby psychiatric testimony will be sought in a commitment hearing. First, a psychotherapist may seek a commitment against a client who initiated treatment voluntarily. Second, a psychotherapist, usually a psychiatrist, may evaluate a patient solely for the purpose of rendering an opinion to the court concerning the advisability of a commitment. Finally, a court may ask a psychotherapist treating an involuntary patient to testify at a judicial review of that commitment (Shuman, 1979). Each of these situations raises questions as to the application of physician-patient or psychotherapist-patient privilege.

The greatest discrepancy in state policies occurs when a psychotherapist initiates a commitment against a person who had voluntarily sought treatment. An exception to the privilege in this situation would harm the effectiveness of psychotherapy. Nevertheless, the legislature must weigh the harm done to psychotherapy against the potential for harm to the patient or society. Several states have statutes that specifically waive the privilege in any civil commitment hearing, regardless of whether the patient had once voluntarily sought treatment. Most other states have no such provision, resulting in the need for judicial interpretation of these laws.

The judicial interpretation in this situation has been mixed. Pennsylvania, for example, would waive the privilege in civil commitments, noting that to do otherwise would thwart the purpose of the commitment laws (*Commonwealth ex rel. Platt v. Platt,* 1979). This contrasts to *People v. Taylor* (1980) where the Colorado court refused to waive the privilege. The court noted that "civil commitment statutes . . . must be strictly construed so that no limit is placed on one's right to seek voluntary treatment" (pp. 1130-1131).

We believe that it is appropriate for the courts to admit testimony in these situations if the statutory requirements for commitment are sufficiently high and require imminent danger of harm to human life or physical safety. Recent court rulings in several states (e.g., *Tarasoff v. Regents of University of California,* 1976; *McIntosh v. Milano,* 1979) have held that psychotherapists have an affirmative duty to act to protect third persons when their patients present imminent danger (see reviews of these cases by Knapp and VandeCreek, 1982; Knapp, VandeCreek, and Herzog, in press; VandeCreek and Knapp, 1984): "Discharge of such duty may require the therapist to take one or more of various steps, depending on the nature of the case, including warning the intended victim or others likely to apprise the victim of the danger, notifying the police, or taking whatever steps are reasonably necessary under the circumstances" (*Tarasoff v. Regents of University of California,* p. 334). One of the most common and reasonable steps has been to seek an involuntary civil commitment. It would make little sense to require psychotherapists to initiate a civil commitment and then prohibit them from testifying at that hearing.

On the other hand, it would thwart the purpose of the privilege law to create an exception to the privilege when the statutory requirement of the commitment is only that the patient needs treatment. Such an exception would deter voluntary patients who fear such a loss of control over their treatment and daily lives. This unusual exception to confidentiality can be justified when a patient poses a threat of harm to others. It should be noted that the petition to commit Taylor in *People v. Taylor* did not allege dangerousness. A petition with a dangerous patient may have resulted in a different outcome.

On other occasions, the psychiatrist may interview the patient only for the purpose of providing information to the civil commitment hearing. In this situation, all courts have held that the privilege is waived even if the waiver is not specifically mentioned in the statute. The common law tradition makes information acquired in court-ordered examinations available to the courts. This evaluation does not harm the psychotherapist-patient relationship because the evaluation is done for diagnosis and recommendations and does not involve treatment.

Most courts hold that the Fifth Amendment privilege against self-incrimination is not violated through the psychiatric examination even if the patient was not warned of the right to remain silent. The common rationale is that patients cannot incriminate themselves "so long as proceedings do not engage person in any criminal prosecution" (*In re Beverly,* 1977, p. 482). A minority of courts have ruled differently and held that the examiner must give a warning (see review by Sarno, 1983). Although constitutional grounds are usually cited for the warning, Texas statutory law requires that the patient be told that the communications of the evaluation are not privileged (e.g., *Brown v. State,* 1981).

Consequently the examiner should inform the patient of the purpose of the examination before it begins so the patient will not misconstrue the relationship as involving treatment. In some situations, this may be a meaningless exercise because psychotic patients may not understand this distinction. Other patients, such as psychopathic sexual deviants, are quite capable of understanding the distinction. Even in the absence of statutory distinction, it is ethical for psychotherapists to provide those warnings (Rappeport, 1982; American Psychological Association, 1981).

Finally, privileged communication issues have been raised in cases involving the review of committed persons. These situations mix the therapeutic and examining functions of the mental health professional. Generally the courts have admitted the testimony even in the absence of a specific statutory exception. For example, in *State v. Kupchun* (1977), the court noted that invoking the privilege in the recommitment hearing of a criminally insane offender would not promote treatment. Consequently the court allowed the psychotherapist of the offender to testify. The court, however, held that the testimony would be secret and would involve no public disclosure. Furthermore, the court limited the testimony of the psychotherapist to opinions as to mental condition and would not admit statements relating to the original guilt of the offender. In other words, the court tried to protect the privacy of the psychotherapeutic relationship as much as possible while still authorizing an exception to the privilege. Similar findings have been noted elsewhere (e.g., *State v. Hungerford,* 1978).

The state of Washington had an unusual situation where the statutes were not clear as to whether the physician-patient privilege applied in certain judicial reviews of involuntarily committed patients. It was not clear whether the law allowed the treating physician to testify, or whether it required an examination by a specially appointed outside physician. The court in *In the matter of R* (1982) attempted to interpret the law according to the inferred wishes of the legislature. It ruled that the physician-patient privilege would not apply in proceedings for the continuation of commitments. The court noted that the legislature wished to provide for continuity of treatment for persons with serious mental disorders. At the same time, it wished to protect the rights of the committed as much as possible.

In deciding this matter, the court held that the recognition of the privilege in recommitment hearings would not advance treatment or further the function of the physician-patient privilege. The court noted that "it is apparent from the very fact that these persons are hospitalized against their will, they are unable to recognize their need for help" (p. 706). Consequently the privilege would not promote voluntary treatment. Furthermore, the court noted that the evaluating physician would have access to the patient records anyway, thus violating the privilege by that fact alone. Finally, the court noted that the short supply of psychiatrists at public facilities means that some psychiatrists would be diverted from treating patients to evaluating them for recommitment alone.

PRIVILEGE AND HEALTH REGULATORY BOARDS

Health regulatory boards such as state licensing boards and individual hospital review committees may have occasion to inspect records to monitor the quality of treatment. At times, when health providers have been the patient, the board will seek the records on the health provider to determine if the provider can still practice without restriction. In other situations, the boards will seek the record of patients to determine that they have received adequate treatment.

Health Providers as Patients

Courts have reached different results concerning the authority of health regulatory boards to acquire otherwise confidential treatment records. In *County of Riverside v. Superior Court* (1974), the California State Board of Chiropractic Examiners sought the treatment records of a chiropractor to determine if his "habitual intemperance in the use of ardent spirits" incapacitated him in "the performance of his professional duties" (p. 887). The California court refused to allow the records to be subpoenaed, noting that the legislature had no exception to the confidentiality of mental health records that allowed its disclosure to administrative agencies. A contrary result was found in *State Board v. New York State Commissioner of Mental Hygiene* (1978). Here the court held that the board for professional medical conduct could acquire the psychiatric records of a physician. The court noted that the board had received previous complaints about the physician, and it could carry out its statutory mandate to investigate these complaints only if it had access to the doctor's records. The compelling state interest in the production of records prevailed because the relevant statute was silent on this issue.

Access to Patient Records

Several courts have decided the issue of whether professional review boards investigating physicians could have access to patient records to determine if the patients were receiving adequate treatment. In *Board of Medical Review Investigation* (1983), the Rhode Island court had to determine if the power of the board to investigate medical conduct conflicted with the physician-patient privilege. One statute appeared to permit the disclosure, while the other appeared to prohibit it. The court held that

> it seems apparent that the injury to society's interest in probity within the medical profession is much greater than the injury done to the patient's interest in the privacy of his medical records. A physician under investigation for professional misconduct subverts rather than supports the rights of patients by distorting the patient's privilege to serve his own ends. Indeed, it is highly questionable whether the petitioner has the standing to invoke the patient's privilege. Consequently, the overall legislative policy would best be implemented by disclosure to the board. (p. 1376).

In *Klinge v. Lutheran Medical Center of St. Louis* (1974), the court had to determine if the staff hospital review committee could examine patient records to determine if the physician was competent and qualified. The court permitted the review committee to view the records. In part, the decision was based on the policy of public interest: "The public's interest in the disclosure of the information to the internal staff of the hospital care outweighs the patient's interest in concealment" (p. 166). In addition, the court noted that the hospital records are not kept completely confidential but are seen and copied by staff members and employees. Thus the lack of complete confidentiality of the hospital records suggests that they were not intended as completely privileged. Finally, the court noted that it must interpret physician-patient privileges in the light of recent federal laws, which require Medicare providers to evaluate staff competency.

Two California cases have dealt with the issue of allowing quality assurance boards to have access to patient records. In *Board of Medical Quality Assurance v. Gheradini* (1979), the court held that the investigators could not have access to patient records. It commented that California's recent constitutional amendment on privacy had been interpreted to put the physician-patient relationship within its ambit. The government could not enter that zone unless the patient provided a waiver or the government demonstrated that it entered the zone with good cause and entered no further than necessary to achieve its purpose. The privileged area cannot be entered just because "the government wants assurance the law is not violated or a doctor is not negligent in treatment of his patient" (p. 62).

A subsequent California case remedied the shortcomings of the investigators of *Gheradini.* In *Board of Medical Quality Assurance v. Hazel Hawkins Memorial Hospital* (1982), the court ruled that the investigators could have the limited access to the patient records they requested. This access was highly specific and limited to charts relevant to the activities of the board. In addition, the investigators took precautions to ensure the privacy of patients by disclosing neither patients' names nor identifying medical information.

Chapter 8

Special Applications of Privilege to Criminal Proceedings

This chapter will review the application of the privilege in criminal courts. In numerous criminal cases, the courts will ask psychotherapists to testify concerning their clients. For the most part, the same criteria apply to the privilege in criminal as in civil courts. The first section will describe some exceptions to this general rule.

Also, mental health professionals are often used as expert witnesses to examine defendants in criminal trials. The court may appoint them, or private attorneys may employ them for an independent opinion. Generally the privilege will not apply in these situations because the examinations are designed to provide information to the court or the attorney and not to provide treatment. The criminal defendants have other shields of confidentiality, however, which may be based on constitutional grounds or on statutory grounds, especially the attorney-client privilege. Although these shields are distinct from the psychotherapist-client privileges, they are an area that may concern psychotherapists at some time. This chapter provides an overview of the shields in court-related examinations.

Finally, the last section of this chapter will deal with psychotherapists charged with crimes. The most common lawsuits occur when mental health professionals are charged with welfare fraud or abuse. The exact parameters of the privilege in these investigations has become quite controversial.

PSYCHOTHERAPIST-PATIENT PRIVILEGE IN CRIMINAL LAW

Most of the laws and case decisions regarding psychotherapist-patient privileges apply equally to criminal and civil law. On occasion, the statutory law may contain unique wording when applied to criminal law. In California, the privilege applies only to psychiatrists and psychologists in criminal cases. Social workers, school psychologists, and marriage, family, and child counselors have no privilege in criminal cases. In Virginia, the physician-patient and psychologist-patient privileges apply only in civil cases (Virginia Code §8.01-399, 1977 and §8.01-400.2, 1983; *Gibson v. Commonwealth,* 1976). Indiana makes an exception to the privilege "in trials for homicide when the disclosure relates directly to the fact or immediate circumstances of said homicide" (Indiana Code Annotates, §25-33-1-17 (1), 1985). The District of Columbia makes an exception to "evidence in criminal cases where the accused is charged with causing the death of, or inflicting injuries upon, a human being, and the disclosure is required in the interests of public justice" (District of Columbia Annotates, §14-307 (b) (1), 1985). The Washington, D.C., exception does not apply, however, to "civil cases involving wrongful death or injuries to another person" (*Simpson v. Braider,* 1985, p. 519).

Other special circumstances regarding the privilege and criminal law have been described elsewhere. Chapter 7 described the application of child abuse crimes to the privilege. The future crimes exception will be discussed next.

Future Crimes Exception

The privilege will not extend to communications that the patient makes in furtherance of a crime. It is well established in common law precedents with attorneys that communications to implement criminal activities are not privileged (Cleary, 1984). States that follow the attorney-client model in the psychotherapist-patient privilege law have a precedent to follow. The proposed but rejected Federal Rule of Evidence 504 has no specific clause stating a future crimes exception to the privilege. A reasonable reading of Rule 504, however, allows a future crimes interpretation. The rule creates the privilege for the diagnosis or treatment of a mental or emotional condition, including drug or alcohol addiction. It would not constitute treatment to aid the client in the furtherance of a crime. These activities may actually do the opposite of treating mental illness; they may further it. Even without specific statutory authority, courts have properly found grounds to create a future crimes exception.

The most common situation in which a future crimes exception is found is when patients use deceit to procure controlled drugs. Patients have lied about their health, altered prescriptions, or stolen prescriptions in order to obtain controlled drugs (e.g., *People v. Emanuel,* 1980; *People v. Johnson,* 1982; *State v. Thomale,* 1982; *State v. Treadway,* 1974). Even without specific statutory exceptions, courts have obtained evidence in these kinds of cases under various theories, including the theory that the privilege in this case would not create a just and reasonable result (*State v. Garrett,* 1983). Also, evidence has been admitted because the communications were not used to further the treatment of the patient (*Finney v. State,* 1981). Another court, *People v. Dean* (1984), used a strict interpretation of the privilege and allowed the physician to verify if the patient was telling the truth about her prescription but did not require him to reveal any direct statements.

In addition to drug abuse, the future crimes issue has arisen in some welfare abuse cases. In *People v. O'Gorman* (1977), the privilege could not be claimed because the communication of false information was fraud against the state when a client lied to her social worker about her eligibility for welfare benefits. That communication was a crime because it was fraud against the state and no social worker-client privilege would apply. *O'Gorman* is distinguished from *Community Service Society v. Welfare Inspector General* (1978). Here the client gave false information to the welfare agency in order to receive benefits, but the privilege was not waived. The discovery of the client's false statements occurred while she was a client in a demonstration project to rehabilitate welfare recipients. There was no exception to the privilege because the client was reporting a past crime to the social worker in the rehabilitation project and was not trying to further a crime through the social worker.

The future crimes exception should not include instances in which, in the course of treatment, the patient shares thoughts or fantasies of an antisocial or criminal nature. The communication to the psychotherapist does not further the completion of these acts. Such instances are clinical material to be resolved in therapy.

This issue was raised in *Mutual of Omaha Insurance Company v. American National Bank and Trust Company* (1985). In this case, a heavily insured woman died of an apparent homicide. The insurance company resisted paying proceeds and investigated her half-brother (and beneficiary) for fraudulently procuring the policies and considered him a suspect in their investigation of her death. They tried to obtain the psychiatric records of the half-brother because it was thought they might have information relevant to the investigation. The company argued that the future crimes exception should apply. The court rejected this argument and distinguished this situation from the future crimes exception: "The patient's purpose in divulging such thoughts may well be to obtain treatment rather than aid in furtherance or concealment of a crime" (p. 549). The court also distinguished this situation from others where a duty to protect third persons arises. (See discussion of *Tarasoff v. Regents of University of California et al.* in Chapter

12.) "The policy to encourage doctors to warn to prevent injuries to others is not implicated so much where injury has already occurred. Disclosure in this case is now unrelated to any existing need to warn" (p. 550).

Privilege with Dangerous Patients

In several cases, psychotherapists have had contact with the patient shortly before or after the commission of a serious crime. In a number of these situations, the patients have requested that the psychotherapist get them help or report them to the police. The majority of courts have held that the patient's request to divulge the information abrogates the privilege. This is an appropriate interpretation because the privilege should not apply when the psychotherapist is asked to be an intermediary.

For example, in *State v. Martin* (1979) a client called his social worker, Mr. Lawlor, and told him, "I have killed somebody." Lawlor told his client that he would have to call the police, and the client agreed and even gave the social worker the address. The social worker arrived with the police and entered the house with the apparent permission of the client.

The South Dakota court correctly held that the communications to Lawlor were not privileged. Although licensed social workers are protected by statute in South Dakota, the court held that the communications are privileged only if they are intended to be confidential. The willingness of the client to allow Lawlor to call the police and his subsequent behavior after the social worker and police arrived indicated that he did not expect the communications to be made in confidence.

Other cases with similar controlling facts have reached identical conclusions. For example, in *People v. Fentress* (1980), a client waived the privilege by asking his attorney to notify the police of his homicide act. And in *People v. Christopher* (1984), the client told a psychiatric nurse of his intention to turn himself in. Subsequently he asked the army chaplain to discuss his problems with the police and medical officials to get him the help he needed. The court would not consider his statements to the nurse or chaplain as privileged. In order for the privilege to apply, the "communication must have been confidential in nature and the patient must have contemplated that it would be kept so" (p. 642).

One Texas court held differently (*Tumlinson v. State,* 1983). An air force sergeant on leave spoke to Dr. Murray, a licensed Texas psychologist, and revealed that he feared he might have killed someone. He described a vision of a woman with a rope around her neck and stated that he had just spent three days with such a woman. He gave the psychologist the name and address of the woman, and the psychologist, with the sergeant's permission, called the police. Later the sergeant was indicted for the murder and found guilty.

On appeal, the sergeant argued that his communications to Murray and the contents of the telephone calls to the police should have been privileged. The appeals court agreed, noting that there was no statutory exception to the privilege found in the law. The court noted that the "duty to warn" portion of Texas confidentiality law refers only to extrajudicial disclosures and not to courtroom testimony. The waiver must be done in writing to the court.

It appears that the Texas court followed the letter of the law to the detriment of the spirit. Communications to third persons should be privileged only if the third persons are necessary to further the treatment of the patient. The Dallas police were not, and the sergeant's authorized communications to them should have waived the privilege.

THE SHIELD OF CONFIDENTIALITY IN CRIMINAL COURT EXAMINATIONS

This section examines the mechanisms that protect confidentiality in criminal court examinations. Although no psychotherapist-patient privilege exists in court-ordered examinations, other shields can restrict or control the access of information to courts. Although these shields do not rest on the psychotherapist-patient privileges, they may interest some readers. (Interested readers can consult more detailed sources for more information: e.g., Allis, 1977; Meister, 1975; New, 1982; Note, 1976*b*).

These confidentiality protections are important because of the wide use that courts make of mental health testimony in criminal cases. The courts may request psychiatric information to determine if the accused is incompetent to stand trial, if the accused was sufficiently sane to be held legally responsible for the alleged crimes, if the witnesses are credible or competent to testify, if there is any risk of suicide while in pretrial detentions, or as an aid in sentencing. A mental health professional who examines a defendant or witness for any one purpose may, of course, acquire information relevant to another aspect of the case. For example, a psychiatrist who examines a patient to determine sanity at the time of the alleged crime may unearth material relevant to the guilt or innocence of the defendant.

The rules regarding the communications between professional and patient can be unusually complex because they may involve several relevant doctrines or laws that will apply depending upon the facts of the case. The case may involve the physician-patient or psychotherapist-patient privilege, the attorney-client privilege, and possibly the constitutional guarantees of the Fifth Amendment (freedom from self-incrimination), Sixth Amendment (right to a fair trial and effective counsel), or Fourteenth Amendment (due process within a trial). These rules provide a shield of confidentiality around defendants that allows them to conduct their defense free from unfair inhibition.

Constitutional Protections

The Fifth Amendment states that "no person . . . shall be compelled in any criminal case to be a witness against himself." In addition, various state constitutions have similar self-incrimination provisions. The federal rules, however, are of primary importance because they were made applicable to the states in *Miranda v. Arizona* (1966). The *Miranda* decision interpreted the Fourteenth Amendment requiring states to follow due process for its citizens to mean that the Fifth Amendment should apply to criminal cases. Defendants should be informed of their right to remain silent, that the information could be used against them in court, and of the right to counsel.

The Fifth Amendment has traditionally been applied to thwart compelled confessions during policy custody and interrogation. The privilege extends not only to direct confessions, but "likewise embraces those which would furnish a link in the chain of evidence needed to prosecute" (*Hoffman v. United States,* 1951, p. 486). Other kinds of physical information, such as fingerprints or blood tests (Cleary, 1984), are not privileged.

The Fifth Amendment can also apply to court-ordered treatment or examinations. It serves "to protect persons in all settings in which their freedom of action is curtailed in any significant way" (*Estelle v. Smith,* 1981, p. 466). The possibility of self-incrimination can occur "from interrogation conducted by a court appointed psychiatrist as well as a police officer" (*Battie v. Estelle,* 1981, p. 669). The Fifth Amendment, however, is limited to criminal and not civil cases. It will not apply to proceedings for civil commitments, proceedings to terminate marital rights, or to pretrial evaluations to determine competency to stand trial.

The Sixth and Fourteenth amendments may also apply. The Sixth Amendment guarantees the effective assistance of counsel. Often counsel can provide effective assistance only if they are allowed to conduct a factual investigation and prepare adequate defense. At times this requires the use of a psychiatric expert.

The Fourteenth Amendment requires equal protection or equal treatment for defendants. It has been raised as an issue when publicly trained mental health experts have been required to reveal information that would not have been required of privately trained experts. In addition, the Fourteenth Amendment requires due process. These due process provisions include procedural safeguards that ensure that the rights of the defendant are not being violated.

Power of Courts to Compel Examinations

Courts have consistently held that they have the right to order compulsory psychiatric examinations of criminal defendants. They have based their rationale on specific statutory authorization, inherent judicial powers, or the interests in maintaining a balance between the state and individuals in litigation. Without compulsory examinations, it could be argued, the prosecution would be unable to prove sanity beyond a reasonable doubt. Because defense psychiatrists have access to the defendant, prosecution psychiatrists should have the same access.

These compulsory examinations do not violate the spirit of the psychotherapist-patient privilege. The requisite psychotherapist-patient relationship does not exist in court-ordered examinations because these interviews are not intended as treatment but only to provide information to the court, and no pretext of confidentiality is assumed. The right of the courts to compel these examinations does not harm the psychotherapist-patient relationship. A compelled examination does not harm an existing relationship or deter defendants from seeking treatment from other professionals. In fact, compulsory examinations may strengthen the privilege because they provide courts with the opportunity to acquire psychiatric information from sources other than an ongoing relationship. In addition to ordering psychiatric examinations, the courts may order physical examinations (*Clark v. Indiana,* 1982). Courts may order supplementary examinations such as an electroencephalogram (EEG) or computed axial tomography (CAT) scan if they are necessary to complete the psychiatric examination (*Commonwealth v. Marshall,* 1977).

Failure to comply with a court-ordered examination could have adverse consequences for the defendant. Defendants are presumed sane until they can demonstrate otherwise. Failure to cooperate with a court-ordered examination could mean that defendants are barred from presenting their own medical evidence of sanity (e.g., *State v. Jackson,* 1982). Also, it could be grounds for a contempt of court citation (e.g., *Pyles v. State,* 1975).

Application of Constitutional Shield to Court-Ordered Examinations

One concern with court-ordered examinations is that defendants may incriminate themselves. Their statements may implicate them in the crime charged, or they may provide evidence concerning their mental condition that could be used to establish the *mens rea* ("guilty mind") necessary for the crime charged. The rule established either through statute or court interpretation is that a court may not use the defendant's statements in these interviews to determine guilt. Instead, these interviews are usually started with a *Miranda*-type warning concerning their purpose. Even if the defendants still incriminate themselves in these interviews, the courts can exclude incriminating evidence from the interviewer's testimony.

United States v. Albright (1968) was one of the most cited cases dealing with the application of the Fifth Amendment. In this case, the defendant was charged with multiple counts of forging U.S. postal money orders. The court found him guilty and rejected his defense of insanity. Albright appealed, in part because he claimed that the court-ordered examination violated his Fifth Amendment rights.

The U.S. District Court rejected Albright's appeal. It noted that it had the statutory authority to inquire into the mental status of a defendant (18 U.S.C.A. §4244). Even without this authority, the court noted that it had the inherent power to require an examination, whose purpose was to provide evidence relating to sanity and "not to determine whether a defendant did or did not do the criminal acts charged" (p. 725). Consequently the court ruled that the defendant's Fifth Amendment rights against self-incrimination were not violated.

The *Albright* ruling has been typical of the decisions by the federal judiciary in other circuits. Subsequent decisions have clarified or amplified *Albright,* but all have followed its lead. For example, in *United States v. Greene* (1974), the defendant was not informed of his right to remain silent during the examination by the government psychiatrists. Nevertheless, the Fifth Amendment was not violated because the psychiatrist only presented evidence in rebuttal of the issue of sanity. There can be no violation of the right against self-incrimination when no self-incrimination is involved. In *Ronson v. Commissioner of Correction of State of New York* (1982), it was held that the Fifth Amendment was not violated when the prosecuting attorney was present at the examination. There was no showing that the defendant made any incriminating remarks later used against him. In *United States v. Williams* (1972), the characterization of the defendant as an "antisocial type" during testimony regarding his sanity was not an incriminating statement but "merely an attempt to speak precisely of Williams's psychological condition" (p. 218).

A final example of the subsequent court clarifications can be found in *Booker v. Wainwright* (1983). Here the information derived from the psychiatric examination was used to impeach (impugn the credibility) the defendant during the penalty phase of the trial. The court held that this use of the information did not violate the Fifth Amendment. The court relied on a previous Supreme Court decision for its opinion. The Supreme Court wrote in *Harris v. New York* (1971) that "every criminal defendant is privileged to testify in his own defense, or to refuse to do so. But that privilege cannot be construed to include the right to commit perjury" (p. 222).

State courts have generally followed the lead of the federal courts in applying the Fifth Amendment to compel psychiatric examinations (e.g., *Gibson v. Zahradnick,* 1978; *People v. Stevens,* 1977; *State v. McGautha,*

1981; *State v. Obstein*, 1968). As stated in *Williamson v. State*, 1976), "The defendant should not fear that what he says may be used against him in a trial where the issue is his guilt or innocence of the offense charged" (p. 275).

The Supreme Court ruled on the applicability of the Fifth Amendment to psychiatric examinations in *Estelle v. Smith* (1981). In this case, Smith was tried for a capital murder that occurred during an armed robbery of a liquor store. Before consulting with Smith's attorney, the trial judge ordered Smith to be evaluated by a psychiatrist, Dr. Grigson, to determine competency to stand trial. Grigson wrote to the judge that Smith was competent. Smith was subsequently found guilty, and Grigson was again called to testify concerning Smith at the sentencing stage of the proceedings. Grigson concluded that Smith was a "very severe sociopath" who had "no remorse or sorrow for what he has done" (pp. 459-460). Grigson also stated that Smith "is going to go ahead and commit other similar or same criminal acts if given the opportunity to so do" (p. 460). Grigson's testimony was based in part on Smith's account of his crime.

The Supreme Court overruled the trial court on the basis of the Fifth and Sixth amendments. The state had relied on the Texas criminal statute, which held that no statements made by the defendant may be entered into determining the issue of guilt. The Supreme Court, however, held that "we can discern no basis to distinguish between the guilt and penalty phases of respondent's capital murder trial so far as the protection of the Fifth Amendment is concerned" (1981, pp. 462-463). The possible consequences to Smith were literally a matter of life and death, and these determined the applicability of the Fifth Amendment. In addition, the court noted that Smith had been evaluated without the benefit of consulting with counsel beforehand, indicating that the Sixth Amendment right to counsel at critical stages of the trial was denied: "The State used respondent's own statements unwittingly made without an awareness that he was assisting the State's efforts to obtain the death penalty" (p. 466).

Mental Health Professionals and the Attorney-Client Privilege

The attorney-client privilege has its roots in the common law and now receives further protection through statutory enactments. The rationale is that the administration of justice is improved because clients feel free to discuss their cases with their attorneys without fear that the information could be used against them later in court.

Sometimes it is unclear how far the attorney-client privilege will extend to the agents or employees of an attorney. The attorney-client privilege covers the services of receptionists, secretaries, messengers, and clerks. It would make little sense to protect the communications made by the clients to their attorneys but then require the secretary who typed the dictation to testify in court as to the nature of the private communication.

In addition to the agents who transcribe or relay information, attorneys also rely on the advice of independent professionals to provide information necessary for the effective development of the case. These agents may also fall within the attorney-client privilege if they are necessary for the effective development of a case or if they further the attorneys' development of the case. This principle was articulated in the case of *United States v. Kovel* (1961) where an accountant working for an attorney was held to fall under the attorney-client privilege. The court compared the need for an accountant in this case with the need for having an interpreter for a foreign speaking client:

> Accounting concepts are a foreign language to some lawyers in almost all cases, and to almost all lawyers in some cases. Hence the presence of an accountant, where hired by the lawyer or by the client, while the client is relating a complicated tax story to the lawyer, ought not destroy the privilege any more than would that of the linguist... the presence of the accountant is necessary, or at least highly useful for the effective consultation between the client and the lawyer which the privilege is designed to permit. (p. 123)

The court went on to comment that "what is vital to the privilege is that the communication be made in confidence for the purpose of obtaining legal advice from the lawyer" (p. 123).

These precedents concerning agents of attorneys have relevance to mental health professionals who work as agents of the attorneys. For example, an attorney may seek advice concerning a case in which the mental health of the client was an issue in litigation. Obviously the attorney alone could not provide much useful information concerning an insanity defense but would require a mental health professional to evaluate the client and provide advice concerning the feasibility of a defense: "Only a foolhardy lawyer would determine tactical and evidentiary strategy in a case with psychiatric issues without the guidance and interpretation of psychiatrists and others skilled in this field" (*United States ex rel. Edney v. Smith,* 1976, p. 1047).

Under most circumstances, the relationship of the mental health professional under the attorney-client privilege is clear-cut. The clients could allow the mental health professional to testify if they waived the privilege. Also clients could bar the mental health professional from testifying if they decided not to enter mental health as an issue in the defense.

The extent of the psychotherapist-defendant privilege becomes controversial when clients introduce their mental health into the proceeding or request expert testimony but then wish to keep certain mental health professionals with adverse testimony off the stand. This could occur, for example, if a client looked into the feasibility of an insanity defense. The first mental health professional might argue against such a defense. The attorney could then seek the advice of another mental health professional who might favor such a defense. If the defense attorney admitted the second psychiatrist on the stand, could the prosecution also require the testimony of the first psychiatrist? This has been the major issue arising out of the application of the attorney-client privilege to mental health professionals.

The majority of courts have held that defense-retained mental health professionals (usually psychiatrists) will not be called upon to testify unless the defense specifically calls them to the stand. In some of these cases, the defendant was still found guilty on the basis of other evidence, and the error was harmless (*Houston v. State,* 1979; *People ex rel. Bowman v. Woodward,* 1976; *People v. Lines,* 1975; *Pouncy v. State,* 1977; *State v. Kociolek,* 1957; *State v. Moore,* 1980; *State v. Pratt,* 1979; *State v. Toste,* 1979; *United States v. White,* 1980; *Ursury v. Florida,* 1983). The popularity of this stand is being eroded, however.

The most commonly cited case advocating this position is *United States v. Alvarez* (1975). In this case, a trial judge held an indigent criminal competent to stand trial but authorized the defendant to retain Dr. Sadoff, a psychiatrist, for an insanity examination. Then, under a mutual discovery order, the prosecution obtained a copy of Sadoff's report, which concluded that the defendant was sane. Subsequently the prosecution subpoenaed Sadoff over the objections of the defense. The defendant was convicted in part on the basis of Sadoff's testimony concerning his sanity and on the basis of the defendant's incriminating statements within that report.

The court reversed the conviction and granted a new trial. The major issue was the use of Sadoff's testimony. The court found that the psychiatrist was protected from disclosure. It held that the defense had not waived confidentiality by asserting a mental capacity defense. Also, the court held that both the attorney-client privilege and the existing federal rules of procedure protected the statements to the defense counsel. The court presented arguments for its decision:

> The effective assistance of counsel with respect to the preparation of an insanity defense demands recognition that the defendant be as free to communicate with a psychiatric expert as with the attorney he is assisting. If the expert is later used as a witness on behalf of the defendant, obviously the cloak of the privilege ends. But when . . . the defendant does not call the expert the same privilege applies with respect to communications from the defendant as applies to such communications to the attorney himself. (p. 1046)

The *Alvarez* court further argued that

> disclosures made to the attorney cannot be used to furnish proof in the government's case. Disclosures made to the attorney's expert should be equally unavailable, at least until he is placed on the witness stand. The attorney must be free to make an informed judgement with respect to the best course for the defense without creating a potential government witness. . . . The attorney should not be inhibited from consulting one or more experts, with possibly conflicting views, by the fear that in doing so he may be assisting the government in meeting its burden of proof. (p. 1047)

A subsequent Maryland decision, *Pratt v. State* (1978) (later affirmed in *State v. Pratt* 1979), provided additional reasoning behind this decision. *Pratt* noted that calling a psychiatrist previously hired by the defense but not called "tends to add undue weight to his testimony" (p. 784). It also tried to rebut the argument that this rule "allows the defense to suppress unfavorable experts while shopping around for an expert that supports its position" (784). Although this may occur, *Pratt* argued that it does not significantly impair the state, which has access to its share of experts as well.

United States ex rel. Edney v. Smith. For many years the case *United States ex rel. Edney v. Smith* (1976) stood out as a single contrary decision, but it has received a more favorable response from courts recently. The decision held that the prosecution could have access to records and testimony of any defense-retained psychiatrist when defendants entered their mental health into litigation. The extent of the privilege exception is narrow and does not apply to incriminating evidence. There is widespread agreement, however, that this would violate the defendant's right against self-incrimination.

Edney was charged with kidnapping and killing the 8-year-old daughter of his ex-girlfriend. The fact that he committed the crime was never in dispute. The dispute occurred over the sanity of Edney at the time of the crime. Edney claimed that he heard voices telling him that God wanted the little girl. He claimed to have drunk large quantities of alcohol and to have smoked marijuana, and he claimed to have had a blackout and to have no recollection of the murder.

Edney's lawyer had arranged for two psychiatric evaluations. The first psychiatrist, Dr. Schwartz, had determined that Edney was not insane at the time of the murder. The second psychiatrist opined that Edney was mentally ill and insane at the time of the murder. The defense called the second psychiatrist to the stand. The prosecution called Schwartz to the stand to rebut the testimony. Edney was found guilty. The major issue in the appeal was the calling of Schwartz to the stand.

In the appeal, the defense argued that the physician-patient and attorney-client privileges should have protected the evidence. The court properly dismissed the physician-patient privilege argument. This privilege exists only to provide encouragement for treatment, an element that was lacking in this case. Furthermore, Edney had waived that privilege by entering his mental health into litigation. The appeals court also rejected the attorney-client argument and upheld the conviction.

Edney appealed to federal courts on the basis that the New York rule violated the Sixth Amendment guarantee of effective counsel. Judge Weinstein, an expert on the law of evidence and procedure, gave an excellent and thorough decision. He showed sympathy for Edney's arguments, but the appeal was limited to constitutional grounds, and Weinstein had to rule accordingly: "Even assuming that such an extension is desirable—and we have no doubt that it is—that does not answer the question before us. We must determine whether it is constitutionally compelled, whether the attorney-client privilege is embodied in the Sixth Amendment, at least to the extent of the facts in this case" (p. 1048).

Judge Weinstein gave compelling arguments for his refusal to find constitutional grounds for this extension of the attorney-client privilege:

> It seems undesirable at this time to canonize the majority rule on the attorney-psychiatrist-client privilege and freeze it into a constitutional form not amenable to change by rule, statute, or further case law development. Were we to force the State into the rigid format suggested by the petitioner in this case . . . we could cut off further experimentation in this area—not only by this state, but by all state and federal courts and legislatures. We cannot say what the ultimate consensus, if any, will be on these policy issues. But it appears inappropriate and unwise at this stage to block potential branches of evolution. (pp. 1054-1055)

Consequently Judge Weinstein let the decision of the New York Appeals Court stand.

Recent Directions. Several recent courts have followed the lead of the New York Appeals Court in *Edney* (*Granviel v. Estelle,* 1981; *Noggle v. Marshall,* 1983; *People v. Sorna,* 1979; *State v. Carter,* 1982; *State v. Craney,* 1984; *State v. Dodis,* 1982). At times, they have provided more affirmative reasons for their results than merely stating that the *Edney* rule was constitutionally permissible. Instead they have often emphasized the need for full disclosure of acts before the court. *People v. Sorna* clarified a previous decision by the Michigan Supreme Court (*People v. Hilliker,* 1971). In *Hilliker,* the prosecution acquired reports of the defense psychiatrist and used them to attack the truthfulness of the defendant, although they excluded incriminating materials. In *Sorna,* the defense was allowed to have access to the defense psychiatrist's report but only for purposes of determining sanity. The Michigan court noted that this purpose was consistent with a recently enacted Michigan law that allowed exchange of reports for purposes of determining sanity. According to *Sorna,* the chilling effect of this law on the defendant-psychiatrist relationship was not the only consideration: "This position ignores the fundamental purpose of a criminal trial: The fair ascertainment of the truth. . . . A necessary concomitant of this goal is the reasonable balancing of advantages and a lessening of a vehemently adversary climate at trial" (p. 895).

A similar finding was made in *State v. Dodis* (1982), where the court also noted the Minnesota statute allowing an exchange of reports dealing with the issue of insanity: "Any other result suppresses evidence that a court or jury needs to know to formulate a just determination concerning the mental illness defense" (p. 240).

State v. Craney (1984) was noted for the tone of argument, if not for its strength. *Craney* noted that the adversarial relationship should not result in truth being withheld from the courts. It rejected the "sporting" theory of justice that allows the concealment of evidence: "We think Alvarez reflects the bygone philosophy that for an attorney's investigation to be effective they must be shrouded in secrecy" (p. 677).

The attorney-psychiatrist-client (or psychiatrist-defendant) relationship is unlike other privileged relationships for mental health professionals in that its rationale does not rest on promoting treatment. Instead its justification comes from the rationale underlying the attorney-client relationship. Like the major rationales for the psychotherapist-patient relationship, the rationale for the attorney-client relationship is utilitarian. Unlike the psychotherapist-patient relationship, no privacy interests are involved: "The proposition is that the detriment to justice from a power to shut off inquiry into pertinent facts in court will be outweighted by the benefits to justice (not to the client) from a franker disclosure in the lawyer's office" (Cleary, 1984, p. 205).

In the long run, does the application of the attorney-client privilege in this situation further the truth-finding capacity of the court? Saltzburg (1980), in a seminal article on privileged communication, supports the conclusions of the New York Court of Appeals in *United States ex rel. Edney v. Smith*, although he claims that the decision could have been made more persuasively. Saltzburg presented four additional reasons for making an exception to the attorney-client privilege in this situation. First, he noted that no privacy interests were involved because the patient had already entered mental health into litigation. Second, the prosecution's substitute examination could not be an adequate substitute for an earlier defense-related examination. Several courts have had to deal with directly obstructive clients who fail to cooperate with mental health examinations. These refusals are overt and obvious, but there is an adequate way to measure covertly noncooperative patients: "a patient who refuses to cooperate, or withholds or distorts information, denies the prosecution of a fair opportunity to conduct a full examination" (Saltzburg, 1980, p. 636). Third, the defense-related psychiatrist will usually get to the defendant first, thus seeing the patient closer to the time of the crime, with less intervening time to alter the mental state. Finally, a defendant may benefit from undergoing several examinations and from examining reports of different psychiatrists even though they may be unfavorable toward the defense. This psychiatric training may be informal and coincidental, but it could occur even when ethical attorneys and psychiatrists are involved.

Saltzburg acknowledges that some steps should be taken so that the defense is not unduly harmed by this rule. The judge should prevent counsel from arguing about the significance of the retention by the prosecution of a psychiatrist originally employed by the defense. This has been noted in several cases (*State v. Moore,* 1980; *Pratt v. State,* 1978) and can be limited through special instructions by the judge to the jury. Also, Saltzburg claimed that the privilege should apply if the defendant abandons the insanity defense or otherwise withholds mental health from litigation. In that way, the defense will not be penalized for making an inquiry into the insanity defense.

Examination of Witnesses

At times, the need of the courts to investigate the competency or credibility of witnesses will conflict with privileged information. The terms *competency* and *credibility* are related but distinct. *Competency* is the threshold test for acceptance as a witness as determined by the judge. *Credibility* refers to the weight the jury gives to the witness's testimonies. Judges follow no absolute rule to determine competency, but the traditional test is whether the individual is sensible enough to report facts accurately and to appreciate the duty to tell the truth. "Is his capacity to observe, remember, and recount, such that he can probably bring added knowledge of the facts?" (Cleary, 1984, p. 156). There is a presumption of the competency to testify, and the burden to overcome this presumption rests with the opponents of the witness.

Credibility refers to the degree of weight the jury gives to the testimony of witnesses. Should the jury disregard the testimony or give it absolute acceptance? Several commentators have noted the effect that certain mental health problems may have on the veracity of certain witnesses. For example, a paranoid person may interpret a reality skewed with suspicion, fantasies, or delusions. Trivial events may become huge injustices, and chance happenings may become eloquent proof of conspiracy. An individual with an antisocial personality may blatantly lie without guilt and do so in a convincing manner.

Most states hold that judges in criminal cases have the right to order psychiatric examinations of key prosecution witnesses when evidence questions their competency or credibility. Like competency, no absolute tests tell judges when an examination should be ordered. The criteria for ordering an examination are high. The exact phrases vary, at least semantically, and include phrases such as "compelling reason" and "substantial showing of need and justification." The trial judge must determine if the benefits to the truth-seeking function of the court will justify the time and distraction taken to assess witness credibility. Also, the judges realize that the examination may invade the privacy of the witness, risking subsequent humiliation. Such examinations, if done routinely, would reduce the willingness of witnesses to testify.

No privilege exists for the results of psychiatric examinations ordered by the court to determine witness credibility or competency. At times, however, opponents of witnesses will try to introduce past mental health records to challenge their credibility. In the past, privileged communication laws, if literally construed, provided a barrier to the discovery of this information (*People v. Lapsley,* 1970). This general rule has undergone modification following recent Supreme Court decisions, which implicate Sixth Amendment rights to confront witnesses. According to the Sixth Amendment, criminal defendants have the right to a fair trial and to confront adverse witnesses. At times this right to confront adverse witnesses may conflict with privileged communication laws. (The case law was described in Chapter 2.)

Privileged Communications and Rape Victims

The examination of witnesses is an important issue in rape or other sexual assault cases. In these cases, the key witness for the prosecution is usually also the victim. In recent years, legislators have tried to balance the need for vigorous prosecution of rape cases with the need to protect the rights of the accused.

Rape is underreported, and it is believed that this is due in part to the behavior of the police or other members of the judicial system who have shown subtle or overt disrespect, callousness, or hostility toward the victims. Many state legislators believed that the number of reported rapes would increase if greater concern were shown for the rights and privacy of the women victims. Consequently most states have passed rape shield laws that limit the rights of the accused to interrogate the victim concerning her sexual history. Other states have forbid the pretrial psychiatric examination of victims in sex offense-related cases.

Privileged communication has arisen as a concern in situations in which the victim has sought the aid of a psychotherapist or a rape crisis counselor. Two issues have arisen in these cases. First, most of the staff at rape crisis centers are volunteers or paraprofessionals who are not covered by privileged communication laws. Second, even with a privilege law, the information might become available to the defense if it conflicted with the Sixth Amendment right to confront witnesses (Stouder, 1982).

Currently, only Pennsylvania, Minnesota, Illinois, California, Massachusetts, Connecticut, Florida, Maine, and New Jersey have privileged communication laws for rape crisis counselors. These rape crisis counselors provide an important service, especially for women of lower-class backgrounds who cannot afford licensed psychotherapists. Except for counselors in the nine states, other rape counselors practice without a privilege.

The status of nonprofessional rape crisis volunteers was an issue in the case of *Matter of Pittsburgh Action Against Rape* (1981), a Pennsylvania case before the passage of the privilege law. A man was charged with rape, involuntary deviate sexual intercourse, indecent assault, simple assault, and terroristic threats. During the cross-examination of the victim-complainant, the defense counsel asked to examine the records of the volunteer rape crisis counselor to determine if the victim had made any statements to her counselors inconsistent with her trial testimony. The executive director of the counseling service, Pittsburgh Action Against Rape (PAAR), refused to comply with that order and was held in contempt of court.

The Supreme Court of Pennsylvania ruled in the contempt order. The majority opinion held that the court could admit statements of the alleged victim to her rape crisis counselor. The court restricted the released information only to those statements and would not admit any interpretations by the counselor. Furthermore, the court ordered an *in camera* review of the records before they would be released to the defense. When the defense uses these files, the use must be restricted. The court noted that "statements contained in such file may have no bearing whatsoever on facts of alleged offense and may relate instead only to counselling services provided by the center, and, therefore, such statements reflecting counseling are to be withheld from defense inspection" (p. 127). In addition, the court noted that it would issue protective orders against the improper discovery by defense. The majority decision was joined by two concurring decisions that upheld the results but added that they believed that Pennsylvania's constitution provided a right to privacy that was involved in this decision and should have been noted in the decision.

The decision also had a notable dissent by Justice Larsen, which reviewed the literature concerning the bias of the judicial system against rape victims and the effects of the rape trauma syndrome. He then considered a privilege for rape crisis counselors according to Wigmore's four criteria and found that the need for such a privilege existed. Larsen concluded his dissent with a plea to the legislature: "Since my position is, alas, only a dissent, I appeal to our legislature to take cognizance of the rape victim's plight and to act promptly and compassionately in legislatively enacting a rape victim/rape crisis counselor testimonial privilege" (p. 150). The plea did not fall on deaf ears. The Pennsylvania legislature subsequently passed such a privilege law.

The rape counselor-rape victim privilege is well justified on both intrinsic and utilitarian grounds. The intrinsic rationale appears especially compelling in this situation. There appears something harsh or even cruel about using the spontaneous words of a trauma victim seeking help against herself in a criminal trial against her assailant. The utilitarian grounds are also clear. In the counselor-victim relationship, the communications are made with the expectation of privacy. Society should sedulously foster this relationship because it aids victims of violent crimes and increases the likelihood of the prosecution of violent offenders. Also, the counselor-victim relationship would be harmed substantially without a privilege. This harm was demonstrated in an aftermath of the publicity generated in the case of *Matter of Pittsburgh Action Against Rape* (1981), where rape crisis centers saw a large decrease in referrals apparently because victims feared that their requests for help would ultimately backfire and harm them in case of future litigation. Finally, the court would not be impaired in its truth-seeking purpose, especially considering the two qualifications we place on the proposed legislation.

The proposed counselor-victim privilege would have two qualifications. First, it would allow courts to waive the privilege if the Sixth Amendment rights of the defendants were jeopardized. Courts would allow a limited waiver of the privilege if, through an *in camera* inspection of the records, the judge found that the information requested was essential to the defense, relevant, material, and unavailable from other sources (Williamson, 1984). Currently most states provide no statutory direction for handling conflicts between the privilege and the Sixth Amendment. Consequently these statutes are vulnerable to a consitutional challenge. Other states, however, provide statutory remedies to handle potential conflicts. Maine allows waiver of the privilege if the judge "deems the disclosure necessary to the sound administration of justice" (Maine Rules of Evidence, Rule 503, 1985). Minnesota and California statutes allow the courts to weigh the effects on the victim, treatment relationship, the treatment services against the public interest, or probative value of the evidence.

The second qualification is that the counselor-victim privilege would apply only to proceedings (including civil cases) arising out of assault or sexual crimes. It would not be a general privilege like the psychotherapist-patient privilege, which would apply theoretically in any proceeding. Rape crisis counselors are highly trained in one area: treatment of rape trauma victims. They should not be recognized as functional equivalents of psychotherapists who can treat a wide range of disorders.

MENTAL HEALTH PROFESSIONALS CHARGED WITH CRIMES

The privilege is designed to protect the privacy of patients and to encourage their participation in treatment. At times, psychotherapists or hospital employees have attempted to assert the privilege when they (and not the patients) have been charged with a crime.

Investigations of Welfare Fraud and Abuse

This is an era of fiscal responsibility. Both Democratic and Republican politicians are concerned about the rapid increase in Medicare and Medicaid costs. Although reasonable persons may disagree about certain aspects of Medicare/Medicaid funding, all agree that the government should reduce welfare fraud and abuse as much as possible. To this end, Congress passed Public Law 95-142, which locates a unit within the Department of Justice to investigate and prosecute physicians and other health professionals who abuse or defraud the Medicare/Medicaid systems.

The nature of these abuses and frauds has been documented in more detail elsewhere (Pontell, Jesilow, and Geis, 1982). Among the fraudulent practices are billing for services never provided; upgrading (billing for a more extensive service than was actually provided); ping-ponging (making unnecessary and reciprocal referrals to other health providers); and ganging (billing services to members of the same family on the same day). These and other procedures have led to the creation of medicaid mills, which annually milk taxpayers of millions of dollars.

Psychiatrists especially have been affected by medical benefits investigations. Although psychiatrists constitute only about 8% of the physicians, they represent 18% of the number of physicians suspended from the program because of fraudulent or abusive practices (Geis et al., 1985). In part, this may be because it is easier to monitor the abuses of psychiatrists than those of other physicians. Unfortunately, the laudable attempt to crack down on fraud and abuse has led to a clash of rights. Medical (especially psychiatric) patients have a need for privacy, which government investigators may, under certain circumstances, violate in their pursuit of fraudulent physicians.

In one of the earlier cases dealing with Medicaid investigation, the court found the government excessively zealous in its activities (*Hawaii Psychiatric Association v. Ariyoshi,* 1979). The attorney general of Hawaii went to the office of a clinical psychologist and copied all the records of his Medicaid patients. The monitoring was routine, and the psychologist was under no suspicion of fraud. The psychologist joined with the Hawaii Psychiatric Association and argued that the practice violated the privacy of his patients.

Although the court did not mention privileged communication laws per se, its ruling has implications for them. The court held that the communications of the psychotherapist to his patients fell under the protection of the constitutional right to privacy. It based its rulings on precedents in the Supreme Court's decisions on privacy in reproductive and family issues (*Roe v. Wade,* 1973; *Whalen v. Roe,* 1977). It stated that "no area could be more deserving of protection than communications between a psychiatrist and his patient. Such communications often include problems in precisely the areas previously recognized by the [Supreme] Court as within the zone of protected privacy, including family, marriage, parenthood, human sexuality, and physical problems" (p. 1038).

The court followed traditional rules and acknowledged that the right to privacy was not absolute and may be entered if the state has a narrowly drawn compelling interest. Here the government had an interest in controlling welfare fraud. The intrusion, however, was not narrowly drawn. The government could have found less intrusive means to investigate fraud than to copy all of the psychologist's records. Furthermore, this kind of investigation should not be done routinely but only when there is "individual articulable suspicion." Even when the government does initiate justifiable investigations, it should take precautions to protect the privacy of client records.

Other, and mostly more recent, cases have supported the efforts of the government to investigate welfare fraud and abuse. Often these efforts rely on the common law interpretation that the confidentiality of the psychotherapist-patient relationship is not violated by the mere disclosure of the name, date, time, and place of treatment. Such a limited disclosure constitutes "neither an invidious discrimination as between indigent and nonindigent patients, nor an undue intrusion into the privacy of Medicaid recipients" (*Gabor v. Hyland,* 1979, p. 993). Other cases have supported this interpretation (*Camperlengo v. Blum,* 1982; *Chidester v. Needles,* 1984; *Doe v. Hynes,* 1980; *In re Grand Jury Investigation,* 1982; *McKirdy v. Superior Court of San Francisco,* 1982; *Reynaud v. Superior Court,* 1982; *State v. Washington,* 1978; *State Department of Social and Health Services v. Latta,* 1979).

The majority of cases are distinguished from *Ariyoshi* because of the limited amount of the intrusion to obtain only information absolutely necessary to achieve the government's purpose. In those cases, the government rejected state privileged communication laws as being overridden by federal laws (*In re Grand Jury Investigation,* 1982). Also, any constitutional right to privacy was balanced by the compelling state need and the limited nature of the intrusion.

The case law in this area is far from being settled. The controversy centers on the extent to which Medicaid investigators can probe into patient records. One recent case illustrates potential difficulties in these cases. In the case of *Commonwealth v. Kobrin* (1985), a psychotherapist was being investigated by a Medicaid fraud unit. The court held that the dialogue of the psychotherapist and patients was privileged and that the Medicaid unit could investigate only "objective data." The judge would review the patients' records and expunge the privileged matter from the record.

The decision sounds reasonable, except that the court took an expansive approach to the term *objective data.* It stated that the objective data could include, among other things, the objective accounts of the patients' past medical and psychiatric history (e.g., past treatments, hospitalizations, and diagnoses), objective information of the symptoms or emotional disturbance, the use of any somatic therapies (e.g., chemotherapy or electroshock therapy), and treatment plans and diagnoses. Certainly this definition expands previous decisions, which held that merely the fact of being a client is privileged. Although the information requested by the court may be objective (or factual), it is highly sensitive and personal. One has to wonder if the investigators required all this information.

Crimes Against Patients

Several New York cases have ruled on the admission of hospital patient records in disciplinary actions against employees. For example, in *Civil Service Employees Association v. Soper* (1981), a hospital aide was charged with the physical abuse of residents at a state-operated developmental center. The state attempted to introduce the testimony of one of the injured residents, but the aide's attorney questioned the testimonial capability of the resident. The defense requested the entire medical history of the resident before they would be satisfied that she was a credible witness. The hospital refused. The arbitrator precluded the resident from testifying unless the defense had access to her records. Consequently the case was adjudicated in favor of the aide. In other New York cases, the court ruled that the confidentiality of patient records had to give way to the needs of a fair trial of civil service employees (*Civil Service Employees Association v. Director, Manhattan Psychiatric Center,* 1979; *Office of Mental Retardation and Developmental Disabilities v. Mastracci,* 1980).

An Illinois court faced a similar issue when a former patient was the primary witness against an employee charged with abuse (*Laurent v. Brelji,* 1979). Here the court authorized an *in camera* inspection of the court records. The limited waiver was justified because the patient should not be asked to "run the risk of having his entire mental history drug out and exposed before a public hearing for the ostensible purpose of questioning his perceptive capabilities" (pp. 932-933).

CONCLUSION

Clearly the control of client information in criminal trials has unique features. These include constitutional protections and the protection where the mental health professional works as an agent of the attorney. In addition, the laws may include special exceptions in criminal cases, or protections for victims of rape through special counselor-victim laws. These factors make the need for close cooperation with a highly expert attorney especially important.

Chapter 9

Other Privilege Laws for Mental Health Professionals

Mental health professionals are most affected by privilege laws dealing with the diagnosis or treatment of mental disorders. They may, however, be affected by other privilege laws, such as those dealing with peer review committees or with the researcher-subject privilege.

PRIVILEGE AND PEER REVIEW COMMITTEES

Peer review refers to an organized system of assessing quality of services. It requires judgment of professional practice by other practitioners within the profession. Peer review has its origins in the informal practices of case conferences, supervision of treatment by senior practitioners, problem-oriented record systems, and inpatient medical review boards.

Today most peer review systems are implemented for more than one purpose. Quality of services is one major purpose. It is reasonable to ensure that all patients are receiving adequate and necessary services. Cost containment is another function of many peer review systems, especially when third-party payers are involved. Peer review may also fulfill a policing function to uncover fraudulent practices. Finally, peer review serves an educational function when feedback is given to providers in an effort to raise the level of professional expertise.

In inpatient psychiatric and general medicine hospital settings, peer review committees may oversee several functions, including utilization review, medical audit, tissue review, and credential review. The utilization review committee may attempt to prevent the unnecessary utilization of facilities by Medicare patients by monitoring the use of facilities according to the medical necessity of the length of patient stay. The medical audit committee reviews the actual quality of care by reviewing the physicians' medical records of their patients. Tissue committees review surgical procedures. The credentials committee reviews the qualifications of physicians and other professionals seeking hospital privileges and will recommend the curtailment or exclusion of staff privileges when indicated.

Since 1965 the federal government has encouraged hospitals to meet qualifications of the Joint Commission on Accreditation of Hospitals because this enables them to receive federal Medicare reimbursements automatically. In addition, the peer review process may encourage the hospital to provide economical and efficient health services. Such incentives are increasingly important because of prospective reimbursement.

In order to ensure honest and critical evaluation of health care by the peer review committee, courts and legislatures have promulgated laws to provide special protection from litigation. The rationale for the confidentiality of peer review functions was stated in the case *Bredice v. Doctors Hospital* (1970):

> Confidentiality is essential to effective functioning of these staff meetings; and these meetings are essential to the continued improvement in the care and treatment of patients. Candid and conscientious evaluation of clinical practice is a *sine qua non* of adequate hospital care. To subject these discussions and deliberations to the discovery process, without showing of exceptional necessity, would result in terminating such deliberation. Constructive professional criticism cannot occur in an atmosphere of apprehension that one doctor's suggestion will be used as a denunciation of a colleague's conduct in a malpractice suit. (p. 250)

Despite these protections, the 1970s saw numerous lawsuits by patients or other injured parties trying to acquire documents for purposes of litigation. Few cases actually dealt with psychiatry, which is to be expected because psychiatrists represent only 8% of the physicians and have relatively low rates of malpractice.

Litigants will seek information from the peer review process in two common types of cases: suits by physicians who perceive themselves harmed because the peer review process questioned their qualifications or credentials and malpractice suits by patients. As a practical matter, the subject matter of peer review committees is not as relevant to litigation as some patients may think. Often the information covered in peer review committees deals with the totality of patient care and not the case of any one patient.

Yet the demand for hospital peer review records is likely to increase in medical malpractice cases because plaintiffs may consider suing the hospital as well as the individual physician under the principle of *respondent superior* or corporate negligence.

Peer Review Statutes

To protect peer review committees from invasion of the freedom of their activity, 46 states have enacted legislation that in some ways protects the information generated by the peer review process. The statutes among the states, however, have little in common. Instead, they constitute a patchwork quilt of statutes, which lack judicial trends or consistency (Dunn and Holbrook, 1981; Roach, 1981, 1984; Roach and Chernoff, 1984).

The application of the statutes depends on two major questions. First, it depends on the expansiveness of the statutory definition of a peer review committee. Although the statutory definition of peer review may not include staff conferences or hospital incident reports, they may fulfill some of the same functions as peer review committees. For example, a court interpreted Maryland's peer review statute broadly to include the transcripts of case conferences at a private psychiatric facility. In *Kappas v. Chestnut Lodge* (1983), the sister of a deceased patient brought a malpractice suit against Chestnut Lodge. The plaintiff lost the initial case and appealed, in part because the trial court refused to admit into evidence certain transcripts of conferences at the treatment center. The U.S. Fourth Circuit Court of Appeals, applying Maryland law in a diversity case, held that the transcripts fell within the definition of peer review practices of the statutes. Other courts have interpreted the laws more strictly and defined peer review committees more literally.

A second feature is the type of action for which the records are being sought. Within the same state, depending on the wording of the statute, the court may allow limited discovery of records for one type of lawsuit but not another. For example, courts in Florida have allowed the privilege to stand in a malpractice suit against physicians but not against suits for defamation. The Florida statute protected peer review records from being introduced as evidence in civil actions relating to the quality of professional services (e.g., a malpractice suit). The court held that a defamation suit would not fall into this category (Roach and Chernoff, 1984).

In some states, courts have considered the issue of whether they could recognize a privilege in the absence of a statute on public policy grounds. This was the case in the Kansas court where the court considered a qualified privilege even in the absence of a protective statute. The court adopted a middle ground between complete discovery and complete protection: "The court must balance the litigant's interest in obtaining the requested information with the resisting party's interest, as well as the public interest in maintaining the confidentiality of the material" (*Berst v. Chipman,* 1982, p. 114). The attempt at balance was also shown in *Gillman v. United States* (1971) where a court protected the conclusions and recommendations of the investigating hospital committee but held that the original testimony was not privileged.

Most courts, however, will not adopt a privilege without statutory direction. Such was the case in *Cronin v. Strayer* (1984), where a physician sought committee records in a defamation suit. A physician was reported to the disciplinary committee for alcohol and drug abuse. No action was taken against the physician, and he subsequently brought a defamation suit against the physician who wrote the letter reporting him to the committee. The court noted the lack of statutory protection and refused to create a privilege on public policy grounds.

Guidelines for Federal Courts

Federal courts will follow Rule 501 of the Federal Rules of Evidence in determining issues of privilege in peer review committees. Rule 501 requires that the federal courts determine privileges on the basis of "reason and experience." Often, on the basis of analogy or comity, the federal courts will follow the lead of the state courts in deciding privileges in peer review. Comity is a practice by which one court will follow the direction of another court on a specific question, although they are not required by the law of precedents to do so. The comity between federal and state laws has the benefit of providing consistent rules. Consequently when a "state holds out the expectation of protection to its citizens, they should not be disappointed by a mechanical or unnecessary application of federal rule" (*Lora v. Board of Education,* 1977, p. 576). "A strong policy of comity between state and federal sovereignties impels federal courts to recognize state privileges where this can be accomplished at no substantial cost to federal substantive and procedural policy" (*United States v. King,* 1976, p. 105).

In specific cases, the federal courts have allowed qualified privileges in medical malpractice decisions (*Bredice v. Doctors Hospital, Inc.,* 1970; *Gillman v. United States,* 1971). But the courts have not recognized a privilege in other actions where the privilege does not directly act to promote the quality of health care such as an antitrust suit against physicians (*Memorial Hospital for McHenry County v. Shadur,* 1981), an age discrimination action (*Schafer v. Parkview Memorial Hospital,* 1984), or allegation that constitutional rights were being violated (*Ott v. St. Luke Hospital of Campbell County,* 1981).

To date, no prevailing trend has developed concerning the legislative writing or judicial interpretation of peer review laws. Some courts will apply statutes liberally to protect peer review or similar monitoring committees, and others will adopt a strict interpretation of the laws. Courts also differ on how they define peer review committees, as well as the type of legal action in which they will permit the privilege to apply. As more cases develop, a clear judicial trend may emerge. Roach and Chernoff (1984) predict that courts will continue to uphold peer review privilege laws but will interpret them narrowly.

RESEARCHER-SUBJECT PRIVILEGE

The psychotherapist-patient privilege is designed for the treatment of mental health problems. Consequently it should not be used to protect communications for other purposes such as for research. This does not mean that a research-subject privilege cannot be justified, only that its justification, if any, should have a separate rationale from the psychotherapist-patient privilege and should come from separate statutory authority. The only exception would be if a research project simultaneously involved treatment of an emotional problem such as in a psychotherapy or a psychiatric treatment outcome study. In those situations, the psychotherapist-patient privilege should apply because the psychotherapist is treating an emotional disorder, and any research outcome was incidental from the standpoint of the patient.

The basis for a researcher-subject privilege can rest only on utilitarian grounds. This differs from the psychotherapist-patient privilege, which has been justified both on utilitarian grounds and on the grounds of the intrinsic desirability of privacy in certain intimate personal relationships (see Chapter 1). Participation in a research project does not typically enhance or fulfill the subject's life in a meaningful manner. Usually participants receive only small remuneration for participation, a sense of helping the researcher, or an intrinsic pleasure at discussing an aspect of their life.

A researcher-subject privilege can be analyzed according to Wigmore's criteria: (1) the communications must originate in confidence that they will not be disclosed; (2) the element of confidentiality is essential to the full and satisfactory maintenance of the relationship; (3) the activity must be one that, in the opinion of society, ought to be promoted strongly; and (4) the injury to the privileged activity from disclosure of the communication would be greater than the benefit of society from the correct disposal of litigation.

First, the data in social science research are confidential according to the ethical standards of the mental health professional associations. They are not to be discussed outside the research project, and researchers must make an effort to protect the anonymity of the respondents. This is especially true in sensitive areas, such as mental health treatment, alcohol or drug abuse, and criminal behavior.

Second, the lack of confidentiality may harm the research. Researchers need to protect the anonymity of their respondents in order to increase the likelihood of an honest response. Failure to maintain confidentiality could lead potential subjects to avoid the research entirely or to give "fluff" answers (socially acceptable answers that may be distorted or blatantly false). The problems of response bias increase as fear of disclosure increases or as the potential for harm to the subject increases.

Confidentiality thus becomes extremely important as the potential for harm to the subject increases. In areas such as criminal behavior, alcohol or drug abuse, or sexual activities, the subject could suffer from prosecution by authorities or public embarrassment if the results were disclosed. Failure to protect the confidentiality of the subjects in these situations would cause these areas to dry up, leaving nothing of interest to the courts or the researchers.

Third, scientific research is fostered strongly by society in general. Many colleges and universities require faculty members to publish scholarly research before considerations are given to tenure or promotion. Also, social science research is sponsored by state, federal, and private funds. The benefits of this support are obvious in the fields of mental health. Publicly supported research has led to advances in chemotherapy, psychotherapy, and behavior therapy. The researcher-subject privilege is unique from other privileges in that it artificially creates or acquires knowledge that would not exist otherwise.

Wigmore's final criterion is that the harm done to the courts must be offset by the advantage to the relationship through the protection of the research. No doubt a researcher-subject privilege could cost the court some information. But the cost to the researcher-subject relationship, especially for research into criminal activities, would be fatal. A lack of privilege in drug- or criminal-related research would cause potential subjects to stay away or cause them to provide false responses to avoid prosecution. Research conducted without confidentiality would produce useless results.

Relevant Federal Statutes

The federal government has several statutes that provide some form of privilege to certain investigators. One federal law empowers the secretary of health and human services to

> authorize persons engaged in research on mental health, including research on the use and effect of alcohol and other psychoactive drugs, to protect the privacy of individuals who are subjects of the research by withholding from all persons not connected with the conduct of such research the names or other identifying characteristics of such individuals. Persons so authorized may not be compelled in any Federal, State, or local civil, criminal, administrative, legislative or other proceeding to identify such individuals. (42 U.S.C. §242a (a) (Supp. V 1975))

Although the term *mental health* is used, it is not defined, thus requiring administrators to determine the scope of the statute. The research project need not be sponsored by the Department of Health and Human Services to qualify for the privilege.

Another federal statute permits the U.S. attorney general to

> authorize persons engaged in research to withhold the names and other identifying characteristics of persons who are the subjects of such [drug abuse] research. Persons who obtain this authorization may not be compelled in any Federal, State, or local civil, criminal, administrative, legislative, or other proceeding to identify the subjects of research for which such authorization obtained. (21 U.S.C. §872 (c) (1970)

Like the mental health research privilege, this does not require the researcher to have received the grant from the federal government. This statute has been upheld in the courts (*People v. Newman,* 1973). This drug research privilege should not be confused with the federal privilege, which applies to persons receiving treatment under the Drug Abuse Office and Treatment Act of 1972. (The provisions of this law were discussed in Chapter 4.)

A final federal statute that may be applicable to mental health professionals authorizes researchers who have received funding from the Law Enforcement Assistance Agency to receive a limited privilege:

> Except as provided by Federal law other than this chapter, no officer or employee of the Federal Government, nor any recipient of assistance under the provisions of this chapter shall use or reveal any research or statistical information furnished under this chapter by any person identifiable to any specific private person for any purpose other than the purpose for which it was obtained in accordance with this chapter. Copies of such information shall be immune from legal process, and shall not, without the consent of the person furnishing such information, be admitted as evidence or used for any purpose in any action, suit, or other judicial or administrative proceedings. (42 U.S.C. §3771 (a) (Supp. V 1975))

Relevant State Statutes

In addition to the federal statutes, legislators in several states have created research privileges. As of 1978, 37 states had adopted a model statute (or a close variation) proposed by the National Conference of Commissioners on Uniform State Laws regarding drug abuse research. These laws typically require drug researchers to apply to proper authorities within each state for protection. An inquiry by Knerr and Carroll (1978) revealed that these provisions are rarely utilized and many state officials reported that no investigators had utilized the statutory shield. A few other state laws provide researchers privileges in unique situations such as epidemiological research, researchers under grants from the department of Juvenile services (Maryland), and scientific investigation (New Hampshire).

We found one decision in which a federal court applied New York State Law to a research privilege. In *In re Love Canal* (1982), the defendants in the Love Canal litigation were unable to acquire the confidential reports of the state department of health concerning their investigations into the health (including psychiatric health) of Love Canal residents. The court noted the relevant state law, which provides a privilege for emergency health studies and concluded that "the privilege granted by the legislature was not meant to be a myth" (p. 135, citing *Yaron v. Yaron,* 1975, p. 518). The defendants, however, could attempt to acquire the same information from sources other than the state department of public health.

To date, there is no coordinated effort to acquire a comprehensive researcher-subject privilege in the federal courts. The Privacy Protection Study Commission (1977), however, did suggest that such a privilege could be useful although limited. The commission suggested that controlled access to the data should be permitted when the researcher is engaged in an illegal act and access to the data is the only way to prove it. This would include, for example, a researcher suspected of fraud. In addition, the privilege should not be used to bar or impede a legitimate audit of the research project. Finally, the commission recommended that the privilege should not prevent a researcher from reporting imminent acts of violence.

It is not likely that state courts will create common law privileges to protect the researcher-subject relationship. Some authors have argued that a researcher-subject privilege should be found within the First Amendment (Day, 1983; Nejelski and Lerman, 1971). But we could find no state appellate court decision addressing the issue of a privilege for mental health professionals doing research without a protective federal statute.

It is conceivable that federal courts could interpret Rule 501 of the Federal Rules of Evidence to allow a privilege. This rule allows courts to find privileges on the basis of "reason and experience." No court to date has upheld an academic research privilege, although a court may limit discovery (*Buchanan v. American Motors Corporation,* 1983).

One case (*In re Grand Jury Subpoena,* 1983) specifically dealt with research in social science. A grand jury was convened to investigate a mysterious fire that destroyed a Long Island restaurant. It subpoenaed a Ph.D. candidate in sociology who was doing research on the sociology of the American restaurant. The court did not reject the possibility of finding a researcher-subject privilege, although it held that his particular study did not meet the necessary criteria:

> Surely the application of a scholar's privilege, if it exists, requires a threshold showing consisting of a detailed description of the nature and seriousness of the scholarly

> study in question, of the methodology employed, of the need for assurances of confidentiality to various sources to conduct the study, and of the fact that the disclosure required by the subpoena will seriously impinge upon that confidentiality. (p. 225)

Here, the researcher could support none of these threshold criteria. Rather, the court learned only that he promised confidentiality to some people. The court however, did allow the scholar to amplify his assertion of privilege and make a good-faith designation of those portions of his work that were arguably covered by the scholar's privilege. Noncovered portions of his work had to be disclosed, and covered portions were subjected to an *in camera* inspection. The court added, however, that "actual observation of criminal activity is not subject to a claim of privilege" (p. 226).

Chapter 10

Psychotherapist Liability for the Unauthorized Release of Information

The psychotherapist-patient privilege is only one of the shields that provides for the privacy of mental patients. Statutory and ethical provisions protect extrajudicial breaches of confidence. Also, patients could initiate criminal or tort actions against psychotherapists who divulge information illegally. This chapter will review the case law dealing with illegal disclosures.

EXTRAJUDICIAL DISCLOSURES

For many years, psychotherapists had a low incidence of lawsuits initiated against them. Psychiatrists had rates lower than the average physician, and the rates for psychologists were "very few in number and inconsequential in economic extent" (Wright, 1981, p. 1485). Although professional liability rates are still small compared to those for physicians, they have been increasing. Lawsuits for unauthorized disclosure of client information are not common and represent only a miniscule percentage of the total lawsuits against psychiatrists (Slawson and Guggenheim, 1984). Lawsuits against psychologists for unauthorized disclosures are also relatively infrequent. These "allege some form of violation of confidence or invasion of privacy such as confirming (in a divorce action) that a husband is no longer in psychotherapy; or the transmittal of various kinds of information to various agencies, as in reporting to a court or informing other persons or agencies as to any information that *the plaintiff* considered to be privileged" (Wright, 1981, p. 1487).

In part, the low incidence may be attributed to training programs that have conscientiously instilled respect for the privacy of psychotherapy clients. Also, clients are reluctant as a rule to bring lawsuits against their psychotherapists (Knapp and VandeCreek, 1981). Many of the rules regarding the unauthorized disclosure of information by psychotherapists are consequently borrowed from cases involving physicians (Liability of Physician for Breach of Confidential Relationship, 1980; Schiffers, 1968).

No single law or legal theory covers liability for unauthorized disclosures: "While psychotherapists have been innovative and daring in choice of treatment, so too have attorneys in choosing theories of liability" (Harris, 1973, p. 411). Lawsuits for unauthorized disclosures of confidential information have been based on breach of statutory duty, breach of fiduciary duty, invasion of privacy, defamation, and breach of contract. All of these legal theories (except breach of implied contract) are based on tort law. "A tort is a civil wrong, other than breach of contract, for which the court will provide a remedy in the form of an action from damage" (Prosser, 1971, p. 2).

Damages based on breach of statutory duty are relatively new since confidentiality laws are also recent. Confidentiality laws were based on the ethical principles of the American Medical Association, the American Psychological Association, the National Association of Social Workers, and the American Association of Counseling and Development (formerly American Personnel and Guidance Association). These ethical codes were unanimous in requiring psychotherapists to protect the privacy of their clients. These rules have obtained legal status through subsequent legislation or administrative regulations that make psychotherapists liable for the unauthorized disclosure of information.

Cases have also been predicated on the theory that psychotherapists have a fiduciary duty of confidentiality. The term *fiduciary relation* denotes a relationship wherein patients place their trust in the psychotherapists with the understanding that the information will be used only to benefit treatment. Violations of confidences by psychotherapists will breach the fiduciary relationship.

A complaint of invasion of privacy is also a means to seek redress. Although there are four subcategories of this tort, only one applies to breach of confidentiality: the public disclosure of private facts. In order for an invasion of privacy breach to be maintained, the facts must have been intended as private, must have been made public, and must have caused outrage, humiliation, or offense to a person of ordinary sensibilities.

Defamation is a written or oral communication to someone other than the person defamed that tends to injure the patient's reputation. Psychotherapeutic information could be involved in defamation because its disclosure could harm someone in the eyes of the community.

The final common legal action is breach of an implied contract. It differs from the other actions in that it is not a tort but a form of breach of contract. Although the psychotherapist relationship is a professional one, it resembles a contractual relationship in several ways. The patient pays the psychotherapist to provide therapy in accordance with acceptable professional standards. These professional standards include adherence to norms requiring the confidentiality of communications (Eger, 1976; Lamb, 1983; Schiffers, 1968).

One famous example of psychotherapist liability was the case of *Doe v. Roe* (1977), which was decided on the basis of breach of contract (as well as invasion of privacy). The court barred the psychiatrist from the further distribution of a book based on a lengthy analysis of her patient. The court noted that all physicians have an implied contract: "A physician who enters into an agreement with a patient to provide medical attention, impliedly covenants to keep in confidence all disclosures made by the patient concerning the patient's physical or mental condition as well as matters discovered by the physician in the course of examination or treatment" (p. 674). The court noted that the book did not disguise adequately the identity of the patient. In addition, the patient had not given written consent for the book to be written.

Often a plaintiff will base a lawsuit on several different legal theories. Although the court may reject one theory, it could find liability on the basis of another. For example, in *Logan v. District of Columbia* (1978), the court found that the aggrieved client could sue on the basis of invasion of privacy but rejected all other theories as inapplicable to that jurisdiction and case. In *Silberstein v. County of Westchester* (1983), a former patient brought action against a county mental health agency for the alleged unauthorized release of information. The court rejected the pleas of breach of contract and dismissed the case, noting that it would have considered the case to have more merit if it had been presented as a tort action.

From the standpoint of the prosecution attorney, each of the legal theories of liability has advantages and disadvantages. For example, the invasion of privacy tort has the advantage that the patient may receive compensation for mental anguish. No such compensation is available under the breach of contract theory because the purpose of contract law is only to restore patients financially to their status before treatment. Invasion of privacy has the disadvantage that the disclosure must have caused offense in the eyes of the ordinary person. This bars liability for apparently innocuous disclosures. Breach of contract has no such requirement (Eger, 1976). The theory of liability advocated in any specific case will depend on the factual situations of the case, the laws of the state, the common law precedents of the case, and recent trends in the law (see review by DeKraai and Sales, 1984). Given the nature of the penalties involved, it behooves psychotherapists to follow ethical and legal guidelines in treating their clients' information.

In certain situations, the confidentiality rules may appear confusing. For example, the role of psychotherapists in breaching confidentiality to protect third parties is one area of uncertainty. (The general rule and case law dealing with the duty to protect are discussed in detail in Chapter 12.) For the purposes of this chapter, it can be said that the issue surrounds whether psychotherapists would be violating the confidentiality of their patients if they breached confidence in an attempt to protect innocent third persons from imminent harm.

The majority of cases dealing with this issue hold that psychotherapists have an affirmative responsibility to act to protect third persons even if it means violating the confidence of others. In two cases, however, courts have held that the psychotherapists could not make such a warning without violations confidentiality laws. Both cases have unique circumstance that greatly limit their relevance. In *Shaw v. Glickman* (1980), a psychotherapy team was sued for failure to warn. The court noted that the team had no basis by which to determine that their patient was going to harm someone. Absent this imminent threat, the psychotherapists could not be held liable for failure to warn. To support their conclusions protecting the psychotherapists, the court noted that Maryland's law did not allow exception to confidentiality for warning third persons.

In the second case, *Hopewell v. Adebimpe* (1982), the psychiatrist apparently overreacted to the threatening statements of his client and issued a warning when the danger was not imminent. Although the report of the case was scanty, the psychiatrist had apparently not exhausted traditional therapeutic strategies before issuing the warning. The court noted that the psychiatrist was liable because he breached the confidentiality of the patient. In both cases, the psychotherapists apparently lacked sufficient reason to breach confidentiality. It is probable that the psychotherapists would not be liable for breaches of confidence if they were appropriately issued to protect third persons.

Psychotherapists incur no liability when they breach confidentiality to report suspected child abuse. These reports are mandated by law, and no professionals will be found liable for fulfilling their statutory responsibility. The only conceivable exception would be if professionals made malicious reports that they knew to be false. Such a situation would be highly improbable and extremely difficult to prove. Fear of legal reprisals should never deter a psychotherapist from reporting suspected child abuse (Education Commission of the States, 1979). In the only case we could find addressing this issue, a federal court dismissed charges against a high school guidance counselor who, among other actions, made a referral to the county child welfare program. The court wrote that the "counselor was entitled to good-faith immunity under Law's presumption of good faith against claims of civil rights violations in referral and recommendation" (*Roman v. Appleby,* 1983, p. 451).

On the contrary, the greatest area of liability comes from the failure to report suspected child abuse (*Groff v. State,* 1980; *Landeros v. Flood,* 1976; *State v. Groff,* 1982). For example, in *Landeros v. Flood* a physician had examined an 11-month-old child for bruises and other injuries sustained in a beating. It was alleged that the physician did not diagnose the injuries as battered child syndrome and failed to report her injuries to the appropriate child abuse authorities. The child was further abused and later placed in the custody of child welfare. The child sued the physician through a guardian *ad litem,* and it was held that the physician could be liable if he had actually diagnosed the abuse and then negligently failed to report it.

Suits have been initiated when disclosures have been made to family members without the consent of the identified patients. These cases are not likely to occur in the context of family therapy with all the family members present on a regular basis. It is true that in these family therapy situations, some family members may seek to make secret alliances or share exclusive information with the family therapist. Margolin (1982) suggests that family therapists should establish a rule at the beginning of therapy that they could reveal any information shared with them at their discretion. This should place the alliance seekers on notice that their secrets may become disclosed. The suits are more likely to occur when a family member is customarily seen individually and the disclosure is made without the consent of the identified patient.

Generally there is no liability for the sharing of information concerning children or minors with their parents. Although the parent may have a legal right to all information, the psychotherapist can use discretion in what information to reveal or when to reveal it. There is a recent trend under minor treatment statutes in which minors may in some states seek treatment independent of their parents' wishes (Melton, 1981; Roach and Kunde, 1983). In these situations where the minor seeks treatment independently, it is logical that the minor should control the release of information. No cases dealing with this situation have arisen yet.

Suits arising out of the unauthorized release of information are most likely to occur when family relationships are strained or when one spouse is contemplating a divorce, property settlement, or child custody case against the other. The judicial response in these situations is not predictable because only a few cases relating to these situations have appeared in the literature. For example, in *Pennison v. Provident Life and Accident Insurance Company* (1963), a woman sought damages against a physician and insurance company who gave information to her husband that later was used against her in a divorce proceeding. Among other reasons, the court noted that "the husband, during the marriage, has a right to a full report from his wife's doctor. He is head and master of the [marital] community and responsible for its debts" (p. 618). A New York case reached a similar conclusion (*Curry v. Corn,* 1966). These decisions reflect paternal theories of the husband-wife relationship.

A different result was found in a more recent case (*MacDonald v. Clinger,* 1982). In part, the difference in interpretation could be due to changing social values. Husbands are no longer viewed as de facto and de jure heads of households. The court noted that medical information may be released to spouses under certain circumstances but that "a more stringent standard should apply with respect to psychiatric information. . . . To permit the disclosure to the other spouse in the absence of an overriding concern would deter the one in need from obtaining the help required" (p. 805).

LIABILITY FOR CONTENTS OF JUDICIAL DISCLOSURES

The law grants immunity for the contents of the testimony of mental health professionals who testify in court. At times the professionals may make comments in court that their patients perceive as inaccurate, defaming, or adverse to the case. Such comments on the witness stand have the defense of absolute privilege. Here the term *privilege* is used in a different sense from a privileged communication. This particular privilege rests on the concept "that conduct which otherwise would be actionable is to escape liability because the defendant is acting in furtherance of some interest of social importance, which is entitled to protection even at the expense of uncompensated harm to the plaintiff's reputation" (Prosser, 1971, p. 776). In the United States, situations such as executive communications, legislative proceedings, and judicial proceedings involve absolute privilege because of the great harm that could occur to the truth-seeking process if witnesses felt intimated in their testimony because of the fear of a lawsuit.

The few attempts to find mental health professionals liable for their statements on the witness stand have failed. In *Clark v. Grigson* (1979), a psychiatrist had performed a court-ordered evaluation of a criminal defendant and recommended the death penalty. The sentenced man sued the psychiatrist, alleging that the evaluation was negligent and that the psychiatrist should have warned him about the adverse nature of the testimony. The court disagreed, noting that "any communication made in the course of judicial proceedings is absolutely privileged and immune from civil liability for damages [and this rule] applies to opinions of expert witnesses as well as to any other testimony in judicial proceedings" (p. 263).

In another case, *Jordan v. Kelly* (1984), the court granted a summary judgment (immediate dismissal) of a case against two psychiatrists for an allegedly unauthorized disclosure of medical information. The psychiatrists had been called by the would-be plaintiffs to testify in a child custody suit. After giving their testimony at the request of the plaintiffs, the psychiatrists were sued for a breach of confidence. The court showed no sympathy for the plaintiffs: "It is like being hit and held at the same time. . . . Here the party who is suing them is the party who put them in that position to begin with" (p. 3). Other courts have reached similar conclusions (e.g., *Bond v. Pecaut,* 1983; *James v. Brown,* 1981; *North Carolina v. Taylor,* 1981).

American courts grant immunity as long as the statements are in some way relevant or pertinent to the case. Relevancy is interpreted loosely, and the witnesses are not required to understand the technical courtroom rules of evidence. The general standard is one of good faith, and the statement must have some reasonable relevance to the subject of inquiry. This rule avoids the situation in which a person might conceivably use the witness stand as a vehicle to defame an individual with comments of no relevance or bearing on the proceedings. If there is a question of the relevance of the testimony to the proceeding, the benefit of the doubt goes to the witness (Prosser, 1971).

Mental health professionals are not expected to be experts in the laws of court procedure. They are not liable for breaches of confidentiality when their testimony is admitted into the court through an error in court procedure. In *Doyle v. Shlensky* (1983), a psychiatrist had examined a married couple pursuant to a court order in a divorce proceeding. Later the disgruntled husband sued the psychiatrist for medical malpractice on the grounds that the court order had been improperly obtained. The court rejected this complaint and held that the order was issued properly. Even if the order had been issued improperly, the court would not have permitted liability against the psychiatrist: "To find merit in such contention would attach to each physician acting under court order the burden of ascertaining whether the order was obtained in full compliance with all procedural requirements. . . . Clearly this would produce an undesirable result" (p. 1122).

These rules regarding the immunity of witnesses are well established in common law; no case could be found in which a physician or mental health professional was successfully sued for comments on the witness stand. This immunity, however, applies only to judicial statements. Statements or communications outside the courtroom have no such immunity.

Psychotherapists need to be careful when communicating to parties antagonistic or adverse to their patient's interests. In *Schaffer v. Spicer* (1974), a psychiatrist was liable for a tort action when he sent a detailed letter about his patient to her opposing attorney. It appeared as if the psychiatrist assumed the material would be introduced into court, but the mother had not waived her privileged communication rights, and she did not intend to enter the material into evidence. In *Anker v. Brodnitz* (1979), the court ruled that a cause of action could be maintained against a physician who disclosed information about his patient before the court ruled that the privilege had been waived. The court also stated that any interview with the physician should be through procedures established by courtroom discovery principles. Private or informal interviews should not occur. The court reasoned that such a ruling would insulate the doctors from pressure from adversary insurance companies to comply with their requests for interviews. Also, the court noted that the issue of "whether a physical or mental condition is in controversy often requires a careful judicial scrutiny and not a mere cursory reading of the complaint" (p. 585). The defense attorneys cannot determine on their own if the privilege is waived.

The *Anker* court noted that other courts in other states may rule differently. For example, in *Adams v. Peck* (1979), the pretrial disclosures of the psychiatrist were not grounds for liability because the patient had waived the privilege and the records of the psychiatrists were soon to be made public in court anyway.

Other cases have dealt with the same issue. In *Alexander v. Knight* (1962), a Pennsylvania court noted that the physician should not have communicated to the opposing attorney even though the physician-patient privilege did not apply in this case. The court noted:

> We are of the opinion that members of a profession, especially the medical profession, stand in a confidential or fiduciary capacity as to their patients. They owe their patients more than just medical care for which payment is exacted; there is a duty of total care; that includes and comprehends a duty to aid the patient in litigation, to render reports when necessary and to attend court when needed. That further includes a duty to refuse affirmative assistance to the patient's antagonist in litigation. (p. 146)

Although the court found liability on other grounds, it denounced the actions of the physician. Also, in *Panko v. Consolidated Mutual Insurance Company* (1970), a federal court refused to find the physician liable for disclosures in the courtroom during a personal injury suit. The physician, however, had made pretrial disclosures to the patient's opposing attorneys. The *Panko* court refused to answer the question whether the pretrial disclosures constituted grounds for liability and instead referred to a pending case in state courts on that issue.

The pretrial disclosures to opposing attorneys may constitute a ground for liability. Although some states may exonerate the psychotherapists if the waiver is eventually made, any such disclosures are made at the risk to the psychotherapist. The most prudent behavior would be to refuse any requests for information that occur outside regular courtroom procedures.

Chapter 11

Recommendations and Model Statute

The need for evidence in court has been emphasized throughout this book. Legislators should grant privileges only in unusual circumstances for relationships of overriding social importance. We believe that the psychotherapist-patient relationship deserves such protection.

Ideally, legislators should be able to match the provisions of a privilege law to the prevailing data on the effects of a privilege. Unfortunately the lack of detailed data makes this impossible. The evidence suggests that the disclosure necessary for effective psychotherapy requires a shield of confidentiality. Privileged communication laws are an important shield, but it is unclear as to how porous the privilege law can become before psychotherapy becomes adversely effected. Judgment and intuition must prevail where empirical evidence is lacking.

Most mental health professionals and legal scholars recognize the need for some privilege for psychotherapy. The attorney-client privilege model does not provide adequate statutory protection for psychotherapy patients. The attorney-client and psychotherapist-client relationships differ too much to make the analogy useful. Issues such as court-ordered treatment, involuntary psychiatric hospitalization, and family therapy do not have equivalent functions for attorneys, thus forcing the courts to rule without clear statutory guidance.

A second model that warrants more serious consideration is the judicial discretion model. This model exists in North Carolina and has been endorsed by Cleary (1984). It allows a privilege unless the court determines that the evidence is needed for the proper administration of justice. It attempts to provide a privilege without unduly harming psychotherapy. Unfortunately, the appellate case law using this approach is scanty, and it is unknown how the law is actually applied by the trial courts. Although we do not endorse this model, we cannot dismiss it. Future research on its actual implementation may alter our view of its desirability.

We endorse a third model based largely on the provisions of Rule 504 of the proposed but rejected Federal Rules of Evidence (see Chapter 4). The modifications we endorse include a constriction of the privilege in cases where human life is jeopardized, such as in cases of suspected child abuse or for trials for homicide, but we endorse an expansion of the privilege for all qualified psychotherapists who perform the function of psychotherapy.

Proposed Rule 504 has several positive features. One salient feature of Rule 504 is the restriction of the privilege to the diagnosis or treatment of a mental, alcohol, or drug problem. The psychotherapist-patient privilege should be separate from any researcher-subject privilege. Also, Rule 504 has an implied future crimes exception. Because the privilege is restricted to diagnosis or treatment, it will not cover activities or communications by patients that further crimes (such as fradulently attempting to acquire controlled drugs) because they do not promote treatment.

The client controls the privilege, although a psychotherapist or agency may invoke the privilege in the absence of a client. Such a provision appears necessary because, at times, client records may be entered into litigation without their knowledge. (See Chapter 6 for a review of cases where clients are not parties to a suit.) Rule 504 maintains the privilege for psychotherapy or diagnosis with third persons present to further treatment such as psychotherapy assistants, other family members, or group therapy members.

Finally, Rule 504 provides several important exceptions, such as for court-ordered examinations or when clients enter their mental health as an element of a claim. Also, Rule 504 provides an exception for proceedings for involuntary psychiatric hospitalizations. We believe that the involuntary psychiatric hospitalization exception should apply only when the statutes require dangerousness as a criterion for hospitalization. The privilege should be maintained when the need for treatment only is the criterion.

We propose several modifications to Rule 504. The first modifications include additional exceptions to the privilege. One additional exception, for child abuse cases, is found in almost every statutory code, although not usually within the psychotherapist-patient privilege. Chapter 7 reviewed two controversies concerning the abrogation of the privilege in case of suspected child abuse: the admissibility of evidence into criminal trials of abusing adults and the admissibility of indirect evidence into placement decisions for abused children.

Those issues should be addressed by statutory law, thus providing the courts with clear direction. The proposed law would treat the initial report of abuse differently from other information. It would admit the initial report of abuse into any proceeding for child abuse or neglect, including the criminal prosecution of adults. Otherwise the proposed law would keep the privilege for information obtained in court-ordered treatment or for other treatment that the abusing parents sought on their own. It could not be used in criminal cases against them. Thus parents would not convict themselves by their participation in therapy.

We advocate another exception—for trials for homicide—that has not received much statutory support, although it is codified in the psychotherapist-patient privilege statutes in Indiana, the District of Columbia, and Wisconsin and in the social worker-client statute of Illinois.

This exception is consistent with the theme we have attempted to follow in allowing other exceptions (involuntary psychiatric hospitalization, child abuse) when physical harm to others becomes likely. Clearly the release of a murderer can threaten other members of society.

The final suggested modification concerns the issue of a functional approach. Privileged communications for psychotherapists differ from other privileges. Usually one profession monopolizes the privileged function. Only attorneys are qualified to practice law, and only physicians are qualified to practice medicine. However, social workers, counselors, psychologists, psychiatrists, and other professionals all conduct psychotherapy, and privileged communication laws often fail to protect all of these professions.

Courts tend to interpret privilege laws strictly and will refuse to recognize privileges outside the professions specifically enumerated in the statutes. One general consequence of such unequal protection has been to deny equal privacy to clients with lower incomes or to clients in rural areas. These clients often use the public mental health facilities that are staffed primarily by social workers, psychiatric nurses, or unlicensed psychologists who are less likely to be covered by the privilege. More affluent clients who have access to privately licensed psychiatrists or psychologist usually receive the privilege; less affluent or rural patients who have access primarily to community mental health facilities usually do not (Stroube, 1979). In addition, the unequal status may give an unfair economic advantage of mental health professionals with the privilege over mental health professionals without it (DeKraai and Sales, 1982).

The intent of privileged communication laws is to encourage persons to participate in psychotherapy. This intent is not completely fulfilled if certain professions receive the privilege and others do not. The proposed alternative would be to extend the privilege to all professionals who perform the function of psychotherapy. Although such a functional privilege has been often endorsed, it has rarely been implemented (Fisher, 1964; Foster, 1976;

Geiser and Rheingold, 1964; Heffernan, 1980; Kennedy, 1973; Shah, 1969; Smith, 1980; Stroube, 1979).

A functional statute should include psychiatrists and psychologists. In addition, states that license social workers, mental health counselors, pastoral counselors, marriage and family therapists, and others could include them in a functional privilege law. Finally, the law should protect all direct service employees of the public mental health system. The functional privilege should protect the clients of all qualified mental health professionals. Although public mental health employees may not have the credentials to be in independent practice, the quality of service can be assured through state regulations and external supervision. It would not reflect a consistent state policy to offer mental health services to the public and then deny the clients the statutory protection offered to clients of independent practitioners.

In this chapter we have made recommendations for statutory provisions based on the cumulative experiences of courts and legislatures and on research. We hope that subsequent research will provide more information on which to frame future statutes. Ideally that research would not only clarify the effects of privilege but would also help guide specific provisions of the law by identifying categories or subcategories of clients that may be more sensitive to the effects of a privilege.

Chapter 12

Overview of Confidentiality

This chapter reviews the current status of confidentiality in the mental health professions. Confidentiality is distinguished from privileged communications. To review, *privileged communications* refers to the legal right that exempts clients—under certain circumstances—from having their disclosures revealed in court without their permission. Privileged communication laws are derived primarily from statutory authority and are an exception to the common law tradition that requires that the courts have access to all available information.

Confidentiality is based on professional ethics and indicates a promise to reveal nothing about clients without their consent or as allowed by law. It has now gained legal status through licensing laws that describe the betrayal of confidences as unprofessional conduct and as grounds for revocation of licenses. For example, in *Morra v. State Board of Examiners of Psychologists* (1973), the court found that an obligation to comply with professional ethical standards was implied by the state licensing statute. Also, many states have laws or administrative regulations governing the disclosure of information within state agencies (DeKraai and Sales, 1984). Finally, some case law has found psychotherapists liable for unauthorized releases of client information.

Psychotherapy by its nature creates an implied contract between therapist and client. Among other things, this contract implies that the venture will benefit the client. By virtue of their expertise, therapists are obligated to protect the welfare of their clients and to advise them about risks related to the contract. Clients usually anticipate confidentiality in psychotherapy (Appelbaum et al., 1984; Schmid et al., 1983). They have a right to be informed whenever their secrets are endangered through their own actions (threats to others), through the actions of their therapists (reports to other professionals; writing about clients), or through the actions of other parties (data banks that collect information from third-party payers). Therapists should inform clients whenever they anticipate a change in the contract regarding confidentiality; however, maintaining confidentiality in psychotherapy can be a complicated process, and at times the rules are not simple. A balancing act may ensue between the opposing forces of maintaining secrecy for the client and meeting the demands to know by others.

MANAGEMENT OF CLIENT INFORMATION

Some psychotherapists may assume that confidentiality is threatened only in unusual situations. This may not necessarily be true. At times confidentiality may be breached unnecessarily because of the way the psychotherapist handles (or mishandles) client information on a day-by-day basis.

In-House Confidentiality

Psychotherapists know many obvious situations that jeopardize confidentiality. Psychotherapists should not discuss details of their clients with family, friends, or others who have no duty to maintain silence. Probably psychotherapists breach confidentiality most frequently within the work setting. Bystanders may overhear indiscreet conversations with colleagues in elevators, restrooms, or hallways, or they may overhear incoming telephone calls where names are used. Even if the listeners do not spread the information further, they have been alerted to the failure to maintain confidentiality and may lose trust in the agency or psychologist.

Of course, psychologists may discuss cases with supervisors, consultants, and colleagues when they intend to improve the quality of their service to the client. Some facilities use a team or case conference approach in which clients' problems and progress are reviewed. In such instances, several persons may have access to client information. Psychotherapists should inform clients if the team approach is used within their agency.

Weihofen (1972) has discussed several guidelines for maintaining in-house confidentiality. Agency rules should specify which personnel may have access to records. The general staff should not have access to records of clients who become employees or who are well known in the community. Someone in the setting should be responsible for training and monitoring the procedures for maintaining confidentiality. Personnel should keep records in secure places and should not take them home or leave them lying on desks.

Contents of Records

Szasz (1965) proposed that psychotherapists solve the problem of confidentiality by keeping no records; what does not exist cannot be shared. This course has several disadvantages, however. A record exists for both the benefit of the client, now and in the future, and for the protection of the therapist. A court may interpret an inadequate record as an indicator of poor care (e.g., *Whitree v. New York,* 1968). Slovenko (1979) encourages mental health professionals to keep better records, and he cited several reasons for exercising more care: accountability to the client, documentation for peer review and third-party payers, and legal protection for the therapist. A good record should contain, among other things, a summary of client problems, treatment plans, notes about progress and problems, and records of consultations with colleagues. Records should not include clinically irrelevant details of past behaviors that might needlessly embarrass the clients or jeopardize their welfare if the records were subpoenaed or viewed by third parties (Shutz, 1982).

Some commentators (Beigler, 1981; Shutz, 1982) recommend keeping a separate set of personal notes on clients in which more sensitive material is recorded. This mechanism is now incorporated into law in Illinois and Washington, D.C. The Illinois statute has been upheld twice in court tests (Shutz, 1982). Without statutory provisions, however, such notes would likely be subject to subpoena.

Because client records exist in part for the benefit of the client, psychologists may not destroy them indiscriminately. The retirement or death of a psychologist or the sale of a practice does not relieve the psychologist or estate of liability for the protection of the confidences of the records. Clients should be informed about the rationale and eventual destruction of records and given the option of requesting that they be maintained or a copy released to a practitioner of their choice. Providers may not solicit the clients of a deceased or retired provider. Rather, clients should be notified that the practice has been terminated and that records will be sent to any provider the client names. It is also wise to retain the original records for at least five years in case of future litigation (Beigler, 1981).

Client Access to Records

The record is routinely regarded as the property of the provider, not of the client, although the material is kept for the client's benefit (e.g., *In re*

Culbertson's Will, 1968). Clients, however, own the test materials that they have created, such as drawings and answer sheets to psychological tests. The psychologist owns the profiles and summaries of these materials. In instances in which psychologists complete work for another professional or agency, the materials belong to the other party, and the third party may view the psychologist's report only with the client's permission.

In recent years, several states have enacted legislation granting clients access to their own records (Wynstra, 1980). Previously professionals argued that this was needless and potentially threatening to clients. Now the awareness of the risk to clients of inaccurate information and of abuse of records in the past (Privacy Protection Study Commission, 1977) has led citizens to demand access to any and all information about themselves. That records may pose a threat to clients was dramatically reaffirmed by the court in *Wolfe v. Beal* (1978) in which an ex-client successfully brought suit to expunge and destroy the records of her hospitalization on the ground that the record resulted from an illegal commitment. The court agreed that the continued existence of the record, even though held in confidence by the facility, posed a continual threat to her reputation.

Most access statutes permit the correction of misinformation and the inclusion of a statement from the client about differences of opinion about validity of information. Many such statutes exempt from disclosure any information judged detrimental to the client or that would betray a confidence made to the therapist. Research with psychiatric inpatients (Roth, Wolford, and Meisel, 1980; Stein, et al., 1979) who were granted access to their records indicated that many records contained errors. Nonetheless, both clients and staff viewed client access as a positive experience.

Requests for Release of Information

Several guidelines are available when clients consent to permit a psychologist to release information to other parties. Slovenko and Usdin (1961) stated that oral consent suffices, but the *Ethical Principles* of the American Psychological Association (1981) and position statements by the American Medical Record Association (1977) and the American Orthopsychiatric Association (1975) require written consent, as do some state statutes. In addition, written consent gives proof and protection to the psychologist. The clients must give consent if they are of age and competent or an emancipated minor (married, or single and living separate and independent). Guardians may sign if the client is a minor or incompetent. An executor or administrator of an estate may sign for a deceased client (Weihofen, 1972).

Clients are sometimes asked to sign blanket or open-ended authorizations with wording such as "furnish any and all information of request," but many authorities have taken a dim view of this practice (Privacy Protection Study

Commission, 1977). Blanket release forms can be so broad and vague that clients cannot reasonably and knowingly sign them. The following language was once used by an insurance company: "I authorize all physicians, hospitals, clinics, dispensaries, sanitariums, druggists, employers, and all other agencies to disclose and release any information regarding the medical history, physical or mental condition of me or my dependents to ______." It is hard to believe that collecting such extensive data is necessary for the company to protect its interests. Rather, a release form should specify the exact data that are needed and the purpose for collecting them. Prospective requests signed prior to receiving services cannot be considered valid because the client is under duress when searching for service and there is no way of knowing in advance what data will be produced.

The therapist must discuss with the client the implications of releasing or refusing to release the requested information. This discussion should be led by the therapist and not the setting's receptionist. Only the therapist understands the implications of the data in the case file and the potential ramifications of releasing information. The client should also understand whether the receiving party has the right to pass the information on to a third party. The client has the right to specify that this not be done without consent. Although most releases are time limited and revokable, court waivers of the privilege are not. A recent exception to this general rule was played out in an Ohio court (Fulero, 1984). Just prior to filing for divorce, a couple consulted a psychologist. The husband refused to participate after an initial introduction, but his wife completed several therapy sessions. During the later divorce proceeding, the wife voluntarily signed a release form permitting her psychologist to disclose limited information from her treatment record. The husband's attorney then requested even more information, but the wife now refused. Since the earlier release form had contained a clause permitting her to revoke the authority to release, she now presented a written revocation of the consent. The husband's attorney asked the court to overrule her revocation. He argued that once the wife's mental health had been voluntarily entered into the court proceeding, she could not withdraw it or provide only selected information. The court agreed, although a compromise was reached in which only some relevant information was released (the husband's attorney had demanded to review the entire file). Whenever possible, psychotherapists must inform their clients of risks to releasing their records.

A release of information form should be considered valid only if the form contains several specific items: (1) the name of the practitioner/agency seeking the client's signature; (2) the date the form is prepared; (3) the name and related identifying information of the party to whom the disclosure will be made; (4) a description of the exact material to be released; (5) the purpose for the release (how the information will be used); (6) limitations imposed upon the receiving party as to how it may use the material and whether it may be released to third parties; (7) an indication of the time period during which the release is valid; (8) a statement that the implications of the release have been discussed; (9) a place for the client's signature and the date of signing; and (10) a place for the signature of a witness (if the client is unable to sign, two witnesses should sign).

Copies of the signed form should be given to the practitioner or agency who obtained the client's signature and the party to whom information is being disclosed or from whom information is being sought. Some agencies may have additional requirements for their release forms. For example, drug and alcohol agencies assisted by the federal government must follow special confidentiality regulations.

If the consent has been based on full information, then the psychologist has no right to refuse to communicate the specified information (Shah, 1969). Noll and Hanlon (1976) found in a survey that none of the mental health agencies contacted refused to comply with requests. Curran (1969), however, reported that 13 of the 116 colleges and universities he contacted had refused to release information to graduate schools or agencies even when written permission was given. This resistance to release of information may be based on the belief that the use of such data may constitute an unwarranted invasion of privacy (Shah, 1969). Noll (1974) has advocated that mental health professionals should actively seek the removal of all questions, or requests for information, about past psychotherapy from application forms. Unfortunately, according to Rosen (1977), clients almost universally can be induced to authorize disclosure, even to agencies unrelated to their treatment.

If and when disclosures are made, psychologists should release only that information which is specifically requested and needed (Shah, 1969). The actual records themselves (test materials, treatment summaries, etc.) should not ordinarily be copied. Such information should be given only in summary form. Authorization could be granted for an appropriate person to examine the actual record in the setting, but this should be permitted only under the supervision of a staff member competent to interpret the materials (Weihofen, 1972).

THREATS TO CONFIDENTIALITY

Psychologists will frequently encounter instances in which clients appear to have granted an informed consent for release of information but where, in fact, the sharing of information may not be in the client's best interest. Both clients and therapists may be naive about the eventual use of the released data, or both may fear that the information will be used against the client. Such situations are especially distressing when the client did not foresee during therapy the prospect of the future request for treatment data. The client then cannot change either the fact of treatment or its content.

Application Forms and Employment

Frequently psychotherapists receive requests for information about prior clients from potential employers and insurers (Menninger and English, 1965; Noll, 1974; Shaevitz, 1971). A survey of California psychiatrists found that 89% of the respondents had received inquires from insurance companies, 56% from schools, and 49% from prospective employers (Privacy Protection Study Commission, 1977).

Application forms sometimes ask some variation of the question: "Have you ever received treatment for an emotional problem?" Such questions place both the applicant and later the therapist in an untenable position. Applicants may answer "yes" to the question, but they may thereby begin a self-incrimination process. They will likely be asked to sign a release form to be sent to the therapist, and their prospects for obtaining the job may be jeopardized. Weinstock and Hoft (1974) reported from a survey that regardless of the type of position under question, rejection rates of up to 77% could result for applicants who were in psychotherapy. On the other hand, if clients lie and answer "no" to the question, they risk being fired later for providing inaccurate information. The risks of this lie being uncovered have increased with the advent of central data banks, which may well contain information about prior medical and mental health treatment.

Psychotherapists are faced with an equally serious dilemma when they receive a signed release form from a client's prospective employer or insurer. Noll (1974, 1976) and Halleck (1971) have written extensively about the problem of therapists becoming double agents in this situation. Unless the therapist can write honestly about some highly commendable qualities of the client, the therapist may face a choice of lying or revealing unfavorable information that may prevent the client from obtaining the job or insurance policy. The truth may also place the client in an "extra-premium class" of insurance coverage (Noll, 1974). Sharfstein, Towery, and Milowe (1980) reported that psychotherapists distort claims information submitted to insurance companies because of fear of the negative impact of the data. While no data exist, it is possible that the psychologists do the same when their clients become applicants for new jobs or insurance policies. Because an unreasonable stigma is still attached to mental health treatment, psychologists may conclude that their obligation to act in the best interest of their clients requires the disclosing of only information that would benefit the client.

Such requests for information frequently warrant discussion with the client about preferred courses of action. Therapists should be cautious about guessing what the client may prefer. Possibly the therapist can simply assert that therapy was not relevant to the client's employment. Psychologists should also pressure employers and insurers to replace such general questions on application forms with questions about relevant current health and functioning.

While psychologists agonize over what information to disclose, the courts have held that any and all relevant information may be released. It is not proper for a client to request that a therapist mislead an employer by withholding essential information. For example, in *Clark v. Geraci* (1960), a family physician was requested by the employee to notify his employer that a medical condition was the cause of absenteeism. The physician did so on several occasions, but the physician eventually learned that the patient's condition was caused in part by alcohol abuse. When the employer eventually requested more detailed information about the employee's health problems, the physician informed the employer about the alcohol abuse against the advice of the patient. In a later suit, the court upheld the physician's actions, stating that a patient cannot request the doctor to tell only part of the truth when all of it is relevant to the condition.

Third-Party Payers

Without a doubt, the availability of third-party reimbursement for psychotherapy for psychologists has increased the availability of psychotherapy, but with this benefit has come the necessity to share data with the payer. Abuses of confidential information by insurance companies have been widely reported (Beigler, 1981; Slovenko, 1975). Clients have received word of their diagnoses from well-meaning friends in the personnel office or from receiving a copy of an insurance payment form. Employees have been dismissed from jobs and denied promotions. Others have been denied credit and mortgage money. Some clients opt to pay for their own services because they fear exposure.

While it may be tempting to argue that third-party payers have no need for confidential information and that the professional judgment of the psychotherapist should suffice (Bent, 1982), there are justifications for the sharing of at least some information with payers. Data about diagnoses, types and duration of treatment, and other client-risk variables are essential from an actuarial stand. Carriers base premium costs on data about projected expenses, and when they are in doubt about their data base, they can be expected to ask for more information. As an example, Blue Cross-Blue Shield of Washington, D.C., developed a special claims form in 1975 to permit the development of a comprehensive picture of utilization and costs, as well as guidelines for identifying unusual cases that might require closer inspection (Beigler, 1981). The claims form, however, requested information that led providers and clients to protest and to threaten a class action suit. Patients reportedly terminated treatment, and others refused to enter treatment. Finally the claims forms were replaced by simpler ones, which continue to be used for about 90% of all claims. The remainder require more information and involve other quality control mechanisms such as peer review. In other instances, insurance carriers have requested to review entire records based on blanket release of information forms (Everstine et al., 1980). When carriers determine that it is impossible to obtain a reliable data base for utilization of certain services such as psychotherapy, they may cut coverage to protect themselves. Thus psychologists and their clients face a serious dilemma of desiring more insurance reimbursement but resisting the process because of threats to confidentiality.

One area of risk is that of disclosure by the office personnel who process the claims forms. Insurance office personnel may not have the same appreciation for confidentiality as psychotherapists, although insurance companies have reportedly instituted stronger measures to train their personnel in this regard. Whenever possible, claims forms should be routed directly to the insurance company without passing through the employer.

Psychotherapists may participate unwittingly in the release of information in facilities that require clients to sign blanket release of information forms upon admission. Such forms sometimes permit the facility to make periodic reports from their records to insurance companies. Clients may have no basis at that time on which to give an informed consent. In one survey (Grossman, 1971), nine of ten hospitals surveyed routinely forwarded such information without the physician's approval or the client's awareness.

The processing of claims forms can trap psychotherapists who are not familiar with standard reporting procedures. Failure to provide standard information often produces a request for more information. At the same time, the principle of confidentiality enjoins the psychotherapists to provide as little information as necessary. Attaching copies of psychological reports or statements justifying treatment is usually unnecessary and unwise.

Psychotherapists should obtain the participation of the client when requests for more information threaten confidentiality. Clients have a right to refuse further disclosure, and psychotherapists should be cautious about supplying more information in order to ensure reimbursement. Clear boundaries should be established with the client on what information can be disclosed before a decision should be made to abandon the claims process. With the client's permission, some requests for more information can be successfully expedited by a call to a claims manager or by replying that a detailed answer would violate confidentiality (Beigler, 1981).

Data Banks

Information supplied by clients and their therapists on application forms and reimbursement claims may find its way into a system with potential for even broader dissemination than that of the personnel office or insurer. Many insurance companies pool their knowledge about clients in massive data banks that other subscribing companies share. Information about a client in psychotherapy that is placed on a reimbursement form may suddenly have national visibility (Westin, 1976). To make matters worse, the data banks' computer systems have been demonstrated to be vulnerable to criminal manipulation. Beigler (1978) described an example of a person who returned home from a stay in a hospital to find his auto insurance already cancelled apparently because a data bank had identified him as a high risk. Similarly, the Privacy Commission reported on a Denver operation in which insurance companies knowingly purchased unauthorized and fraudulent access to hospital records. And in Chicago, unethical lawyers looking for potential malpractice cases arranged for unauthorized access to hospital records. Confidentiality problems with data banks are especially serious for psychiatric patients because of the continuing stigma attached to receiving psychotherapy. An example is that of a Pennsylvania woman who had been rejected for major medical insurance based on a data bank's inaccurate statement that she was an alcoholic.

Generally two kinds of agencies collect information on citizens: credit bureaus and consumer investigation agencies. Credit bureaus collect and report information to clients (department stores, credit card companies) about bill paying habits. Consumer investigation agencies collect and sell reports on applicants for various kinds of insurance and employment. At one time, these reports purported to describe, among other things, the character, style of life, and drinking and sexual habits of persons. One of the largest such agencies is the Medical Information Bureau (MIB). This clearinghouse holds data on 11 million or 12 million people and is tapped by some 700 insurance companies (Kennedy and Jacobs, 1981; Whiteside, 1975). These information agencies are now subject to more regulations about the content and release of data. The MIB now claims that it places on file only information received from doctors' medical findings (no neighborhood investigators are used), and data are automatically erased seven years from date of entry. Clients, however, may still be unaware of this extensive network that compiles and shares their health profile. Psychotherapists are obliged to share a minimum of information about their clients.

Peer Review and Quality Assurance

The topic of peer review has already been discussed in Chapter 9 in the context of privileged communication. Here we discuss peer review only as it relates to the broader principle of confidentiality. Peer review was initially implemented in 1972 by Congress to review the quality, necessity, and appropriateness of services delivered in Medicare, Medicaid, and maternal and child health programs (Young, 1982). Currently the rationale for peer review has been expanded to include the functions of policing, continuing education, and quality assurance. Sechrest and Hoffman (1982) have described peer review as "the *sine qua non* of a mature profession" (p. 17). In spite of these lofty claims, psychotherapists have not always accepted peer review with enthusiasm. Many equate peer review with insurance company claims procedures in which nonprofessionals review and make decisions about reimbursement. In spite of this lackluster response, various forms of peer review are being incorporated into third-party systems of mental health delivery, and many regard peer review as a preferred mechanism to government oversight.

Peer review typically involves inspection of written records, and, as with insurance claims procedures, the more information that is made available, the more productive the review can be. Consequently the review process requires some personal information about clients; however, such sensitive information can be kept separate from other claims procedures and destroyed as soon as the review is completed (Bent, 1982). Whether such practices actually occur, however, is less clear, as evidenced by the following example cited by Lassen (1982). In a Social Security Administration-sponsored demonstration project, it was discovered that Blue Cross/Blue Shield, part of an independent peer review system, was routinely microfilming all documents, including highly personal information, from client treatment plans. These microfilmed records could be released to other parties with the earlier blanket release ("release all records") signed naively by the client.

One wonders how clients would react if they could follow their records through the maze. Would they embark on therapy in the same manner if they knew in advance the threats to confidentiality of their records?

CONFIDENTIALITY AND DANGEROUS PERSONS

Psychotherapists are bound to hold confidential all information about the past crimes of their clients. Therapists should not report even serious crimes unless these crimes are included within the bounds of a mandated report or are in furtherance of the duty to protect. The law requires physicians to report a variety of health-related situations such as gunshot wounds and certain contagious diseases. Mental health professionals will be affected most by mandatory child abuse reporting laws. Unfortunately, many psychotherapists know little about the existence of these mandatory reporting provisions, let alone the intracies of their state's law or the specific reporting procedures (Muehleman and Kimmons, 1981; Swoboda et al., 1978).

Child Abuse Reporting

Child abuse is a generic term that covers the areas of nonaccidental injury, neglect, sexual molestation, and mental injury. States define these elements differently, yet each combines two or more of them in their reporting laws. In an attempt to identify abusing families, every state has established laws requiring certain persons to report suspected child abuse. The first mandated reporting laws were restricted to physicians or other medical personnel. Now many states require a wide variety of mental health professionals as mandated reporters or include them through phrases that require "any person" suspecting the abuse to report it. Of course, even without a statutory duty, psychotherapists have an ethical responsibility to report suspected child abuse (Education Commission of the States, 1979).

The laws protect mandated reporters by providing immunity from liability for those who report suspected child abuse in good faith (defined as a sincere belief that the abuse had occurred). Also, the failure to report suspected child abuse may result in criminal or civil liability. Psychotherapists should familiarize themselves with the clinical signs of child abuse and should understand their state laws and reporting procedures.

The Duty to Protect

Psychotherapists may have to breach confidentiality when their patients become imminently dangerous to others. The issue of protecting third persons received national attention in the case of *Tarasoff v. Regents of the University of California* (1976). Despite the importance of the *Tarasoff* decision, it has "led to much commentary but little understanding" (VandeCreek and Knapp, 1984, p. 53). It is important for psychotherapists to understand what the *Tarasoff* court did and did not say.

The details of *Tarasoff* have been discussed in more detail elsewhere (Knapp, 1980; Knapp and VandeCreek, 1982; Knapp, VandeCreek, and Herzog, in press; Slovenko, 1975), and only necessary background information will be provided here. Prosjenit Poddar was an outpatient who expressed his intent to kill his former girlfriend, Tatiana Tarasoff, when she returned from her summer vacation. The psychologist believed the threat and asked the campus police to commit Poddar. The campus police interviewed Poddar but released him when he appeared rational and promised to stay away from Tarasoff. Poddar discontinued treatment, and the psychologist was instructed by his superiors to do no more to deter Poddar. Two months later, Poddar killed Tarasoff when she returned from vacation.

The California court supported the claim of Tarasoff's parents, stating that the psychologist should have done more to prevent the murder. The court ruled that the confidentiality of the psychotherapeutic relationship was important but that the "protective privilege ends where the public peril begins" (p. 337). Because warning the intended victim is the most obvious form of protection, some have referred to this ruling as the "duty to warn." The court decision did not limit the protective actions to warnings, however.

For the most part, subsequent California courts have followed the *Tarasoff* decision strictly, and reasonably consistent guidelines have been developed. It is important for psychotherapists to understand the circumstances under which the duty to protect may arise and the limits to that duty. The duty to protect is invoked whenever a patient presents a danger to others even though a specific threat has not yet been issued. Idle threats that are not taken literally do not invoke the duty to protect. "A therapist should not be encouraged routinely to reveal such threats . . . unless such disclosure is necessary to avert danger to others" (p. 347). But other clinical indicators, even in the absence of a direct threat, may invoke the duty to protect. In *Jablonski v. United States* (1983), a federal court applying California law held that the psychiatrist could be liable for failure to warn his client's girlfriend of his dangerousness. Although the client had not directly threatened his girlfriend, if the psychiatrist had obtained the client's previous records, he would have been aware of a past history of violence toward lovers.

The duty to protect does not require psychotherapists to interrogate their clients or conduct an independent investigation when the identity of the victim is unknown. Rather, the duty to protect arises only when the victim is identified or could be identified upon a "moment's reflection" (*Tarasoff,* p. 345; *Mavroudis v. Superior Court for County of San Mateo,* 1980).

Finally, the duty to protect does not require that warning the intended victim is the only response when danger arises. On the contrary, warning intended victims may become superfluous or counterproductive under certain circumstances (Appelbaum, 1985). Instead the *Tarasoff* court stated that the "discharge of such duty may require the therapist to take one or more of various steps, depending on the nature of the case, including warning the intended victim" (p. 334). The psychotherapist may attempt an involuntary commitment, notify the police, or take other steps to deter violence. In many situations, however, psychotherapists can prevent violence through the use of sound psychotherapeutic techniques.

The duty to protect did take an extension in California in *Hedlund v. Superior Court of Orange County* (1983). Here a woman was shot by her lover who had expressed intentions of violence against his girlfriend. The court concluded that the psychotherapist should have warned the victim. In addition, the court agreed that the duty to protect should have extended to the victim's infant son who was with his mother and was traumatized by the shooting. The court stated, "Nor is it unreasonable to recognize the existence of a duty to persons in close relationship to the object of a patient's threat" (p. 47). The implications of this extension are not clear. What is meant by "close relationship"? For example, if an elementary school teacher is a potential victim, should the therapist warn other school officials and/or the children in addition to the teacher?

The *Tarasoff* decision is binding only in California. Courts in other states will have to decide if the *Tarasoff* principles apply to their state. To date, court decisions have indicated that *Tarasoff* would apply in New Jersey (*McIntosh v. Milano,* 1979) and Nebraska (*Lipari v. Sears,* 1980). A Maryland court, however, has held that *Tarasoff* would not apply in that state (*Shaw v. Glickman,* 1980). (The unusual circumstances of the *Shaw* case were described in Chapter 10.)

Even in states that have adopted *Tarasoff,* psychotherapists should not overreact to this decision. Nothing in it tells psychotherapists that they have to forsake their clinical judgment in treating potentially violent outpatients. The duty to protect is invoked only when the danger to human life is imminent and other therapeutic interventions do not have a reasonable chance to circumvent it.

Several commentators point to other acceptable ways to handle potentially violent clients. Wexler (1980) has suggested that continued psychotherapy can often diffuse the threat, and Roth and Meisel (1977) have documented how social or environmental manipulations can reduce the risk of danger. The duty to warn applies only when the psychotherapist has determined that other options are not viable. Furthermore, the psychotherapist should use standard procedures in assessing danger. Verbal threats, hostile fantasies, or angry outbursts do not necessarily indicate immediate danger. When in doubt, the psychotherapist can seek professional consultation and indicate in the client's record the rationale for the decision made (Knapp and VandeCreek, 1982). The same principles apply when clients threaten the lives of public officials. The potential for danger should be assessed, and, if necessary, consultation may be sought.

According to the ethical principles of the American Psychological Association (APA, 1981) and the American Psychiatric Association (1979), psychotherapists may breach confidentiality if it is necessary to protect a client from suicide. As with the protection of others, breaches of confidentiality should not be done routinely with suicidal clients but only after other procedures have been exhausted and the potential for suicide becomes imminent (Knapp and VandeCreek, 1983).

To date, no court case has been found in which a mental health professional was successfully sued for breaching confidentiality in order to protect a suicidal person. In contrast to homicidal persons, courts have not extended the right to divulge confidential information about suicidal clients to the level of a duty (*Bellah v. Greenson,* 1978). For example, the *Bellah* court stated that only the safety of third persons, and not threats to self or property, is sufficient to warrant a breach of confidentiality.

It has been suggested that psychologists should inform their clients in advance about subject matter that may warrant disclosure—something similar to a mental health *Miranda* warning (Eger, 1976; Fleming and Maximov, 1974). The disadvantage of this warning is a likely chilling effect on the therapeutic relationship and the refusal of some clients to seek treatment.

Eger (1976) recommended presenting this warning in terms of the therapist's duty to the client. Carrying out this duty to clients involves preventing clients from harming themselves. Therapists therefore have a duty to inform clients that causing harm to others will harm themselves and that the therapist will try to prevent this. Therapists should make every effort to involve the client in the disclosure process, such as by obtaining consent and making the warning in the client's presence. The most prudent course of action for psychotherapists appears to be to keep treatment needs as the first priority, since actual violence is rare among clients, and to pursue all other avenues to reduce the danger before disclosing (Roth and Meisel, 1977).

SPECIAL SITUATIONS

Group and Family Therapy

Problems of confidentiality are inherent in group and family therapy. Although group therapists should routinely stress the rule of not discussing the content of therapy outside the office, Davis (1980) found that many group members discussed confidential information from group sessions with family and friends regardless of requests from leaders not to do so. Clients do not have a professional obligation of confidentiality.

Even more delicate may be the case of family therapy where some therapists may advocate frankness and honesty but where sharing of certain secrets may change the balance of power in the family (Hare-Mustin, 1980). Individual sessions with family members may also elicit information that the member does not wish to share. Such information, if shared, could make a great difference in the family. For example, knowledge of continuing sexual affairs, addictions, or illegal behaviors of children could jeopardize the outcome of therapy.

Margolin (1982) recommends that therapists make their ground rules about confidentiality explicit and indicate that confidentiality between therapist and family members often may not apply although the clients have a right to request confidentiality. Ultimately, however, it is the therapist's discretion, not responsibility, to divulge material.

Children

Psychotherapy with children presents unique problems regarding the disclosure of information to parents. The traditional rule is that the parents—not the child—determine the need for psychotherapy and that the parents have access to information obtained within therapy and the right to authorize the release of information to others. This traditional rule still applies to preteenage children, although, as in family therapy, the psychologist should use discretion on what, when, or how to reveal information to parents. However, the law regarding adolescents appears to show signs of changing in certain instances.

In a few situations, teenagers may legally seek treatment independent of their parent, and if minors can seek treatment independently, they should control the information obtained within psychotherapy (Weinapple and Perr, 1979). Minors may seek treatment independently if they are emancipated (living alone and financially self-supporting, in the armed services, or married). Also, several states have statutes that allow teenagers to seek mental health or drug abuse treatment without parental consent. Finally, a few courts have recognized mature minors who show legal capacity to seek treatment independently. The legal recognition of mature minors is quite rare, and practitioners should not assume that they can routinely treat teenagers who appear mature. Psychotherapists should consult local authorities for their state's laws regarding the treatment of teenagers.

Psychotherapists have the same legal obligations to release information in life-endangering situations with children (homicidal potential, suicidal potential, child abuse) as they do with adult clients. Most children who enter therapy do so with their parents' consent and often at their insistence. Problems of confidentiality arise when parents later request information about their child's progress in therapy. There are no clear ethical guidelines. Common law suggests that parents have absolute rights to access to information of the child's treatment. But many therapists insist that therapy cannot proceed with a child any more than with an adult without the promise of confidentiality. McGuire (1974) found general agreement among a small sample of therapists that one should grant the same degree of confidentiality with children as with adults. His respondents also agreed that the conditions of confidentiality should be thoroughly discussed with the child and that one should not release information about a child without the child's consent even if the adults grant consent. Psychotherapists also must exercise caution when writing reports on their child clients. Reports should be written with the expectation that parents will eventually read the report.

Limitations by Prior Agreement

In several instances, confidentiality may be severely limited or modified by prior agreement. These include court-ordered evaluations, evaluations for government security clearances, evaluations for social security disability and other agencies working with or paying for the care of the client, and evaluations for involuntary hospitalization. In these cases psychotherapists must still honor confidentiality except that, because they are employed by the agency, all relevant information may be shared. Clients need to know that the usual conditions of confidentiality do not exist in this situation.

Another exception to confidentiality exists in the military. All military officials are agents of the military first rather than of the client (Clausen and Daniels, 1966). Every encounter anyone in the military has with a health professional is reported in the health record, and this record may be made available not only to a commanding officer but to promotion boards (Bourne, 1982). In this setting, it becomes doubly important that psychotherapists exercise discretion in determining what to commit to paper.

Writing about Clients

Psychotherapists have a professional obligation to assist in educating other members of the profession and the general public. The use of case material is often the best vehicle in teaching about clinical matters, but what are the implications for confidentiality of client data?

Clients usually do not contract for a course of psychotherapy with the intent or thought of becoming the subject of speeches, books, or popular press exposés. They expect and deserve confidentiality. Writing about clients without breaching confidentiality is no easy matter.

Freud assumed that some of the most relevant and important clinical data were also so unique that the identity of the client might be quite obvious. He also found it unnecessary to obtain their consent. The first of his famous six case histories, a case of hysteria, was turned down by the editor on the grounds that it breached confidentiality (Slovenko, 1983). One case history even used the client's name (Dr. Schreber) who was described as paranoid (a litigious type) and who was a public magistrate. Clearly times have changed.

Freud assumed that his clients would never read his scholarly writings; this should not be assumed today. Publication of material where personal details are essential and where the client might be identified or be harmed by reading it should be viewed as a modification of the contract of psychotherapy. Therapists do not have a right to modify this contract unilaterally unless it is for the benefit of the client or society. Writing about clients is for the therapist's benefit, not the client's benefit. Distress caused by discovery of personal material in writing is grounds for libel, invasion of privacy (if the client's name is used), and malpractice (Slovenko, 1983).

Several guidelines are available for therapist-authors. There is no problem when case material is so brief or so thoroughly camouflaged or so common to the experience of many persons that the client's identity is impossible to ascertain. Another mechanism to camouflage identities is to fictionalize one's name if extensive case material is used or if the nature of one's practice is such that one's unique client cannot be masked. Such a step was taken by the authors of a recent book written for the nonscientific community *Confessions of a Gynecologist* (Anonymous, 1972). Some writers will find this tactic a serious sacrifice or not necessary, however.

The thought of writing about a client may have negative consequences for both the client and the process of psychotherapy. Slovenko (1983) suggested that therapist-authors should ask themselves if they might be tempted to prolong or modify treatment, pursue tangential but gossipy sidelines, or impede therapy by extensive note taking in their efforts to obtain literary material.

Whenever therapists seriously contemplate writing about personal details of a client's life, they should discuss this intention with the client and obtain a current consent. The timing of that request is a matter of discretion. Asking for consent after a highly charged session could frighten the client ("Am I that weird?") and could be harmful to the course of therapy ("I won't share that kind of material again"). Nonetheless, an early consent (called a *prospective waiver*) grants the client sufficient warning that the contract of therapy will now take on a dual purpose and that the implied contract of therapy with confidentiality has been modified. A prospective waiver by itself is still not a sufficient consent and may not withstand a court test (Slovenko, 1983) because the client cannot predict the future course of therapy. Clients also cannot give voluntary consent during the course of therapy because they are still dependent on the therapist for aid. Therefore a retrospective waiver is also needed after termination of treatment. Only with both a prospective and a retrospective consent have both therapist and client been ethically and legally protected.

The ideal situation, and the one offering accuracy in citing case material, is to have the client review the material and attest to its accuracy and consent to its publication. This was the situation with the writing of *Sybil* (Schreiber, 1973), a lengthy and highly personal description of a woman with multiple personality. Sybil (a pseudonym for the client) had several meetings with the author (a professor of English), as did the therapist. Both client and therapist reviewed and contributed to the preparation of the manuscript, and both have attested to its accuracy. It is possible that other clients would be more willing than expected to participate in reviewing their case material when the data are presented in less dramatic form.

Sometimes a collaborative effort may harm the client, or the material could be presented in the context of theoretical formulations that the client would not understand. It also may not be proper to obtain a prospective waiver because of the delicate nature of therapy. In many cases, the decision to describe a certain client is not made until after termination. If it is not appropriate for the client to read the case material, the client should be given a summary of the content plus a clear description of the author's means of masking identity. The client should be granted the option of maximum, not minimum, information in order to make an informed consent.

A recent publication violated all of the above guidelines. The book, *In Search of a Response,* written by a psychiatrist, described many intimate details of a client's life. Although the client was given a pseudonym, she was still identifiable by others. The client had given verbal consent several years prior to the book's publication, but she was not given an opportunity to review or discuss the book's actual content. Following publication, the client brought suit anonymously, charging that the book violated her right of privacy and the confidential nature of the doctor-client relationship. The trial court recommended a unique solution, reminiscent of Freud's contention that clients and the general public rarely read scholarly works, and enjoined only that portion of the book's distribution calculated to reach the nonscientific reader. The appellate court later found no justification for this distinction, perhaps because the book had never been advertised as a scientific publication, and ruled that the client deserved total confidentiality (*Doe v. Roe,* 1977).

Appendix A

State Statutes on Privilege

Statutes Pertaining to:

State	Physicians/ Psychiatrists	Psychologists	Social Workers	Clergy	Other
Alabama	Ala. Code §34-26-2 (Supp. 1984) Psychiatrist	Ala. Code §34-26-2 (Supp. 1984)		Ala. Code tit.12, 21-166 (Supp. 1984)	
Alaska	Al. R. Civ. P. §43(h)(4) (Supp. 1966) Physician	Al. R. Evid. 504		Al. R. Civ. P. §43(h)(3)	
Arizona	Ariz. Rev. Stat. Ann. §12-2235 (1982) Physician	Ariz. Rev. Stat. Ann. §32-2085 (Supp. 1984–1985)		Ariz. Rev. Stat. Ann. §12-2233 (1982)	
Arkansas	Ark. Stat. Ann. §28-1001 Unif. R. Evid. 503 (Supp. 1985) Psychotherapist	Ark. Stat. Ann. §28-1001 Unif. R. Evid. 503 (Supp. 1985) Psychotherapist	Ark. Stat. Ann. §71-2815 (Supp. 1983)	Ark. Stat. Ann. §28-1001 Unif. R. Evid. 505 (Supp. 1985)	
California	Ca. Evid. Code §1014 (Supp. 1985) Psychotherapist	Ca. Evid. Code §1014 (Supp. 1985) Psychotherapist	Ca. Evid. Code §1014 (Supp. 1985) Psychotherapist	Ca. Evid. Code §1034 (Supp. 1985)	Ca. Evid. Code §1035.2 (Supp. 1985) Sex. Assault §1014 (Supp. 1985) Marr. & Family

Colorado	Colo. Rev. Stat. §13-90-107 (Supp. 1983) Physician	Colo. Rev. Stat. §12-43-120 (Supp. 1983)	Colo. Rev. Stat. §12-63.5-115 (1979)	Colo. Rev. Stat. §13-90-107 (Supp. 1983)	Colo. Rev. Stat. §13-90-107 (Supp. 1983) Nurse
Connecticut	Conn. Gen. Stat. Ann. §52-146d (Supp. 1985) Psychiatrist	Conn. Gen. Stat. Ann. §52-146c (Supp. 1985)		Conn. Gen. Stat. Ann. §52-146b (Supp. 1985)	Conn. Gen. Stat. Ann. §52-146k (Supp. 1985) Sex. Assault
Delaware	Del. R. Evid. 503 Psychotherapist	Del. R. Evid. 503 Psychotherapist	Del. Code Ann. tit.24, §3913 (Supp. 1982)	Del. Code Ann. tit.10, §4316	
District of Columbia	D.C. Code Ann. §14-307 (Supp. 1985) Physician	D.C. Code Ann. §2-1704.16 (1981)		D.C. Code Ann. §14-309 (1981)	
Florida	Fla. Stat. Ann. §90.503 (1979) Psychotherapist	Fla. Stat. Ann. §90-503 (1979) Psychotherapist		Fla. Stat. Ann. §90-503 (1979)	Fla. Stat. Ann. §90-5035 (Supp. 1985) Sex. Assault
Georgia	Ga. Code Ann. §24-9-21 (1982) Psychiatrist	Ga. Code Ann. §43-39-16 (1982)		Ga. Code Ann. §24-9-22 (1982)	
Hawaii	Haw. R. Evid. 504 Psychotherapist	Haw. R. Evid. 504 Psychotherapist		Haw. Rev. Stat. §621-20.5 Haw. R. Evid. 506	
Idaho	Idaho Code §9-203.4 (Supp. 1985) Physician	Idaho Code §54-2314 (1979)	Idaho Code §54-3213 (1979)	Idaho Code §9-203.3 (Supp. 1985)	

continued

Statutes Pertaining to: *(continued)*

State	*Physicians/ Psychiatrists*	*Psychologists*	*Social Workers*	*Clergy*	*Other*
Illinois	Ill. Ann. Stat. ch.110 §8-802 (1984) Physician[1]	Ill. Ann. Stat. ch.111 §5306 (Supp. 1985)[1]	Ill. Rev. Stat. ch.111 §6324 (Supp. 1985)[1]	Ill. Rev. Stat. Ch. 51 §48.1 (Supp. 1985)	Ill. Rev. Stat. Ch. 110 §8-802.1 (Supp. 1985) Sex. Assault
Indiana	Ind. Code Ann. §34-1-14-5 (Supp. 1985) Physician	Ind. Code Ann. §25-33-1-17 (Supp. 1985)		Ind. Code Ann. §34-1-14-5 (Supp. 1985)	
Iowa	Iowa Code Ann. §622.10 (Supp. 1985) Physician	Iowa Code Ann. §622.10 (Supp. 1985)[2]	Iowa Code Ann. §622.10 (Supp. 1985)[2]	Iowa Code Ann. §622.10 (Supp. 1985)	Iowa Code Ann. §622.10 (Supp. 1985) Nurse
Kansas	Kan. Stat. §60-427 (Supp. 1983) Physician	Kan. Stat. §74-5323 (Supp. 1984)	Kan. Stat. §75-5360 (1984)	Kan. Stat. §60-429 (Supp. 1983)	
Kentucky	Ky. Rev. Stat. Ann. §421.215 (1984) Psychiatrist	Ky. Rev. Stat. Ann. §319.111 (1984)	Ky. Rev. Stat. Ann. §335.170 (1984)	Ky. Rev. Stat. Ann. §421.210 (1984)	
Louisiana	La. Rev. Stat. Ann. §13:3734 (Supp. 1985) Psychotherapist	La. Rev. Stat. Ann. §13:3734 (Supp. 1985) Psychotherapist	La. Rev. Stat. Ann. §37:2714(B) (1974)	La. Rev. Stat. Ann. §13:3734.1 (Supp. 1985)	La. Rev. Stat. Ann. §13:3734 (Supp. 1985) Nurse
Maine	Me. R. Evid. 503 (Supp. 1985) Psychotherapist	Me. R. Evid. 503 (Supp. 1985) Psycotherapist	Me. Rev. Stat. Ann. tit.32 §7005 (Supp. 1984)	Me. R. Evid. 505 (Supp. 1984)	Me. Rev. Stat. Ann. 16-§8-53-A (Supp. 1985) Sex. Assault

Maryland	Md. Cts. & Jud. Proc. Ann. §9-109 (1984) Psychiatrist	Md. Cts. & Jud. Proc. Ann. §9-109 (1984)	Md. Cts. & Jud. Proc. Ann. §9-121 (1984)	Md. Cts. & Jud. Proc. Ann. §9-111 (1984)	
Massachusetts	Mass. Gen. Laws Ann. ch233 §20B (Suppl 1985) Psychotherapist	Mass. Gen. Laws Ann. ch233 §20B (Supp. 1985) Psychotherapist	Mass. Gen. Laws Ann. ch112 §135 (1983)	Mass. Gen. Laws Ann. ch233 §20A (Supp. 1985)	Mass. Gen. Laws Ann. ch233 §207 (Supp. 1985) Sex. Assault
Michigan	Mi. Comp. Laws Ann. §600.2157 (Supp. 1982) Physician	Mi. Comp. Laws Ann. §333.18237 (Supp. 1982)	Mi. Comp. Laws Ann. §339.1610 (Supp. 1982)	Mi. Comp. Laws Ann. §600.2156 (Supp. 1982)	Mi. Comp. Laws Ann. §551.339 (Supp. 1982) Marr. Couns.
Minnesota	Minn. Stat. Ann. §595.02(d) (Supp. 1985) Physician	Minn. Stat. Ann. §595.02(g) (Supp. 1985)		Minn. Stat. Ann. §595.02(c) (Supp. 1985)	Minn. Stat. Ann. (§595.02(g) (Supp. 1985) Nurse Minn. Stat. Ann. §595.02(j) (Supp. 1985) Sex. Assault
Mississippi	Miss. Code Ann. §13-1-21 (Supp. 1984) Physician	Miss. Code Ann. §73-31-29 (Supp. 1984)		Mis. Code Ann. §13-1-22 (Supp. 1984)	Miss. Code Ann. §13-1-21 (Supp. 1984) Nurse
Missouri	Mo. Ann. Stat. §491.060 (Supp. 1985) Physician	Mo. Ann. Stat. §337.055 (Supp. 1985)		Mo. Ann. Stat. §491.060 (Supp. 1985)	

[1]In the event of a conflict between these sections and the Mental Health and Developmental Disabilities Confidentiality Act (Chapter 91½, §801 et seq.), that act shall control.

[2]The privilege extends to "mental health professionals," defined as registered psychologists, nurses' or persons with Masters degrees in social work or counseling.

continued

Statutes Pertaining to: *(continued)*

State	*Physicians/ Psychiatrists*	*Psychologists*	*Social Workers*	*Clergy*	*Other*
Montana	Mont. Rev. Code Ann. §26-1-805 (Supp. 1983) Physician	Mont. Rev. Code Ann. §26-1-807 (Supp. 1983)	Mont. Rev. Code Ann. §37-22-40 (Supp. 1983)	Mont. Rev. Code Ann. §26-1-804 (Supp. 1983)	Mont. Rev. Code Ann. §26-1-808 (Supp. 1983) Psych. Teachers
Nebraska	Neb. R. Evid. §27-504 (Supp. 1979) Physician	Neb. R. Evid. §27-504 (1979)		Neb. R. Evid. §27-506 (Supp. 1979)	
Nevada	Nev. Rev. Stat. §49.215 (Supp. 1981) Psychotherapist	Nev. Rev. Stat. §49.215 (Supp. 1981) Psychotherapist	Nev. Rev. Stat. §49.215 (Supp. 1981)[3]	Nev. Rev. Stat. §49.255 (Supp. 1981)	
New Hampshire	N.H. Rev. Stat. Ann. §329:26 (Supp. 1983) Physician	N.H. Rev. Stat. Ann. §330-A:19 (Supp. 1983)		N.H. Rev. Stat. Ann. §516.35 (Supp. 1983)	N.H. Rev. Stat. Ann. §330-A:14 (Supp. 1983) Pastoral Couns.
New Jersey	N.J. Stat. Ann. §2A:84A-22.2 (Supp. 1985) Physician	N.J. Stat. Ann. §45:14B-28 (Supp. 1985)		N.J. Stat. Ann. §2A:84A-23 (Supp. 1985)	N.J. Stat. Ann. §2A:84A-22.12 (Supp. 1985) Sex. Assault §45:8B-29 (Supp. 1985) Marriage Couns.

New Mexico	N.M. R. Evid. 504 (1983) Psychotherapist	N.M. R. Evid. 504 (1983) Psychotherapist	N.M. R. Evid. 509 (1983)	N.M. R. Evid. 506 (Supp. 1983)	N.M. R. Evid. 509 (1983) Soc. Serv. Pers. for Status Off.
New York	N.Y. Civ. Prac. Law §4504 (McKin. Supp. 1982) Physician	N.Y. Civ. Prac. Law §4507 (McKin. Supp. 1982)	N.Y. Civ. Prac. Law §4508 (McKin. Supp. 1982)	N.Y. Civ. Prac. Law §4505 (McKin. Supp. 1982)	N.Y. Civ. Prac. Law §4504 (McKin. Supp. 1982) Nurse
North Carolina	N.C. Gen. Stat. §8-53 (Supp. 1983) Physician	N.C. Gen. Stat. §8-53.3 (Supp. 1983)	N.C. Gen. Stat. §8.53-7 (Supp. 1983)	N.C. Gen. Stat. §8-53.2 (Supp. 1983)	N.C. Gen. Stat. §8-53.5 (Supp. 1983) Mar. & Family §8-53.8 M. H. Counselors
North Dakota	N.D. R. Evid. 503 (Supp. 1983) Psychotherapist	N.D. R. Evid. 503 (Supp. 1983) Psychotherapist		N.D. R. Evid. 505	
Ohio	Ohio Rev. Code Ann. §2317.02(B) (Page Supp. 1982) Physician	Ohio Rev. Code Ann. §4732.19 (Page Supp. 1984)	Ohio Rev. Code Ann. §2317.02 (Page Supp. 1984)	Ohio Rev. Code Ann. §2317.02(B) (Page Sup. 1982)	
Oklahoma	Okla. Stat. Ann. Tit. 12, §2503 (Supp. 1984) Psychotherapist	Okla. Stat. Ann. Tit. 12, §2503 (Supp. 1984) Psychotherapist	Okla. Stat. Ann. Tit. 59, §1271.1 (Supp. 1984-85)	Okla. Stat. Ann. Tit. 12, §2505 (Supp. 1984)	
Oregon	Or. Rev. Stat. §40.230 (Supp. 1983) Psychotherapist	Or. Rev. Stat. §40.230 (Supp. 1983) Psychotherapist	Or. Rev. Stat. §40.250 (Supp. 1983)	Or. Rev. Stat. §40.260 (Supp. 1983)	

[3] "A person employed by a public or private agency as a . . . psychiatric social worker."

continued

Statutes Pertaining to: *(continued)*

State	*Physicians/ Psychiatrists*	*Psychologists*	*Social Workers*	*Clergy*	*Other*
Pennsylvania	Pa. Cons. Stat. Ann. §5929 (Pur. Supp. 1983) Physician	Pa. Cons. Stat. Ann. §5944 (Pur. Supp. 1983)		Pa. Cons. Stat. Ann. §5943 (Pur. Supp. 1983)	Pa. Cons. Stat. Ann. §5945.1 (Pur. Supp. 1983) Sex. Assault
Rhode Island	R.I. Gen. Laws §5-37.3-3 (Cum. Supp. 1984) Psychotherapist	R.I. Gen. Laws §5-37.3-3 (Cum. Supp. 1984) Psychotherapist		R.I. Gen. Laws §9-17-23 (Supp. 1982)	
South Carolina				S.C. Code §19-11-90 (Supp. 1976)	
South Dakota	S.D. Compiled Laws Ann. §19-13-6 (Supp. 1984) Psychotherapist	S.D. Compiled Laws Ann. §19-13-6 (Supp. 1984) Psychotherapist	S.D. Compiled Laws Ann. §36-26-30 (Supp. 1984)	S.D. Compiled Laws Ann. §9-13-16 to 18 (Supp. 1984)	S.D. Compiled Laws Ann. §19-13-21-2 (Supp. 1984) College Counselors
Tennessee	Tenn. Code Ann. §24-1-207 (Supp. 1984) Psychiatrist	Tenn. Code Ann. §63-11-213 (Supp. 1984)	Tenn. Code Ann. §63-23-107 (Supp. 1984)	Tenn. Code Ann. §24-1-206 (Supp. 1984)	
Texas	Tex. Rev. Civil Stat. Ann. Art. 4495b §5.08 (Vernon. Supp. 1982) Physician	Tex. Rev. Civil Stat. Ann. Art. 5561h (Vernon Supp. 1982)		Tex. Civil Stat. Tit. 55, Art. 3715(a)	

Utah	Utah Code Ann. §78-24-8(d) (1977) Physician	Utah Code Ann. §58-25-8 (Supp. 1983)	Utah Code Ann. §58-35-10 (1974)	Utah Code Ann. §78-24-8 (Supp. 1983)	Utah Code Ann. §58-31-7 (Supp. 1983) Mar. & Family Th.
Vermont	Vt. Stat. Ann. Tit. 12, §1612 (Supp. 1985) Physician		Vt. R. Evid. §503	Vt. Stat. Ann. Tit. 12, §1607 (Supp. 1984)	V. R. Evid. §503 Nurses M. H. Prof.[4]
Virginia	Va. Code §8.01-399 (1977) Physician	Va. Code §8.01-400.2 (Supp. 1983)	Va. Code §8.01-400.2 (Supp. 1983)	Va. Code §8.01-400 (Supp. 1983)	Va. Code §8.01-400.2 (Supp. 1983) Counselors
Washington	Wash. Rev. Code Ann. §560.060(4) (1981) Physician	Wash. Rev. Code Ann. §18.83110 (1981)		Wash. Rev. Code Ann. §560.060(3) (Supp. 1981)	
West Virginia			W.Va. Code §30-30-12 (Supp. 1985)		
Wisconsin	Wis. Stat. Ann. §905.04 (Wests Supp. 1984) Physician	Wis. Stat. Ann. §905.04 (Wests Supp. 1984)		Wis. Stat. Ann. §905.06 (Wests Supp. 1984)	Wis. Stat. Ann. §905.04 (Supp. 1984) Nurses
Wyoming	Wyo. Stat. §1-12-101 (Supp. 1985) Physician	Wyo. Stat. §33-27-103 (Supp. 1981)		Wyo. Stat. §1-12-101 (Supp. 1985)	Wyo. Stat. §1-12-116 (Supp. 1985) Sex. Assault Fam. Violence Advocate

[4] "A 'mental health professional' is a qualified person designated by the Commissioner of Mental Health."

Appendix B

Rule 504: Psychotherapist-Patient Privilege

(a) Definitions.

(1) A "patient" is a person who consults or is examined or interviewed by a psychotherapist.

(2) A "psychotherapist" is (A) a person authorized to practice medicine in any state or nation, or reasonably believed by the patient so to be, while engaged in the diagnosis or treatment of a mental or emotional condition, including drug addiction, or (B) a person licensed or certified as a psychologist under the laws of any state or nation, while similarly engaged.

(3) A communication is "confidential" if not intended to be disclosed to third persons other than those present to further the interest of the patient in the consultation, examination, or interview, or persons reasonably necessary for the transmission of the communications, or persons who are participating in the diagnosis and treatment under the direction of the psychotherapist, including members of the patient's family.

(b) General rule of privilege—A patient has a privilege to refuse to disclose and to prevent any other person from disclosing confidential communications, made for the purposes of diagnosis or treatment of his mental or emotional condition, including drug addiction, among himself, his psychotherapist, or persons who are participating in the diagnosis or treatment under the direction of the psychotherapist, including members of the patient's family.

(c) Who may claim the privilege—The privilege may be claimed by the patient, by his guardian or conservator, or by the personal representative of a deceased patient. The person who was the psychotherapist may claim the privilege but only on behalf of the patient. His authority so to do is presumed in the absence of evidence to the contrary.

(d) Exceptions.

(1) Proceedings for hospitalization—There is no privilege under this rule for communications relevant to an issue in proceedings to hospitalize the patient for mental illness, if the psychotherapist in the course of diagnosis or treatment has determined that the patient is in need of hospitalization.

(2) Examination by order of the judge—If the judge orders an examination of the mental or emotional condition of the patient, communications made in the course thereof are not privileged under this rule with respect to the particular purpose for which the examination is ordered unless the judge orders otherwise.

(3) Condition an element of claim or defense—There is no privilege under this rule as to communications relevant to an issue of the mental or emotional condition of the patient in any proceeding in which he relies upon the condition as an element of his claim or defense, or, after the patient's death, in any proceeding in which any party relies upon the condition as an element of his claim or defense.

From: 56 *Federal Rules and Decisions* 240, 241.

Appendix C

Federal Regulations Governing Privilege

I. Records in Drug and Alcohol Facilities

1175. Confidentiality of Patient Records

(a) Disclosure authorization.

Records of the identity, diagnosis, prognosis, or treatment of any patient which are maintained in connection with the performance of any drug abuse prevention function conducted, regulated, or directly or indirectly assisted by any department or agency of the United States shall, except as provided in subsection (e) of this section, be confidential and be disclosed only for the purposes and under the circumstances expressly authorized under subsection (b) of this section.

(b) Purposes and circumstances of disclose affecting consenting patient and patient regardless of consent.

(1) The content of any record referred to in subsection (a) of this section may be disclosed in accordance with the prior written consent of the patient with respect to whom such record is maintained, but only to such extent, under such circumstances, and for such purposes as may be allowed under regulations prescribed pursuant to subsection (g) of this section.

(2) Whether or not the patient, with respect to whom any given record referred to in subsection (a) of this section is maintained, gives his

written consent the content of such record may be disclosed as follows:

(A) To medical personnel to the extent necessary to meet a bona fide medical emergency.
(B) To qualified personnel for the purpose of conducting scientific research, management audits, financial audits, or program evaluation, but such personnel may not identify, directly or indirectly, any individual patient in any report of such research, audit, or evaluation, or otherwise disclose patient identities in any manner.
(C) If authorized by an appropriate order of a court of competent jurisdiction granted after application showing good cause therefor. In assessing good cause the court shall weigh the public interest and the need for disclosure against the injury to the patient, to the physician-patient relationship, and to the treatment services. Upon the granting of such order, the court, in determining the extent to which any disclosure of all or part of any record is necessary, shall impose appropriate safeguards against unauthorized disclosure.

(c) Prohibition against use of record in making criminal charges or investigation of patient.

Except as authorized by a court order granted under subsection (b)(2)(c) of this section, no record referred to in subsection (a) of this section may be used to initiate or substantiate any criminal charges against a patient or to conduct any investigation of a patient.

(d) Continuing prohibition against disclosure irrespective of status as patient.

The prohibitions of this section continue to apply to records concerning any individual who has been a patient, irrespective of whether or when he ceases to be a patient.

(e) Armed Forces and Veterans' Administration; interchange of records.

The prohibitions of this section do not apply to any interchange of records—

(1) within the Armed Forces or within those components of the Veterans' Administration furnishing health care to veterans, or
(2) between such components and the Armed Forces.

(f) Penalty for first and subsequent offenses.

Any person who violates any provision of this section or any regulation issued pursuant to this section shall be fined not more than $500 in the case of a first offense, and not more than $5,000 in the case of each subsequent offense.

From: 21 C.F.R. 1175 (1982)

II. Protection of Researchers and Research Subjects in Drug and Alcohol Research

1316.21 Confidentiality of identity of research subjects

(a) Any person conducting a bona fide research project directly related to the enforcement of the laws under the jurisdiction of the Attorney General concerning drugs or other substance which are or may be subject to control under the Controlled Substances Act (84 Stat. 1242; 21 U.S.C. 801) who intends to maintain the confidentiality of the identity of those persons who are the subjects of such research may petition the Administrator of the Drug Enforcement Administration for a grant of confidentiality: Providing, That:

(1) The Attorney General is authorized to carry out such research under the provisions of Section 502(a) (2-6) of the Controlled Substance Act of 1070 (21 U.S.C. 872(a) (2-6); and the research is being conducted with funds provided in whole or part by the Department of Justice; or

(2) The research is of a nature that the Attorney General would be authorized to carry out under the provisions of Section 502(a) (2-6) of the Controlled Substances Act (21 U.S.C. 872(a) 2-6), and is being conducted with funds provided from sources outside the Department of Justice.

(b) All petitions for Grants of Confidentiality shall be addressed to the Administrator, Drug Enforcement Administration, 1405 I Street NW., Washington, D.C. 20537, and shall contain the following:

(1) A statement as to whether the research protocol requires the manufacture, production, import, export, distribution, dispensing, administration, or possession of controlled substances, and if so the researcher's registration number or a statement that an application for such registration has been submitted to DEA;

(2) The location of the research project;

(3) The qualifications of the principal investigator;

(4) A general description of the research or a copy of the research protocol;

(5) The source of funding for the research project;

(6) A statement as to the risks posed to the research subjects by the research procedures and what protection will be afforded to the research subjects;

(7) A statement as to the risks posed to society in general by the research procedures and what measures will be taken to protect the interests of society;

(8) A specific request to withhold the names and/or any other identifying characteristics of the research subjects; and

(9) Statements establishing that a grant of confidentiality is necessary to the successful completion of the research project.

(c) The grant of confidentiality of identity of research subject shall consist of a letter issued by the Administrator, which shall include:

(1) The researcher's name and address.

(2) The researcher's registration number, if applicable.

(3) The title and purpose of the research.

(4) The location of the research project.

(5) An authorization for all persons engaged in the research to withhold the names and identifying characteristics of persons who are the subjects of such research, stating that persons who obtain this authorization may not be compelled in any Federal, State, or local civil, criminal, administrative, legislative, or other proceeding to identify the subjects of such research for which this authorization was obtained.

(6) The limits of this authorization, if any.

(7) A statement to the effect that the grant of confidentiality of identity of research subjects shall be perpetual but shall pertain only to the subjects of the research described in the research protocol, the description of the research submitted to DEA, or as otherwise established by DEA.

(d) Within 30 days of the date of completion of the research project, the researcher shall so notify the Administrator. The Administrator shall issue another letter including the information required in paragraph (c) of this section and stating the starting and finishing dates of the research for which the confidentiality of identity of research subjects was granted; upon receipt of this letter, the research shall return the original letter of exemption.

From: 21 C.F.R. 1316.21 (1984).

References

Allis, N. (1977). Prosecutional discovery of the defense case: The shield of confidentiality. *Southern California Law Review* **50:**461-511.

American Jurisprudence 2d (1976). Rochester, N.Y.: Lawyers Co-operative Publishing Co.

American Medical Records Association (1977). Confidentiality of patient health information: A position statement of the American Medical Records Association. In H. Schuchman, L. Foster, and S. Nye. (1982). *Confidentiality of Health Records.* New York: Gardner Press.

American Orthopsychiatric Association (1975). Position statement on confidentiality of health records. In H. Schuchman, L. Foster, and S. Nye (1982). *Confidentiality of Health Records.* New York: Gardner Press.

American Psychiatric Association (1979). The principle of medical ethics with annotations especially applicable to psychiatry. *American Journal of Psychiatry* **136**:137-147.

American Psychological Association (1981). *Ethical Principles of Psychologists.* Washington, D.C.: Author.

Anderson, W., and Sherr, S. (1969). Confidentiality expectations of college students: Revisited. *Journal of College Student Personnel* **6:**264-269.

Anonymous (1972)*Confessions of a Gynecologist.* Garden City, N.Y.: Doubleday.

Applebaum, P. (1985). Tarasoff and the clinician: Problems in fulfilling the duty to protect. *American Journal of Psychiatry* **142:**425-429.

Appelbaum, P. S.; Kapen, G.; Walters, B.; Lidz, C.; and Roth, L. H. (1984). Confidentiality: An empirical test of the utilitarian perspective. *Bulletin of the American Academy of Psychiatry and Law* **12:**109-116.

Beigler, J. (1978). Psychiatry and confidentiality. *American Journal of Forensic Psychiatry* **1:**7-19.

Beigler, J. (1981). Psychiatric confidentiality and the American legal system: An ethical conflict. In S. Bloch and P. Chodoff (eds.), *Psychiatric Ethics.* New York: Oxford University Press.

Bent, R. J. (1982). Multidimensional model for control of private information. *Professional Psychology* **13:**27-33.

Best, B. (1972). Privilege, in judicial or quasi-judicial proceedings, arising from relationship between psychiatrist or psychologist and patient. *American Law Reports 3d* **44:**24-162.

Black, C. (1975). The marital and physical privileges: A reprint of a letter to a congressman. *Duke Law Journal* **1975:** 45-51.

Bobbie, E. R. (1973). *Survey Research Methods.* Belmont, Calif: Wadsworth.

Bourne, P. G. (1982). Ethical problems of therapists in government and industry. In M. Rosenbaum (ed.), *Ethics and Values in Psychotherapy.* New York: Free Press.

Braman, R. J. (1967). Group therapy and privileged communications. *Indiana Law Review* **43:**93-105.

Brooks, M. G. (1980). Evidence. *North Carolina Law Review* **58:**1456-1470.

Butler, J. (1971). Psychotherapy and *Griswold:* Is confidence a privilege or right. *Connecticut Law Review* **3:**599-606.

Byrnes, T. (1976). Medical privilege in Oregon. *Oregon Law Review* **55:**459-473.

Carraway, N., and Currie, E. (1977). Privileges. *Mississippi Law Journal* **48:**989-1057.

Chafee, Z. (1943). Privileged communications: Is justice served or obstructed by closing the doctor's mouth on the witness stand? *Yale Law Journal* **52:**607-612.

Christensen, E. (1977). Constitutional law—right of privacy—evidence law of privileges—the patient-litigant exception to the psychotherapist-patient privilege. *Loyola of Los Angeles Law Review* **10:**695-708.

Clausen, R. E., and Daniels, A. K. (1966). Role conflicts and their ideological resolution in military psychiatric practice. *American Journal of Psychiatry* **123:**280-287.

Cleary, E. (ed.) (1984). *McCormick's Handbook on the Law of Evidence.* 3d ed. St. Paul: West.

Comment. (1952). Confidential communciations to a psychotherapist: A new testimonial privilege. *Northwestern University Law Review* **47:**384-389.

Comment. (1962). Functional overlap between the lawyer and other professionals: Its implications for the privileged communications doctrine. *Yale Law Journal* **71:**1226-1273.

Comprehensive Alcohol Abuse and Alcoholism, Prevention, Treatment, and Rehabilitation Act of 1970. (1982). *United States Code Annotated* **42:**5101.

Confidentiality of Alcohol and Drug Abuse Patient Records and Child Abuse and Neglect Reporting (Fall 1979). *Alcohol Health and Research Works* **9:**31-34.

Corcoran, J.; Breeskin, J.; and Court, H. L. (1977). Absence of privileged communications and its impact on air force officers. *Air Force Law Review* **17:**51-62.

Cosden, E. (1971). The physician-patient privilege in Oklahoma. *Tulsa Law Journal* **7:**157-180.

Cottle, M. (1956). Witnesses—privilege-communications to psychotherapists. *University of Kansas Law Review* **4:**597-599.

Cross, W. (1970). Privileged communications between participants in group therapy. *Law and Social Order,* 191-211.

Crowe, M. B.; Grogan, J.; Jacobs, R.; Lindsay, C.; and Mark, M. (1985). Delineation of the roles of clinical psychology: A survey of practice in Pennsylvania. *Professional Psychology: Research and Practice* **16:**124-137.

Curd, T. (1938). Privileged communications between the doctor and his patient—an anomaly of the law. *West Virginia Law Review* **44:**165-174.

Curran, W. J. (1969). Policies and practice concerning confidentiality in college mental health services in the United States and Canada. *American Journal of Psychiatry* **125:**1520-1530.

Davis, D. (1971). Evidence—privileged communications—A psychiatrist has no constitutional right to assert an absolute privilege against disclosure of psychotherapeutic communications. *Texas Law Review* **49:**929-942.

Davis, K. (1980). Is confidentiality in group counseling realistic? *Personnel and Guidance Journal* **59:**197-201.

Day, L. (1983). In search of a scholar's privilege. *Communications and the Law* **5:**3-21.

DeKraai, M., and Sales, B. D. (1982). Privileged communications of psychologists. *Professional Psychology* **13:**372-388.

DeKraai, M., and Sales, B. D. (1984). Confidential communications of psychotherapists. *Psychotherapy: Theory, Research and Practice* **21:**293-318.

Dickens, B. (1978). Legal protection of psychiatric confidentiality. *International Journal of Law and Psychiatry* **1:**255-279.

Dillman, D. A. (1978). *Mail and Telephone Surveys: The Total Design Method.* New York: Wiley Interscience.

Dunn, L., and Holbrook, R. (1981). Legal issues concerning peer review documents. *Topics in Health Records Management* **2**(1):9-16.

Education Commission of the States. (1979). *Trends in Child Protection Laws: 1979.* Denver: Author.

Eger, C. L. (1976). Psychotherapists' liability for extrajudicial breaches of confidentiality. *Arizona Law Review* **18:**1061-1094.

Everstine, L.; Everstine, D. S.; Heymann, G. M.; True, R. H.; Frey, D. H.; Johnson, H. G.; and Seiden, R. H. (1980). Privacy and confidentiality in psychotherapy. *American Psychologist* **35:**828-840.

Fisher, R. M. (1964). The psychotherapeutic professions and the law of privileged communications. *Wayne Law Review* **10:**609-654.

Fleming, J. G., and Maximov, B. (1974). The patient or his victim: The therapist's dilemma. *California Law Review* **62:**1025-1068.

Foster, H. H. (1976). An overview of confidentiality and privilege. *Journal of Psychiatry and Law* **4:**393-401.

Foster, H. H. (1978). The devil's advocate. *Bulletin of the American Academy of Psychiatry and the Law* **6:**475-479.

Fulero, S. M. (1984). Waiver to release information is irrevocable, court says. *Ohio Psychologist,* 5.

Geis, G.; Jesilow, P.; Pontell, H.; and O'Brien, M. (1985). Fraud and abuse of government medical benefit programs by psychiatrists. *American Journal of Psychiatry* **142:**231-234.

Geiser, R. L., and Rheingold, P. D. (1964). Psychology and the legal process: Testimonial privileged communications. *American Psychologist* **19:**831-837.

Green, B. (1980). The psychotherapist-patient privilege in Texas. *Houston Law Review* **18:**136-172.

Grossman, M. (1971). Insurance reports as a threat to confidentiality. *Journal of Psychiatry* **128:**64-68.

Guernsey, T. (1981). The psychotherapist-patient privilege in child placement: A relevancy analysis. *Villanova Law Review* **26:**955-996.

Guidry, G. G. (1984). The Louisiana Supreme Court and the physician-patient privilege: *Arsenaux v. Arsenaux. Louisiana Law Review* **44:**1813-1822.

Gumper, L. L. (1984). *Legal Issues in the Practice of Ministry.* Minneapolis, Ministers Life Resources.

Guttmacher, M., and Weihofen, H. (1952). Privileged communications between psychiatrist and patient. *Indiana Law Journal* **28:**32-44.

Hague, W. (1983). The psychotherapist-patient privilege in Washington: Extending the privilege to community mental health clinics. *Washington Law Review* **58:**565-586.

Halleck, S. L. (1971). *The Politics of Therapy.* New York: Science House.

Hare-Mustin, R. T. (1980). Family therapy may be dangerous for your health. *Professional Psychology* **11:**935-938.

Harms, L. M. (June 1981). Confidentiality of drug and alcohol abuse patient records: Part two. *Topics in Health Records Management* **1**(4):85-90.

Harris, M. (1973). Tort liability of the psychotherapists. *University of San Francisco Law Review* **8:**405-436.

Heffernan, P. (1980). The scope of the psychologist-patient testimonial privilege in Utah. *Utah Law Review* **1980:**385-393.

Heller, M. (1957). Some comments to lawyers on the practice of psychiatry. *Temple Law Quarterly* **30:**401-407.

Herst, R. (1979). The psychiatrist-patient privilege in Illinois. *Loyola University Law Journal* **10:**525-550.

Human, D. (January 1983). Release of medical records of alcohol and drug abuse patients: the regulatory maze. *Journal of the American Records Association* **54**(1):21-27.

Jagim, R.; Wittman, W.; and Noll, J. (1978). Mental health professionals' attitudes towards confidentiality, privilege, and third-party disclosure. *Professional Psychology* **9:**458-466.

Kazdin, A. (1978). Evaluating the generality of findings in analogue therapy research. *Journal of Consulting and Clinical Psychology* **46:**673-686.

Kennedy, C. (1973). The psychotherapists' privilege. *Washburn Law Review* **12:**297-315.

Kennedy, W., and Jacobs, E. (1981). Literature review of legal aspects of medical records. *Topics in Health Records Management* **1:**19-32.

Knapp, S. (1980). A primer on malpractice for psychologists. *Professional Psychology* **11:**606-611.

Knapp, S., and VandeCreek, L. (1981). Malpractice as a regulator of psychotherapy. *Psychotherapy: Theory, Research and Practice* **18:**354-358.

Knapp, S., and VandeCreek, L. (1982). Tarasoff: Five years later. *Professional Psychology* **13:**511-516.

Knapp, S., and VandeCreek, L. (1983). Malpractice risks with suicidal patients. *Psychotherapy: Theory, Research, and Practice* **20:**274-280.

Knapp, S., and VandeCreek, L. (1985). Privileged communications for pastoral counseling: Fact or fancy? *Journal of Pastoral Care* **39:**293-300.

Knapp, S.; VandeCreek, L.; and Herzog, C. (In press). The Duty to Protect: Legal Principles and Therapeutic Guidelines.

Knerr, C., and Carroll, J. (1978). Confidentiality and criminological research: The evolving body of law. *Journal of Criminal Law and Criminology* **69:**311-321.

Kobocow, B.; McGuire, J.; and Blau, B. (1983). The influence of confidentiality conditions on self-disclosure of the early adolescent. *Professional Psychology: Research and Practice* **14:**435-443.

Krattenmacher, T. (1973). Testimonial privileges in federal courts: An alternative to the proposed federal rules of evidence. *Georgetown Law Review* **62:**61-123.

Lamb, L. (1983). To tell or not to tell: Physician's liability for disclosure of confidential information about a patient. *Cumberland Law Review* **13:**617-637.

Lassen, C. L. (1982). The Colorado medicare study: Perspective of the peer review committee. *Professional Psychology* **13:**105-111.

Lewis, E. C., and Warman, R. E. (1964). Confidentiality expectations of college students. *Journal of College Student Personnel* **1:**7-11, 20.

Liability of Physician for Breach of Confidential Relationship. (1980). *Negligence Compensation Cases Annotated 4th Series.* Willmette, Ill: Callaghen & Company.

Lindenthal, J. J., and Thomas, C. S. (1980). A comparative study of the handling of confidentiality. *Journal of Nervous and Mental Disease* **158:**361-369.

Lindenthal, J. J., and Thomas, C. S. (1982). Psychiatrists, the public and confidentiality. *Journal of Nervous and Mental Disease* **170:**319-323.

Lindenthal, J. J.; Amaranto, E.; Jordan, T.; and Wepman, B. (1984). Decisions about confidentiality in medical student health settings. *Journal of Counseling Psychology* **31:**573-576.

Lockhart, D. C. (ed.). (1984). *Making Effective Use of Mailed Questionaires.* San Francisco: Jossey-Bass.

Louisell, D. (1956). Confidentiality, conformity and confusion: Privileges in federal court today. *Tulane Law Review* **21:**101-124.

Louisell, D. (1957). The psychologist in today's legal world: Part II. *Minnesota Law Review* **41:**731-750.

Louisell, D., and Sinclair, K. (1971). Foreword: Some reflections on the law of privileged communications—The psychotherapist-patient privilege in perspective. *California Law Review* **59:**30-55.

McGuire, J. (1974). Confidentiality and the child in psychotherapy. *Professional Psychology* **5:**374-379.

McGuire, J.; Toal, P.; and Blau, B. (1985). The adult client's conception of confidentiality in the therapeutic relationship. *Professional Psychology: Research and Practice* **16:**375-384.

Maly, B. (1977). The limits of constitutional privacy in the psychotherapist-patient evidentiary privilege. *Golden Gate University Law Review* **8:**55-67.

Margolin, G. (1982). Ethical and legal considerations in marital and family therapy. *American Psychologist* **37:**788-801.

Meisel, A. (1982). The rights of the mentally ill under state constitutions. *Law and Contemporary Problems* **45:**7-40.

Meister, K. (1975). Miranda on the couch: An approach to problems of self-incrimination, right to counsel, and Miranda warnings in pre-trial psychiatric examinations of criminal defendants. *Columbia Journal of Law and Social Problems* **11:**403-465.

Melton, G. (1981). Effects of state law permitting minor to consent to psychotherapy. *Professional Psychology* **12:**647-654.

Menninger, W. W., and English, J. T. (1965). Confidentiality and the request for psychiatric information for nontherapeutic purposes. *American Journal of Psychiatry* **122:**638-645.

Merluzzi, T. V., and Brischetto, C. S. (1983). Breach of confidentiality and perceived trustworthiness of counselors. *Journal of Counseling Psychology* **30:**245-251.

Messersmith, L. (1984). Evidence: The psychotherapist-patient privilege under Federal Rule of Evidence 501. *Washburn Law Journal* **23:**706-718.

Meyer, R., and Smith, S. (1977). A crisis in group therapy. *American Psychologist* **32:**638-643.

Meyer, R., and Willage, D. (1980). Confidentiality and privileged communication in psychotherapy. In P. Lipsitt and B. Sales (eds.), *New Directions in Psycholegal Research.* New York: Van Nostrand Reinhold.

Miller, D., and Thelen, M. (1986). Knowledge and beliefs about confidentiality in psychotherapy. *Professional Psychology: Theory, Research, and Practice* **17:**15-19.

Morgan, E. (1943). Suggested remedy for obstructions to expert testimony by rules of evidence. *University of Chicago Law Review* **10:**285-298.

Morgan, M. (1978). Must the group get up and testify? An examination of group therapy privilege. *Group* **2:**67-87.

Muehleman, T., and Kimmons, C. (1981). Psychologists' views on child abuse reporting, confidentiality, life, and the law: An exploratory study. *Professional Psychology* **12:**631-638.

Nejelski, P., and Lerman, L. (1971). A researcher-subject testimonial privilege: What to do before the subpoena arrives. *Wisconsin Law Review,* 1085-1148.

New, B. E. (1982). The Fifth Amendment and compelled and psychiatric examinations: Implications of *Estelle v. Smith. The George Washington Law Review* **50:**275-305.

Newman, S. (1981). Privacy in personal medical information: A diagnosis. *University of Florida Law Review* **33:**394-424.

Noll, J. O. (1974). Needed—A bill of rights for clients. *Professional Psychology* **5:**3-12.

Noll, J. O. (1976). The psychotherapist and informed consent. *American Journal of Psychiatry* **133:**1451-1453.

Noll, J. O., and Hanlon, M. J. (1976). Patient privacy and confidentiality at mental health centers. *American Journal of Psychiatry* **133:**1286-1289.

Note (1972). Medical jurisprudence—privileged communications between physician and patient—state regulation and right to privacy. *Tennessee Law Review* **39:**515-525.

Note (1976*a*). Constitutional law: *Davis v. Alaska* applied to hold that physician-patient privilege must give way to accused's right to confrontation. *Minnesota Law Review* **60:**1086-1096.

Note (1976*b*). Protecting the confidentiality of pretrial psychiatric disclosures: A survey of standards. *New York University Law Review* **51:**409-445.

Note (1983). The Arkansas physician-patient privilege re-examined. *Arkansas Law Review* **36:**658-677.

Olson, R. (1973). A look at Indiana Code 34-1-14-5: Indiana's physician-patient privilege. *Valparaiso Law Review* **8:**37-59.

Pontell, H.; Jesilow, P.; and Geis, G. (1982). Policing physicians: Practitioner fraud and abuse in a government medical program. *Social Problems* **30:**117-125.

Privacy Protection Study Commission (1977). *Personal Privacy in an Information Society.* Washington, D.C.: U.S. Govt. Printing Office.

Prosser, W. (1971). *The Law of Torts.* St. Paul: West.

Psychotherapists/Medical Records. (1979). *Medical Liability Reporter* **1:**25.

Purrington, W. (1906). An abused privilege. *Columbia Law Review* **6:**388-422.

Rappeport, J. (1982). Differences between forensic and general psychiatry. *American Journal of Psychiatry* **139:**331-334.

Roach, W. (1981). Discoverability and admissibility of medical staff committee records: A state-by-state analysis. *Topics in Health Records Management* **2**(1):17-28.

Roach, W. (1984). Proposed Uniform Health Care Act and more on discoverability of peer review committee records. *Topics in Health Records Management* **5**(4):83-85.

Roach, W., and Chernoff, S. (1984). Discoverability of peer review committee records: An update. *Topics in Health Records Management* **5**(3):99-104.

Roach, W., and Cosgrove, M. (1981). Substance abuse record confidentiality and child abuse reporting requirements. *Topics in Health Records Management* **1**(3):75-81.

Roach, W., and Harms, L. (1981). Confidentiality of drug and alcohol abuse patient records: Part one. *Topics in Health Records Management* **1**(3):75-81.

Roach, W., and Kunde, K. (1983). Release of and access to minor's medical records. *Topics in Health Records Management* **4**(3):73-78.

Rosen, C. E. (1977). Why clients relinquish their rights to privacy under sign-away pressures. *Professional Psychology* **8:**17-24.

Roth, L. H., and Meisel, A. (1977). Dangerousness, confidentiality and the duty to warn. *American Journal of Psychiatry* **134:**508-511.

Roth, L. H.; Wolford, J.; and Meisel, A. (1980). Patient access to records: Tonic or toxin? *American Journal of Psychiatry* **137:**592-596.

Rothstein, P. (1981). *Evidence: State and Federal Rules.* St. Paul, Minn.: West.

Saltzburg, S. (1980). Privileges and professionals: Lawyers and psychiatrists. *Virginia Law Review* **66:**597-652.

Saltzburg, S., and Redden, K. (1982). *Federal rules of evidence manual.* 3d ed. Charlottesville, Va.: Michie Company.

Sarno, G. (1983). Necessity and sufficiency of statements informing one under investigation for involuntary commitment of right to remain silent. *American Law Reports 4th* **23:**563-582.

Schiffers, I. (1968). Physician's tort liability apart from defamation for unauthorized disclosure of confidential information about patients. *American Law Reports 3d,* **20:**1109-1123.

Schmid, D.; Appelbaum, P. S.; Roth, L. H.; and Lidz, C. (1983). Confidentiality in psychiatry: A study of the patient's view. *Hospital and Community Psychiatry* **34:**353-355.

Schreiber, R. R. (1973). *Sybil.* Chicago: Regnery.

Sechrest, L., and Hoffman, P. E. (1982). The philosophical underpinnings of peer review. *Professional Psychology* **13:**14-18.

Shaevitz, M. H. (1971). Letter to the editor. *APA Monitor* **2**(8):14.

Shah, S. (1969). Privileged communications, confidentiality and privacy: Privileged communications. *Professional Psychology* **1:**56-69.

Sharfstein, S. S.; Towery, O. B.; and Milowe, I. D. (1980). Accuracy of diagnostic information submitted to an insurance company. *American Journal of Psychiatry* **137:**70-73.

Shuman, D. (1979). The road to Bedlam: Evidentiary guideposts in civil commitment proceedings. *Notre Dame Law Review* **55:**53-111.

Shuman, D., and Weiner, M. (1982). The privilege study: An empirical examination of the psychotherapist-patient privilege. *North Carolina Law Review* **60:**893-942.

Shutz, B. M. (1982). *Legal Liability in Psychotherapy.* San Francisco: Jossey-Bass.

Siegel, M. (1979). Privacy, ethics, and confidentiality. *Professional Psychology* **10:**249-258.

Simmons, D. D. (1968). Client attitudes toward release of confidential information without consent. *Journal of Clinical Psychology* **24:**364-365.

Slawson, P., and Guggenheim, P. (1984). Psychiatric malpractice: A review of the national loss experience. *American Journal of Psychiatry* **141:**979-981.

Slovenko, R. (1960). Psychiatry and a second look at the medical privilege. *Wayne Law Review* **6:**174-203.

Slovenko, R. (1974). Psychotherapist-patient testimonial privilege: A picture of misguided hope. *Catholic University Law Review* **23:**649-673.

Slovenko, R. (1975). Psychotherapy and confidentiality. *Cleveland State Law Review* **24:**375-396.

Slovenko, R. (1977). Group psychotherapy: Privileged communication and confidentiality. *Journal of Psychiatry and the Law* **5:**405-466.

Slovenko, R. (1979). On the need for recordkeeping in the practice of psychiatry. *Journal of Psychiatry and the Law* **7:**399-440.

Slovenko, R. (1983). The hazards of writing or disclosing information in psychiatry. *Behavioral Sciences and the Law* **1:**109-127.

Slovenko, R., and Usdin, G. (1961). The psychiatrist and privileged communication. *Archives of General Psychiatry* **4:**431-444.

Smith, S. (1980). Constitutional privacy in psychotherapy. *George Washington Law Review* **40:**1-60.

Stein, E. J.; Furedy, R. L.; Simonton, M. J.; and Neuffer, C. H. (1979). Patient access to medical records on a psychiatric in-patient unit. *American Journal of Psychiatry* **136:**327-329.

Stouder, B. (1982). Pennsylvania establishes new privilege for communications made to a rape center counselor. *Temple Law Quarterly* **55:**1124-1148.

Stroube, M. K. (1979). The psychotherapist-patient privilege: Are some patients more privileged than others? *Pacific Law Journal* **10:**801-824.

Swoboda, J. S.; Elwork, A.; Sales, B. D.; and Levine, D. (1978). Knowledge of and compliance with privileged communication and child-abuse-reporting laws. *Professional Psychology* **9:**457.

Szasz, T. S. (1965). *The Ethics of Psychoanalysis.* New York: Basic Books.

Tillinghast, M., and VandeCreek, L. (1985). Expectations and preferences for confidentiality of client-counselor communications. Paper presented at the Eastern Psychological Association, Baltimore.

VandeCreek, L., and Knapp, S. (1984). Counselors, confidentiality, and life-endangering clients. *Counselor Education and Supervision* **24:**51-57.

Virginia Court ruling stirs concern about confidentiality protections in group therapy (1979). *Hospital and Community Psychiatry* **30:**428.

Warren, S., and Brandeis, L. (1890). The right to privacy. *Harvard Law Review* **4:**193-220.

Weihofen, H. (1972). Confidentiality. In A. Beigel and A. Levenson (eds.). *The Community Mental Health Center: Strategies and Programs.* New York: Basic Books.

Weil, M., and Sanchez, E. (1983). The impact of the Tarasoff decision on clinical social work practice. *Social Service Review* **57:**112-124.

Weinapple, M., and Perr, I. (1979). The rights of minors to confidentiality: An aftermath of *Bartley v. Kremens. Bulletin of the American Academy of Psychiatry and the Law* **9:**247-254.

Weiner, M., and Shuman, D. (1984). Privilege—A comparative study. *Journal of Psychiatry and the Law* **12:**373-384.

Weinstock, M., and Hoft, J. I. (1974). The effect of illness on employment opportunities. *Archives of Environmental Health* **29:**79-83.

Wiesberg, R., and Wald, M. (1984). Confidentiality laws and state efforts to protect abused or neglected children: The need for statutory reform. *Family Law Quarterly* **18:**143-212.

Westin, A. F. (1976). *Computers, Health Records, and Citizen Rights.* NBS Monograph No. 157. Washington, D.C.: U.S. Dept. of Commerce, National Bureau of Standards.

Wexler, D. (1980). Victimology and mental health law: An agenda. *Virginia Law Review* **66:**681-711.

Whiteside, A. (1975). A reporter at large: Anything adverse? *New Yorker* **51:**45-50.

Wigmore, J. H. (1961). *Evidence in Trials at Common Law.* Vol. 8. McNaughton Rev., Boston: Little, Brown.

Williams, R. (1979). Confidential communication privileges under federal and Virginia law. *University of Richmond Law Review* **13:**593-612.

Williamson, K. (1984). Confidentiality of sexual assault victim-counselor communication: A proposed model statute. *Arizona Law Review* **26:**461-488.

Wise, T. (1978). Where the public peril begins: A survey of psychotherapists to determine the effects of Tarasoff. *Stanford Law Review* **31:**165-190.

Woods, K., and McNamara, R. (1980). Confidentiality: Its effect on interviewee behavior. *Professional Psychology* **11:**714-721.

Woods, R. (1978). Evidence: Justification for extension of the psychotherapist privilege. *Washburn Law Review* **17:**672-679.

Wright, R. (1981). Psychologists and professional liability (malpractice) insurance. *American Psychologist* **36:**1485-1493.

Wynstra, N. (1980). Legal review: The dilemma of access versus confidentiality. *Topics in Health Records Management* **1:**89-95.

Young, H. H. (1982). A brief history of quality assurance and peer review. *Professional Psychology* **13:**9-13.

Case Citations

Citations are presented in alphabetical order. The citation numbers are used to identify cases in the Case Citations by State list that follows this chapter.

1. *Adams v. Peck,* 403 A.2d 840 (Md. App. 1979).
2. *Alexander v. Knight,* 197 Pa. Super. 79, 177 A.2d 142 (1962).
3. *Allred v. State,* 554 P.2d 411 (Alaska, 1976).
4. *Amburgery v. Central Kentucky Regional Mental Health Board,* 663 S.W.2d. 952 (Ky. App. 1984).
5. *Anker v. Brodnitz,* 98 Misc.2d 148, 413 N.Y.S.2d 582 (1979).
6. *Application of Do Vidio,* 56 Misc. 2d 79, 288 N.Y.S.2d 21 (Fam. Ct. 1968).
7. *Argonaut Insurance Company v. Peralta,* 358 So.2d 232 (Fla. App. 1978).
8. *Ascherman v. Superior Court,* 62 Cal. Rptr. 547 (Ct. App. 1967).
9. *Atwood v. Atwood,* 550 S.W.2d 465 (Ky. 1976).
10. *Baker v. State,* 637 S.W.2d 522 (Ark. 1982).
11. *Bassil v. Ford Motor Company,* 278 Mich. 173, 270 N.W. 258 (1936).
12. *Battie v. Estelle,* 655 F.2d 692 (5th Cir. 1981).
13. *Bellah v. Greenson,* 81 Cal. App.3d 614, 146 Cal. Rptr. 535 (App. 1978).
14. *Belmont v. State Personnel Board,* 36 Cal. App.3d 518, 111 Cal. Rptr. 607 (App. 1974).
15. *Benoit v. Randall,* 431 S.W.2d 107 (Mo. 1968).
16. *Berst v. Chipman,* 232 Kan. 180, 653 P.2d 107 (1982).
17. *Bieluch v. Bieluch,* 190 Conn. 813, 462 A.2d 1060 (1983).
18. *Binder v. Ruvell,* Civil Docket 52C2535, Circuit Court of Cook County, Illinois,

June 24, 1952; reported in JAMA 150:1241, 1952, and discussed in 47 Nw.U.L. Rev. 384 (1952).

19. *Blue Cross of Northern California v. Superior Court of Yolo County,* 61 Cal. App.3d 798, 132 Cal. Rptr. 635 (1976).
20. *Board of Medical Quality Assurance v. Gheradini,* 93 Cal. App.3d 669, 156 Cal. Rptr. 55 (App. 1979).
21. *Board of Medical Quality Assurance v. Hazel Hawkins Memorial Hospital,* 135 Cal. App.3d 561, 185 Cal. Rptr. 405 (App. 1982).
22. *Board of Medical Review Investigation,* 463 A.2d 1373 (R.I. 1983).
23. *Boggess v. Aetna Life Insurance Company,* 128 Ga. App. 190, 196 S.E.2d 172 (App. 1973).
24. *Boling v. Superior Court,* 105 Cal. App.3d 430, 164 Cal. Rptr. 432 (App. 1980).
25. *Bond v. District Court in and for Denver City,* 682 P.2d 33 (Colo. 1984).
26. *Bond v. Pecaut,* 561 F. Supp. 1037 (N.D., Ill. 1983).
27. *Booker v. Wainwright,* 703 F.2d 1251 (11th Cir. 1983).
28. *Bredice v. Doctors Hospital, Inc.,* 50 F.R.D. 249 (D.D.C. 1970).
29. *Bremer v. State,* 18 Md. App. 291, 307 A.2d 503, cert. den., 415 U.S. 930 (1974).
30. *Britt v. Superior Court of San Diego County,* 20 Cal.3d 844, 143 Cal. Rptr. 695, 574 P.2d 766 (1978).
31. *Brown v. State,* 612 S.W.2d 83 (Tex. Civ. App. 1981).
32. *Buchanan v. American Motors Corp.,* 697 F.2d 151 (6th Cir. 1983).
33. *Caesar v. Mountanos,* 542 F.2d 1064 (9th Cir. 1976).
34. *Campbell v. State,* 105 Misc.2d 204, 431 N.Y.S.2d 977 (Ct. Cl. 1980).
35. *Camperlengo v. Blum,* 436 N.E.2d 1299 (N.Y. 1982).
36. *Carr v. Schmid,* 105 Misc.2d 645, 432 N.Y.S.2d 807 (1980).
37. *Carson v. Jackson,* 466 So.2d 1188 (Fla. App. 4th Dist. 1984).
38. *Chidester v. Needles,* 353 N.W.2d 849 (Iowa, 1984).
39. *Civil Service Employees Association v. Director,* Manhattan Psychiatric Center, 72 A.D. 2d 256, 420 N.Y.S.2d 909 (1979).
40. *Civil Service Employees Association v. Soper,* 84 A.D.2d 927, 447 N.Y.S.2d 62 (1981).
41. *Clark v. Geraci,* 208 N.Y.S.2d 564 (1960).
42. *Clark v. Grigson,* 579 S.W.2d 263 (Tex. 1979).
43. *Clark v. Indiana,* 436 N.E.2d 779 (Ind. 1982).
44. *Clausen v. Clausen,* 675 P.2d 562 (Utah, 1983).
45. *Commissioner of Social Service v. David S.,* 55 N.Y.2d 588, 436 N.E.2d 451 (1982).
46. *Commonwealth ex rel. Platt v. Platt,* 404 A.2d 410 (Pa. Super. 1979).
47. *Commonwealth v. Clemons,* 427 N.E.2d 761 (Mass. App. 1981).
48. *Commonwealth v. Collett,* 387 Mass. 424, 439 N.E.2d 1223 (1982).
49. *Commonwealth v. Kobrin,* 395 Mass. 284, 479 N.E.2d 674 (1985).
50. *Commonwealth v. LeCain,* 477 N.E.2d 207 (Mass. App. 1985).
51. *Commonwealth v. Marshall,* 364 N.E.2d 1237 (Mass. 1977).
52. *Community Hospital Ass'n. v. District Court in and for the County of Boulder,* 570 P.2d 243 (Colo. 1977).
53. *Community Service Society v. Welfare Inspector General,* 91 Misc.2d 383, 398 N.Y.S.2d 92 (Sup. 1977), aff'd 411 N.Y.S.2d 188 (1978).

54. *Corcoran v. S. S. Kresge Co.*, 47 N.E.2d 257 (Mass. 1943).
55. *County of Riverside v. Superior Court,* 116 Cal. Rptr. 886 (App. 1974).
56. *Cranford v. Cranford,* 120 Ga. App. 470, 170 S.E.2d 844 (1969).
57. *Critchlow v. Critchlow,* 347 So.2d 453 (Fla. App. 1977).
58. *Cronin v. Strayer,* 392 Mass. 525, 467 N.E.2d 143 (1984).
59. *Curry v. Corn,* 52 Misc.2d 1035, 277 N.Y.S.2d 470 (Sup. Ct. 1966).
60. *Cynthia B. v. New Rochelle Hospital,* 86 A.D.2d 256, 449 N.Y.S.2d 755 (App. Div. 1982).
61. *Davis v. Alaska,* 415 U.S. 308 (1974).
62. *Denaro v. Prudential Insurance Co.*, 154 App. Div. 840, 139 N.Y.S. 758 (1913).
63. *Dennis v. United States,* 384 U.S. 855 (1966).
64. *Doe v. Bolton,* 410 U.S. 179 (1973).
65. *Doe v. Hynes,* 104 Misc.2d 398, 428 N.Y.S.2d 810 (Sup. Ct. 1980).
66. *Doe v. Roe,* 93 Misc.2d 201, 400 N.Y.S.2d 668 (Sup. Ct. 1977).
67. *Doyle v. Shlensky,* 76 Ill. Dec. 466, 120 Ill. App.3d 807, 458 N.E.2d 1120 (App. 1st Dist. 1983).
68. *Duchess of Kingston's Case,* 20 State Trials 355 (1776).
69. *Eisenstadt v. Baird,* 405 U.S. 438 (1972).
70. *Elliot v. Watkins Trucking Company,* 406 F.2d 90 (7th Cir. 1969).
71. *Ellis v. Ellis,* 472 S.W.2d 741 (Tenn. App. 1971).
72. *Estelle v. Smith,* 451 U.S. 451 (1981).
73. *Ex Parte Day,* 378 So.2d 1159 (Ala. 1979).
74. *Fahlfeder v. Commonwealth of Pennsylvania Board of Probation,* 470 A.2d 1130 (Pa. Comwlth. Ct. 1984).
75. *Falcon v. Alaska Public Offices Com'n,* 570 P.2d 469 (Alaska, 1977).
76. *Felber v. Foote,* 321 F. Supp. 85 (D. Conn. 1970).
77. *Finney v. State,* 3 Ark. App. 180, 623 S.W.2d 847 (App. 1981).
78. *Fitzgibbon v. Fitzgibbon,* 197 N.J. Super. 63, 484 A.2d 46 (Super. Ch. 1984).
79. *Freeman v. State,* 258 Ark. 617, 527 S.W.2d 909 (1975).
80. *Gabor v. Hyland,* 166 N.J. Super. 275, 399 A.2d 993 (Super. 1979).
81. *Gibson v. Commonwealth,* 216 Va. 412, 219 S.E.2d 845 (1975). Cert. den., 425 U.S. 994 (1976).
82. *Gibson v. Zahradnick,* 581 F.2d 75 (4th Cir. 1978).
83. *Gillespie v. Gillespie,* 631 S.W.2d 592 (Tex. Civ. App. 1982).
84. *Gillman v. United States,* 53 F.R.D. 316 (S.D.N.Y. 1971).
85. *Grand Jury Investigation of Onondaga County,* 59 N.Y.S.2d 130, 450 N.E.2d 678 (1983).
86. *Granviel v. Estelle,* 655 F.2d 673 (5th Cir. 1981).
87. *Greene v. Greene,* 15 N.C. App. 314, 190 S.E.2d 258 (1972).
88. *Greene v. New England Mutual Life Insurance Company,* 108 Misc.2d 540, 437 N.Y.S.2d 844 (Sup. Ct. 1981).
89. *Grey v. Los Angeles Superior Court,* 62 Cal. App.3d 698, 133 Cal. Rptr. 318 (App. 1976).
90. *Griswold v. Connecticut,* 381 U.S. 479 (1965).
91. *Groff v. State,* 390 So.2d 361 (Fla. App. 1980).
92. *Grosslight v. Superior Court,* 72 Cal. App.3d 502, 140 Cal. Rptr. 278 (App. 1977).

93. *Hahman v. Hahman,* 129 Ariz. 101, 628 P.2d 984 (App. 1981).
94. *Hamilton v. Verdow,* 287 Md. 544, 414 A.2d 914 (1980).
95. *Hampton v. Hampton,* 405 P.2d 549 (Oreg. 1965).
96. *Harris v. New York,* 91 S.Ct. 643 (1971).
97. *Harris v. State,* 678 P.2d 397 (Alaska App. 1984).
98. *Hawaii Psychiatric Society v. Ariyoshi,* 481 F. Supp. 1028 (D. Hawaii 1979).
99. *Hayerstick V. Banet,* 370 N.E.2d 341 (Ind. 1978).
100. *Hedlund v. Superior Court of Orange County,* 34 Cal.3d 695, 669 P.2d 41 (1983).
101. *Hoffman v. United States,* 341 U.S. 479 (1951).
102. *Hopewell v. Adebimpe,* 130 *Pitt. L. J.* 107 (1982).
103. *Horne v. Patton,* 291 Ala. 701, 287 So.2d 824 (1974).
104. *Horne v. State,* 12 Ark. App. 301, 677 S.W.2d 856 (App. 1984).
105. *Houston v. State,* 602 P.2d 784 (Alaska, 1979).
106. *Huelter v. Superior Court for County of Santa Clara,* 87 Cal. App.3d 544, 151 Cal. Rptr. 138 (App. 1979).
107. *Husgen v. Stussie,* 617 S.W.2d 414 (Mo. App. 1981).
108. *Hyman v. Jewish Chronic Disease Hospital,* 15 N.Y.2d 317, 258 N.Y.S.2d 397 (1965).
109. *Ideal Publishing Corp. v. Creative Features,* 59 A.2d 862, 399 N.Y.S.2d 118 (1977).
110. *In interest of R.D.S.,* 259 N.W.2d 636 (N. Dak. 1977).
111. *In interest of Zappa,* 631 P.2d 1245 (Kan. App. 1981).
112. *In re "B,"* 482 Pa. 471, 394 A.2d 419 (1978).
113. *In re Beverly,* 342 So.2d 481 (Fla. 1977).
114. *In re Board of Medical Review Investigation,* 463 A.2d 1373 (R.I. 1983).
115. *In re Brenda H.,* 169 N.H. 382, 402 A.2d 169 (1979).
116. *In re Courtney S.,* 130 Cal. App.3d 567, 181 Cal. Rptr. 843 (App. 1982).
117. *In re Culbertson's Will,* 57 Misc.2d 391, 292 N.Y.S.2d 806 (Sup. Ct. 1968).
118. *In re Doe,* 711 F.2d 1187 (2d Cir. 1984).
119. *In re Fred J.,* 89 Cal. App.3d 168, 152 Cal. Rptr. 327 (App. 1979).
120. *In re Grand Jury Investigation,* 441 A.2d 525 (R.I. 1982).
121. *In re Grand Jury Subpoena,* 570 F. Supp. 1476 (S.D.N.Y. 1983).
122. *In re Kryschuk v. Zulynik,* 14 D.L.R.2d 676 (Sask. Magis. Ct. 1958).
123. *In re Lifschutz,* 2 Cal.3d 415, 85 Cal. Rptr. 829, 467 P.2d 557 (1970).
124. *In re Love Canal,* 112 Misc.2d 861, 449 N.Y.S.2d 134 (Sup. 1982).
125. *In re Pebsworth,* 705 F.2d 261 (7th Cir. 1983).
126. *In re Sippy,* 97 A.2d 455 (D.C. 1953).
127. *In re T.L.S.,* 481 N.E.2d 1037 (Vt. 1984).
128. *In re Terry W.,* 59 Cal. App. 7545, 130 Cal. Rptr. 913 (App. 1976).
129. *In re Welfare of Dodge,* 29 Wash. App. 486, 628 P.2d 1343 (App. 1981).
130. *In re Zuniga,* 714 F.2d 632 (6th Cir. 1983).
131. *In the matter of Humphrey,* 79 Misc.2d 192, 359 N.Y.S.2d 733 (1974).
132. *In the matter of L.J.M.,* 473 N.E.2d 637 (Ind. App. 4th Dist. 1985).
133. *In the matter of R,* 97 Wash.2d 183, 641 P.2d 704 (1982).
134. *In the matter of the Doe Children,* 402 N.Y.S.2d 958 (Fam. Ct. 1978).
135. *In the matter of Stephen F.,* 118 Misc.2d 655, 460 N.Y.S.2d 856 (Fam. Ct. 1982).
136. *Jablonski v. United States,* 712 F.2d 391 (9th Cir. 1983).

137. *James v. Brown,* 629 S.W.2d 781 (Tex. Civ. App. 1981).
138. *Jennings v. D.H.L. Airlines,* No. 83 C 5789 (N.D. Ill. May 21, 1984), 8 MDLR 467.
139. *Jones v. Department of Human Resources,* 310 S.E.2d 753 (Ga. App. 1983).
140. *Jones v. Prudential Insurance Company,* 388 A.2d 476 (D.C. 1978).
141. *Jones v. Superior Court for County of Alameda,* 119 Cal. App.3d 534, 174 Cal. Rptr. 148 (1981).
142. *Jordan v. Kelly,* 728 F.2d 1 (1st Cir. 1984).
143. *Kappas v. Chestnut Lodge,* 709 F.2d 878 (4th Cir. 1983).
144. *Khairzdah v. Khairzdah,* 464 So.2d 1311 (Fla. App. 4th Dist. 1984).
145. *King v. O'Connor,* 426 N.Y.S.2d 415 (1980).
146. *Klinge v. Lutheran Medical Center of St. Louis,* 518 S.W.2d 157 (Mo. 1974).
147. *Kristensen v. Kristensen,* 406 So.2d 1210 (Fla. 5th DCA 1981).
148. *Kruglikov v. Kruglikov,* 29 Misc.2d 17, 217 N.Y.S.2d 845, ap. dismd. 16 App. Div.2d 735, 226 N.Y.S.2d 931 (1961).
149. *Landeros v. Flood,* 17 Cal.3d 399, 551 P.2d 389, 131 Cal. Rptr. 69 (1976).
150. *Laurent v. Brelji,* 30 Ill. Dec. 164, 74 Ill. App.3d 214, 392 N.E.2d 929 (App. 4th Dist. 1979).
151. *Leach v. Millers Life Insurance Company of Texas,* 400 F.2d 179 (5th Cir. 1968).
152. *LeGore v. LeGore,* 31 Pa. D & C.2d 107, 5 Adams Co. Leg. J. 51 (1963).
153. *Lembke v. Unke,* 171 N.W.2d 837 (N.D. 1969).
154. *Lipari v. Sears, Roebuck & Company,* 497 F. Supp. 185 (D. Neb. 1980).
155. *Lipsey v. State,* 170 Ga. App. 770, 318 S.E.2d 184 (App. 1984).
156. *Lockwood v. McGaskill,* 261 N.C. 754, 136 S.E.2d 67 (1964).
157. *Logan v. District of Columbia,* 447 F. Supp. 1328 (D.D.C. 1978).
158. *Lora v. Board of Education,* 74 F.R.D. 565 (E.D.N.Y. 1977).
159. *Luhdorff v. Superior Court,* 212 Cal. Rptr. 516 (App. 5th Dist. 1985).
160. *Lukaszewicz v. Ortho Pharmaceutical Corporation,* 90 F.R.D. 709 (E.D. Wis. 1981).
161. *Lynch v. Mutual Life Insurance Company of New York,* 55 Misc.2d 179, 284 N.Y.S.2d 768 (1967).
162. *MacDonald v. Clinger,* 84 A.D.2d 482, 446 N.Y.S.2d 801 (App. Div. 1982).
163. *Mahoney v. Superior Court,* 191 Cal. Rptr. 425 (App. 1983).
164. *Matter of A.J.S.,* 630 P.2d 217 (Mont. 1981).
165. *Matter of Atkins,* 112 Mich. App. 528, 316 N.W.2d 477 (App. 1982).
166. *Matter of Baby X,* 293 N.W.2d 736 (Mich. App. 1980).
167. *Matter of Parental Rights of P.P.,* 648 P.2d 512 (Wyo. 1982).
168. *Matter of Pittsburgh Action Against Rape,* 428 A.2d 126 (Pa. 1981).
169. *Mavroudis v. Superior Court for County of San Mateo,* 162 Cal. Rptr. 724 (App. 1980).
170. *McIntosh v. Milano,* 403 A.2d 500 (N.J. Super. Ch. 1979).
171. *McKirdy v. Superior Court of San Francisco,* 188 Cal. Rptr. 14 (1982).
172. *Memorial Hospital for McHenry County v. Shadur,* 664 F.2d 1058 (7th Cir. 1981).
173. *Miller v. Colonial Refrigerated Transportation,* 81 F.R.D. 741 (M.D. Pa. 1979).
174. *Miraglia v. Miraglia,* 462 So.2d 507 (Fla. App. 4th Dist. 1984).
175. *Miranda v. Arizona,* 384 U.S. 436 (1966).
176. *Mohammad v. Mohammad,* 358 So.2d 610 (Fla. App. 1978).
177. *Morra v. State Board of Examiners of Psychologists,* 212 Kan. 103, 510 P.2d 614 (1973).

178. *Mullen v. United States,* 263 F.2d 275 (D.C. 1959).
179. *Mutual of Omaha Insurance Company v. American National Bank and Trust Company,* 610 F. Supp. 546 (D.C. Minn. 1985).
180. *M. v. K.,* 186 N.J. Super. 363, 452 A.2d 704 (Super. 1982).
181. *Myers v. State,* 251 Ga. 883, 310 S.E.2d 504 (1984).
182. *Nagle v. Hooks,* 295 Md. 133, 460 A.2d 49 (1983).
183. *National Health Laboratory v. Mora,* 105 Misc.2d 279, 432 N.Y.S.2d 52 (1980).
184. *New State Ice Co. v. Leibmann,* 285 U.S. 262 (1931).
185. *Noggle v. Marshall,* 706 F.2d 1406 (6th Cir. 1983).
186. *North Carolina v. Taylor,* 283 S.E.2d 761 (N.C. Sup. Ct. 1981).
187. *Office of Mental Retardation and Developmental Disabilities v. Mastracci,* 77 App. Div.2d 73, 433 N.Y.S.2d 946 (App. Div. 1980).
188. *Osterman v. Ehrenworth,* 106 N.J. Super. 515, 256 A.2d 123 (Super. 1969).
189. *Ott v. St. Luke Hospital of Campbell County,* 522 F. Supp. 706 (E.D. Ky. 1981).
190. *Panko v. Consolidated Mutual Insurance Company,* 423 F.2d 41 (3d Cir. 1970).
191. *Pardie v. Pardie,* 158 N.W.2d 641 (Iowa 1968).
192. *Parkson v. Central DuPage Hospital,* 105 Ill. App.3d 850, 61 Ill. Dec. 651, 435 N.E.2d 140 (App. 1982).
193. *Payne v. Howard,* 75 F.R.D. 465 (D.D.C. 1977).
194. *Pearse v. Pearse,* 63 Eng. Rep. 950 (cl 18546).
195. *Pennison v. Provident Life and Accident Insurance Company,* 154 So.2d 617 (La. App. 1963).
196. *People ex rel. Bowman v. Woodward,* 63 Ill.2d 382, 349 N.E.2d 57 (1976).
197. *People v. Battaglia,* 156 Cal. App. 3d 105B, 203 Cal. Rptr. 370 (Cal. App. 2d Dist. 1984).
198. *People v. Christopher,* 476 N.Y.S.2d 640 (A.D. 4th Dept. 1984).
199. *People v. Dean,* 126 Ill. App.3d 631, 81 Ill. Dec. 653, 647 N.E.2d 353 (App. 5th Dist. 1984).
200. *People v. Doe,* 96 Misc.2d 975, 410 N.Y.S.2d 233 (1978).
201. *People v. Doe,* 430 N.E.2d 696 (Ill. App. 1982*a*).
202. *People v. Doe,* 430 N.E.2d 696 (Ill. App. 1982*b*).
203. *People v. John Doe,* 455 N.Y.S.2d 945 (Sup. 1982).
204. *People v. Emanuel,* 98 Mich. App. 163, 295 N.W.2d 875 (1980).
205. *People v. Fentress,* 103 Misc.2d 179 425 N.Y.S.2d 485 (1980).
206. *People v. Gomez,* 185 Cal. Rptr. 155 (App. 1982).
207. *People v. Hilliker,* 29 Mich. App. 543, 185 N.W.2d 831 (App. 1971).
208. *People v. Johnson,* 314 N.W. 2d 631 (Mich. App. 1982).
209. *People v. Lapsley,* 26 Mich. App. 424, 182, N.W.2d 601 (App. 1970).
210. *People v. Lines,* 119 Cal. Rptr. 225, 13 Cal.3d 500, 531 P.2d 793 (1975).
211. *People v. Lobaito,* 133 Mich. App. 547, 351 N.W.2d 233 (App. 1984).
212. *People v. McHugh,* 478 N.Y.S.2d 754 (Sup. 1984).
213. *People v. Newman,* 345 N.Y.S.2d 502 (1973).
214. *People v. O'Gorman,* 91 Misc.2d 539, 398 N.Y.S.2d 336 (1977).
215. *People v. Phillips,* 1 Western L.J. 109 (1813).
216. *People v. Sorna,* 88 Mich. App. 351, 276 N.W.2d 892 (App. 1979).
217. *People v. Stevens,* 386 Mich. 579. 194 N.W.2d 372 (1972).
218. *People v. Stritzinger,* 34 Cal.3d 505, 194 Cal. Rptr. 431, 668 P.2d 738 (1983).
219. *People v. Taylor,* 618 P.2d 1127 (Colo. 1980).

220. *Perry v. Fiumano,* 61 App. Div.2d 512, 403 N.Y.S.2d 382 (App. Div. 4th Dist. 1978).
221. *Pouncy v. State,* 353 So.2d 640 (Fla. Dist. App. 1977).
222. *Pratt v. State,* 39 Md. App. 442, 387 A.2d 779 (App. 1978).
223. *Prink v. Rockefeller Center, Inc.,* 48 N.Y.2d 309, 422 N.Y.S.2d 911, 398 N.E.2d 517 (1979).
224. *Pyles v. State,* 25 Md. 263, 334 A.2d 160 (1975).
225. *Reid v. Moore-McCormack Lines,* 49 F.R.D. 91 (S.D.N.Y. 1970).
226. *Reynaud v. Superior Court,* 138 Cal. App.3d 1, 187 Cal. Rptr. 660 (App. 1982).
227. *Ritt v. Ritt,* 98 N.J. Super. Ct. 590, 238 A.2d 196 (Super. 1967).
228. *Roberts v. Superior Court,* 9 Cal.3d 330, 107 Cal. Rptr. 309, 508 P.2d 309 (1973).
229. *Robinson v. Magovern,* 83 F.R.D. 79 (W.D. Pa, 1979).
230. *Roe v. Doe,* 402 U.S. 307 (1977).
231. *Roe v. Wade,* 410 U.S. 113 (1973).
232. *Roman v. Appleby,* 558 F. Supp. 449 (E.D. Pa. 1983).
233. *Romanowicz v. Romanowicz,* 213 Pa. Super. 382, 248 A.2d 238 (1968).
234. *Ronson v. Commissioner of Correction of State of New York,* 551 F. Supp. 450 (S.D.N.Y. 1982).
235. *Roper v. Roper,* 336 So.2d 654 (Fla. App. 1976).
236. *Rosegay v. Canter,* 187 N.J. Super 652, 455 A.2d 610 (Super. 1982).
237. *Rudnick v. Superior Court of Kern County,* 11 Cal.3d 924, 114 Cal. Rptr. 603, 523 P.2d 643 (1974).
238. *Sampson v. Missouri Pacific R.R.,* 560 S.W.2d 573 (Mo. 1978).
239. *San Francisco v. Superior Court,* 37 Cal.2d 227, 231 P.2d 26 (1951).
240. *Schafer v. Parkview Memorial Hospital,* 593 F. Supp. 61 (N.D. Ill. 1984).
241. *Schaffer v. Spicer,* 88 S.D. 36, 215 N.W.2d 134 (1974).
242. *Scherz v. Scherz,* 110 Misc.2d 137, 442 N.Y.S.2d 41 (Sup. Ct. 1981).
243. *Shaw v. Glickman,* 45 Md. App. 718, 415 A.2d 625 (Md. Ct. Spec. App. 1980).
244. *Shipman v. Division of Social Services,* 442 A.2d 101 (De. Fam. Ct. 1981).
245. *Silberstein v. County of Westchester,* 92 App. Div.2d 867, 459 N.Y.S.2d 838 (App. Div. 1983).
246. *Simpson v. Braider,* 104. F.R.D. 512 (D.D.C. 1985).
247. *Simrin v. Simrin,* 233 Cal. App.2d 90, 43 Cal. Rptr. 376 (1965).
248. *Sims v. State,* 251 Ga. 877, 311 S.E.2d 161 (1984).
249. *Slakan v. Porter,* 737 F.2d 368 (4th Cir. 1984).
250. *Smith v. Superior Court,* 118 Cal. App.3d 136, 173 Cal. Rptr. 145 (1981).
251. *Spencer v. Spencer,* 301 S.E.2d 411 (N.C. App. 1983).
252. *State Board v. New York State Commissioner of Mental Hygiene,* 64 App. Div. 224, 409 N.Y.S.2d 665 (1978).
253. *State Department of Social and Health Services v. Latta,* 92 Wash.2d 812, 601 P.2d 520 (1979).
254. *State ex rel. Calley v. Olsen,* 532 P.2d 230 (Oreg. 1975).
255. *State ex rel. Etc. v. Estate of Stephens,* 426 N.E.2d 116 (Ind. App. 1981).
256. *State ex rel. Hickox v. Hickox,* 410 N.Y.S.2d 81 (1978).
257. *State ex rel. Juvenile Department v. Brown,* 528 P.2d 569 (Or. App. 1974).
258. *State ex rel. Pflaum v. Psychology Examining Board,* 331 N.W.2d 614 (Wis. App. 1983).

259. *State of Georgia v. Reid-Hall,* No. 20149, Super Ct. of Clarke County (Ga. 1984).
260. *State v. Andring,* 342 N.W.2d 128 (Minn. 1984).
261. *State v. Bruno,* 1 Conn. App. 384, 473 A.2d 311 (App. 1984).
262. *State v. Brydon,* 626 S.W.2d 443 (Mo. App. 1981).
263. *State v. Carter,* 641 S.W.2d 54 (Mo. 1982).
264. *State v. Craney,* 347 N.W.2d 668 (Iowa, 1984).
265. *State v. Dodis,* 314 N.W.2d 233 (Minn. Sup. Ct. 1982).
266. *State v. Driscoll,* 53 Wisc.2d 699, 193 N.W.2d 851, 50 ALR 3d 554 (1972).
267. *State v. Enebak,* 272 N.W.2d 27 (Minn. 1978).
268. *State v. Evans,* 104 Ariz. 434, 454 P.2d 976 (1969).
269. *State v. Farrow,* 116 N.H. 731, 366 A.2d 1177 (1976).
270. *State v. Fears,* 659 S.W.2d 370 (Tenn. Cr. App. 1983).
271. *State v. Fouquette,* 67 Nev. 505, 221 P.2d 404, cert. den. 341 U.S. 932 (1950).
272. *State v. Garrett,* 8 Ohio App.3d 244, 456 N.E.2d 1319 (App. 1983).
273. *State v. Gibson,* 3 Wash. App. 596, 476 P.2d 727 (App. 1970).
274. *State v. Gotfrey,* 598 P.2d 1325 (Utah, 1979).
275. *State v. Groff,* 409 So.2d 44 (Fla. App. 1982).
276. *State v. Hembd,* 305 Minn. 120, 232 N.W.2d 872 (1975).
277. *State v. Hoester,* 661 S.W.2d 449 (Mo. banc. 1984).
278. *State v. Hungerford,* 84 Wisc.2d 236, 267 N.W.2d 258 (1978).
279. *State v. Jackson,* 298 S.E.2d 866 (W. Va. 1982).
280. *State v. Kociolek,* 23 N.J. 400, 129 A.2d 417 (1957).
281. *State v. Kupchun,* 117 N.H. 417, 373 A.2d 1325 (1977).
282. *State v. Martin,* 274 N.W.2d 893 (S.D.), cert. den., 444 U.S. 883 (1979).
283. *State v. McGautha,* 617 S.W.2d 554 (Mo. App. 1981).
284. *State v. Miller,* 709 P.2d 225 (Oreg. 1985).
285. *State v. Moore,* 45 Or. 837, 609 P.2d 866 (1980).
286. *State v. Obstein,* 52 N.J. 516, 247 A.2d 5 (1968).
287. *State v. Odenbrett,* 349 N.W.2d 265 (Minn. 1984).
288. *State v. Pratt,* 284 Md. 516, 398 A.2d 421 (1979).
289. *State v. R.H.,* 683 P.2d 269 (Alaska App. 1984).
290. *State v. Roma,* 140 N.J. Super. 582, 357 A.3d 45 (1976), 143 N.J. Super. 504, 363 A.2d 923 (1976).
291. *State v. Sands,* 700 P.2d 1369 (Ariz. App. 1985).
292. *State v. Stotts,* 695 P.2d 1110 (Ariz. 1985).
293. *State v. Sweet,* 149 Vt. 238, 453 A.2d 1131 (1982).
294. *State v. Thomale,* 317 N.W.2d 147 (S.D. 1982).
295. *State v. Thresher,* 122 N.H. 63, 442 A.2d 578 (1982).
296. *State v. Toste,* 178 Conn. 626, 424 A.2d 293 (1979).
297. *State v. Treadway,* 69 Ohio Op. 507, 328 N.E.2d 825 (1974).
298. *State v. Walker,* 639 S.W.2d 854 (Mo. App. 1982).
299. *State v. Washington,* 83 Wis.2d 808, 266 N.W.2d 597 (1978).
300. *Tarasoff v. Regents of the University of California,* 13 Cal.3d 177, 529 P.2d 553 (1974), *vacated,* 17 Cal.3d 425, 131 Cal. RPTR 14, 551 P.2d 34 (1976).
301. *Teperson v. Donato,* 371 So.2d 703 (Fla. App. 1979).
302. *Theodoropoulas v. Theodoropoulas,* 2 All E.R. 722 (Winch, Ass.) (1963).
303. *Touma v. Touma,* 140 N.J. Super. 544, 357 A.2d 25 (Super. 1976).

304. *Town of Lafayette v. City of Chippewa Falls,* 70 Wisc. 2d 610, 235 N.W.2d 435 (1975).
305. *Tucson v. Rowles,* 21 Ariz. App. 424, 520 P.2d 518 (1974).
306. *Tumlinson v. State,* 663 S.W.2d 539 (Tex. Crim. App. 5th Dist. 1983).
307. *Tylitzki v. Triple X Service,* 126 Ill. App.2d 144, 261 N.E.2d. 533 (1970).
308. *United States ex rel. Edney v. Smith,* 39 N.Y.2d 620, 383 N.Y.S.2d 23, 350 N.E.2d 400 (1976).
309. *United States v. Albright,* 388 F.2d 719 (4th Cir. 1968).
310. *United States v. Alvarez,* 519 F.2d 1036 (3d Cir. 1975).
311. *United States v. Bryan,* 339 U.S. 323 (1950).
312. *United States v. Glover,* 588 F.2d 876 (2d Cir. 1978).
313. *United States v. Goffman,* 567 F.2d 960 (10th Cir. 1977).
314. *United States v. Graham,* 548 F.2d 1302 (8th Cir. 1977).
315. *United States v. Greene,* 479 F.2d 1068 (7th Cir. 1974).
316. *United States v. Hooper,* 440 F. Supp. 1208 (D.C. Ill. 1977).
317. *United States v. King,* 73 F.R.D. 103 (E.D.N.Y. 1976).
318. *United States v. Kovel,* 296 F.2d 918, 96 ALR 2d 116 (2d Cir. 1961).
319. *United States v. Layton,* 90 F.R.D. 520 (N.D. Cal. 1981).
320. *United States v. Lindstrom,* 698 F.2d 1154 (11th Cir. 1983).
321. *United States v. Meagher,* 531 F.2d 752 (5th Cir. 1976).
322. *United States v. Nixon,* 418 U.S. 683 (1974).
323. *United States v. Radetsky,* 535 F.2d 556, 569 (10th Cir. 1976).
324. *United States v. White,* 617 F.2d 1131 (5th Cir. 1980).
325. *United States v. Williams,* 456 F.2d 217 (5th Cir. 1972).
326. *United States v. Witt,* 542 F. Supp. 696 (S.D.N.Y. 1982).
327. *Ursury v. Florida,* 428 So.2d 713 (Fla. App. 4th Dist. 1983).
328. *Washington v. State,* 388 U.S. 14 (1967), on remand 417 S.W.2d 278 (Tex. Crim. Ct. App.)
329. *Webb v. Quincy City Lines, Inc.,* 73 Ill. App.2d 405, 219 N.E.2d 165 (App. 1966).
330. *Whalen v. Roe,* 429 U.S. 589 (1977).
331. *Whitree v. New York,* 290 N.Y.S.2d 486 (1968).
332. *Wichansky v. Wichansky,* 126 N.J. Super. 156, 313 A.2d 222 (1973).
333. *Will of Postley,* 125 Misc.2d 416, 479 N.Y.S.2d 464 (1984).
334. *Williams v. Buffalo General Hospital,* 28 App. Div.2d 777, 280 N.Y.S.2d 699 (1967).
335. *Williamson v. State,* 330 So.2d 272 (Miss. 1976).
336. *Wing v. Wing,* 393 So.2d 285 (La. App. 1980).
337. *Wolfe v. Beal,* 384 A.2d 1187 (Pa. 1978).
338. *Wright v. American General Life Insurance Co.,* 297 S.E.2d 910 (N.C. App. 1982).
339. *Yaron v. Yaron,* 83 Misc.2d 276, 372 N.Y.S.2d 518 (Sup. 1975).
340. *Ziegler v. Superior Court in and for the County of Pima,* 134 Ariz. 390, 656 P.2d 1251 (App. 1982).
341. *Zilborg v. Zilborg,* 131 N.Y.S.2d 122 (1954).

Case Citations by State

Numbers refer to case citations in previous chapter.

Alabama	73, 103
Alaska	3, 75, 97, 105, 289
Arizona	93, 268, 291, 292, 305, 340
Arkansas	10, 77, 79, 104
California	8, 13, 14, 19, 20, 21, 24, 30, 55, 89, 92, 100, 106, 116, 119, 123, 128, 141, 149, 159, 163, 169, 171, 197, 206, 210, 218, 226, 228, 237, 239, 247, 250, 300
Colorado	25, 52, 219
Connecticut	17, 76, 261, 296
Delaware	244
District of Columbia	126, 140, 178
Florida	7, 37, 57, 91, 113, 144, 147, 174, 176, 221, 235, 275, 301
Georgia	23, 56, 139, 155, 181, 248, 259
Illinois	18, 67, 150, 192, 196, 199, 202, 307, 329
Indiana	43, 99, 132, 255
Iowa	38, 191, 264
Kansas	16, 111, 177
Kentucky	4, 9
Louisiana	195, 336
Maryland	1, 29, 94, 143, 182, 222, 224, 243, 288

State	Cases
Massachusetts	47, 48, 49, 50, 51, 54, 58
Michigan	11, 130, 165, 166, 204, 207, 208, 209, 211, 216, 217
Minnesota	260, 265, 267, 276, 287
Mississippi	335
Missouri	15, 107, 146, 238, 262, 263, 277, 283, 298
Montana	164
Nevada	271
New Hampshire	115, 269, 281, 295
New Jersey	78, 80, 170, 180, 188, 227, 236, 280, 286, 290, 303, 332
New York	5, 6, 34, 35, 36, 39, 40, 41, 45, 53, 59, 60, 62, 65, 66, 85, 88, 108, 109, 117, 124, 131, 134, 135, 145, 148, 161, 162, 183, 187, 198, 200, 203, 205, 212, 213, 214, 215, 220, 223, 242, 245, 252, 256, 308, 331, 333, 334, 339, 341
North Carolina	87, 156, 186, 251, 338
North Dakota	110, 153
Ohio	272, 297
Oregon	95, 254, 257, 284, 285
Pennsylvania	2, 46, 74, 102, 112, 152, 168, 233, 337
Rhode Island	22, 114, 120
South Dakota	241, 282, 294
Tennessee	71, 270
Texas	31, 42, 83, 137, 151, 306
Utah	44, 274
Vermont	127, 293
Virginia	81
Washington	129, 133, 253, 273
West Virginia	279
Wisconsin	258, 266, 278, 299, 304
Wyoming	167
Federal	12, 26, 27, 28, 32, 33, 61, 63, 64, 69, 70, 72, 82, 84, 86, 90, 96, 98, 101, 118, 121, 125, 130, 136, 138, 142, 143, 151, 154, 157, 158, 160, 172, 173, 175, 178, 179, 184, 185, 189, 190, 193, 225, 229, 230, 231, 232, 234, 240, 246, 249, 309, 310, 311, 312, 313, 314, 315, 316, 317, 318, 319, 320, 321, 322, 323, 324, 325, 326, 327, 328, 330
Foreign	68, 122, 194, 302

INDEX